UNDERSTANDING ENGLISH LANGUAGE

ORDINARY LEVEL (FORM 1-4)

KINDLE DIRECT PUBLISHING (KDP)

BY JOHN EDWARD

©2020 JOHN EDWARD

Copyright © by John Edward

All Rights Reserved

Published by; KINDLE DIRECT PUBLISHING (KDP)

SEATTLE, WASHINGTON- UNITED STATES

ISBN 9798612386520

FOREWORD

Understanding English Language for Ordinary level is among of the best books in English Language for Ordinary level students. It gives us various insights of language skills, its attributes and its development. The distinctive features of this book are being comprehensive, precise and brief. This book has been carefully and thoroughly written to suit ordinary level students. Students will use this book for reference and clarification on different English language perspectives. It uses a helpful method approach for those students who need to use and critically review English language concepts. Hence, it is expected that, students and teachers will find this book as a user friendly guide because it comprises the topics like; Parts of speech, Tenses, Comprehension and summary, Composition, Appreciating of literary work and Vocabulary

PREFACE

This book covers six chapters as indicated in the book. These topics are; Parts of speech, Tenses, Comprehension and summary, Composition, Appreciating of literary work and Vocabulary. This book has been written in a simple language which can make the subject matter more readable and accessible.

This book is unique because has been so carefully designed so that it caters for the needs of various types of learners. The teacher will also find the book very helpful because the examples contained in the book may guide them on what to involve their students in hence will enable them to pass their examinations.

The book presents skills as a process that can be mastered in step by step sequence. It is our hope that this book will be very helpful to all readers together with all students. We cannot pass the examination without reading hence good preparations prevent poor performance.

ACKNOWLEDGEMENTS

The preparation of this book took a long time and involved many people. I would like to express my thanks for their thoughtful comments, advice and suggestions. Some of these fellows are;

- Rev.Prof Donald Mwanjoka& Dyness Mwanjoka
- Ostina Amulike Mwambene
- Mr.&Mrs Fidelis Kanga
- Mr.&Mrs Asubisye Mejala
- Miss. Anna Mejala
- Dr. Charles Raphael
- Mrs Justina Raphael
- Mr. Wilbert Ruta
- Mzee Bethania Lupendza
- Mr.&Mrs Charles Luhwagho
- Mama Agness Msomba
- Shizya Mwazembe
- Liberty Mwazembe

Table of Contents

CHAPTER 1

ENGLISH STRUCTURE

PARTS OF SPEECH

NOUNS

Are the words which are used to name people, animals, places and things e.g. dog, Dar es Salaam and Shadrack.

Noun ending	Examples
-ation	Organization, education.
-er/or	Actor, speaker, pointer.
-ism	Socialism, nationalism.
-ment	Government, environment.
-ness	Happiness, kindness.
-ity	Reality, ability, activity.
-ance	Assistance, abundance.
-ship	Ownership, hardship.

TYPES OF NOUNS;

1. **Common nouns;** are those nouns referring to person, things or places in general sense e.g. people, child, sister, lion and city.
2. **Proper nouns;** are the ones which name specific person, things or places. They must always start with capital letters e.g. John, London, South Africa, Indian Ocean, EAC and UNO.
3. **Collective nouns;** are those nouns that name a collection of things or person are regarded as one e.g. class, army, team, choir and crowd.
4. **Concrete nouns;** are the ones that name anything that can be perceived through atleast one of our five physical senses e.g. book.
5. **Abstract nouns;** are those which name things that cannot be perceived through our five physical senses e.g. fear, regret, love and truth.
6. **Material nouns;** are those which name material or substances which are used for making other things e.g. wood, steel, copper and cotton.
7. **Countable nouns;** are the ones that name things which can be counted e.g. box, pen and pencil.
8. **Uncountable nouns;** are the ones that name things which cannot be counted e.g. milk, water, oil, soil and sugar.

VERBS;

Are the words that express action or used to denote an action of noun or pronoun e.g. write, play, dance, read, darken, differentiate, originate, fasten, beautify, apologize and publicize.

TYPES OF VERBS;

1. **Lexical verbs (main verbs);** are the ones that can stand independently with full dictionary meaning e.g. sing, talk, write and see.
2. **Auxiliary verbs (helping verbs);** are the verbs that help main or lexical verbs to express meaning e.g. Be, have, has, do, am, are, were, can, must, may, could, shall, will, did and should.

ADVERBS;

Are the words that are used to modify verbs, adjectives or they are the words that modify one another e.g. slowly, very, and extremely.

Adjective+ ly = adverb
Kind- kindly
Angry- angrily
Final- finally
Wise- wisely
Nice- nicely

KINDS OF ADVERBS;

1. **Adverbs of time and duration;** tell when or for how long the actions take place e.g. early, soon, now, today, tomorrow, yesterday, often, never, again, late, ago, since, formerly and then.

   Examples;
   - She will bring our money **today.**
   - The president will be visiting our school **soon.**

2. **Adverbs of manner;** are the adverbs that describe how actions are done e.g. fast, quickly, cheerfully, slowly, well, right, wisely, foolishly, badly, nicely, sadly and happily.

   Examples;
   - The headmaster was speaking **sadly.**
   - Children were playing football **happily.**

3. **Adverbs of frequency;** are used to tell how often the action is performed e.g. again, always, once, thrice, twice, occasionally, weekly, sometimes, frequently, annually and usually.

   Examples;
   - The MP **occasionally** visits our school.
   - They meet **annually** to discuss family matters.
   - We do a test **once** a week.

4. **Adverbs of degree;** are used to show how much or to what extent or degree the action is done e.g. too, very, little, much, rather, almost, quite and hardly.

  Examples;
- We have **almost** finished the work.
- They have done **little** to avoid cholera.
- We have **too much** homework today.

5. **Interrogative adverbs;** are used to ask questions and they must appear at the beginning of the sentence e.g. how, when, where and why.

  Examples;
- **How** did you get there?
- **Where** are you going next?
- **Why** do you want to take this class?

6. **Adverbs of certainty;** are the adverbs that affirm the action e.g. surely, truly, definitely and obviously.

  Examples;
- They **definitely** care for their child.
- **Surely,** I will bring the book tomorrow.
- **Obviously,** he loves her.

7. **Conjunctive adverbs;** are the adverbs that join two ideas e.g. otherwise, nevertheless, moreover, however, therefore, besides, in addition, above all, likewise and similarly.

  Examples;
- USA is a rich country, **therefore** should help other countries.
- She was lazy, **however** she passed the exam.
- We need to study hard; **otherwise,** we will fail the exam.

8. **Adverbs of place;** used to answer the question where e.g. here, there, in, out, inside, outside, above, below, far, near, forward, backward, up, down, anywhere and elsewhere.

  Examples;
- Henry lives **here.**
- They are standing **inside** the room.
- Charles is going **there.**

ADJECTIVES;

Are the words that modify nouns or pronouns by describing them e.g. careful, hopeful, careless, hopeless, readable, desirable, incredible, contemptible, childish, boyish, childlike, famous, spacious, windy, handy, friendly and brotherly.

KINDS OF ADJECTIVES;

1. **Adjectives of quantity;** these are words which tell us how much a thing is e.g. much, little, some, any, sufficient, great, several, enough, one and many.

   Examples;
   - I ate **some** chapattis.
   - You have **no** sense.
   - Aisha drinks **little** milk.
   - He has **much** money.
   - We have **sufficient** food.

2. **Adjectives of quality;** describe a thing or tell us what kind a person or thing is e.g. color, shape and texture.

   Orders;
   - Adjective of size e.g. small and big.
   - Adjective of quality e.g. expensive and cheap.
   - Adjective of age e.g. old, young and little.
   - Shape adjective e.g. irregular, round and rectangular.
   - Color adjective e.g. red, blue and white.
   - Material or substance adjective e.g. cotton and wooden.
   - Adjective of origin e.g. Indian and Tanzanian.
   - Adjective of purpose e.g. walking stick, riding boot and killing lion.

3. **Demonstrative adjectives;** these words point out which person or things are meant e.g. this, that, these, those and such.

   Examples;
   - **These** books are mine.
   - I love **such** girls.

4. **Interrogative adjectives;** used for asking questions e.g. which, what, whose and how many.

   Examples;
   - **Which** pen is yours?
   - **What** plans do you make?
   - **Whose** book is this?

5. **Possessive adjectives;** used for indicating ownership or possession e.g. my, its, their, her and his.

   Examples;
   - I have **my** ways of doing things.

- The dog wags **its** tail.
- Dogs like **their** masters.
- One girl has **her** handbag.
- Our teacher uses **his** car.

PRONOUNS;

Are the words that take the place of a noun in a sentence e.g. he, she, it, you and they.

TYPES OF PRONOUNS;

1. **Personal pronouns;** refer to people except for the third person e.g. **he, she, I, we, you** and **they**.
2. **Impersonal pronouns;** bear no relationship with the speaker.
   ### Examples;
   - You never know what may happen.
   - You say that man is a selfish animal.

3. **Intensive pronouns/ emphatic pronouns;** come immediately after the nouns or pronouns they intensify
   ### Examples;
   - I **myself** believe that things will improve.
   - They **themselves** promised to help us in trouble.

4. **Reciprocal pronouns;** are the ones that express the interchangeable or mutual actions among or between individuals in a sentence
   ### Examples;
   - Nancy and John greeted **each other.**
   - Workers in this country need to learn to help **one another.**

5. **Indefinite pronouns;** they stand for individuals or groups in general or in definite way e.g. all, another, any, both, such, each, either, few, many, some, neither, nobody, none, nothing, other, anybody, someone, everybody, anything, everyone and somebody.
   ### Examples;
   - Make sure that you give **everyone** a copy of the book.
   - **All** are my friends.
   - We found **nobody** in the car.
   - **Nothing** is impossible before God.

6. **Demonstrative pronouns;** are used for pointing to the intended things for the listeners to see and understand.
   ### Examples;

- **This** is the book that I was telling you about.
- **These** are furious.

7. **Reflexive pronouns;** such pronouns are formed by suffixing self or selves.
   Examples;
   - I saw **myself** on the TV program.
   - The girl saw **herself** in the mirror.
   - We trained **ourselves** to do the job.
   - They believed in **themselves**.

8. **Possessive Pronouns;** These are pronouns that indicate possession or ownership of particular things. Examples are mine, his, hers, its, ours, yours, and theirs.
   Examples;
   - The book is **mine.**
   - The car is **theirs.**
   - The building is **hers.**
   - This book is **yours.**

9. **Interrogative pronouns;** are the ones that used for asking questions.
   Examples;
   - **Who** said that?
   - **Whom** do you think we should invite?
   - To **whom** did you give the paper?

10. **Numerical Pronouns;** you use these to show the number or position a thing or a subject occupies in a scheme of arrangement e.g. one, two, three, first, second and third.
    Examples;
    - Many people were invited but only **two** will be interviewed.
    - My father has **two** houses, the **first** is in Lagos and the **second** is in Ibadan.

11. **Relative pronouns;** refer to people and object.
    a) **WHO;** is used to for saying exactly which person or what kind of person you are talking about.
       Examples;
       - He **who** hesitates is lost.
       - The man **who** is honest is trusted.
       - The boy **who** came here yesterday is my friend.

    b) **WHOM;** is used instead of who as the object of a verb or preposition.
       Examples;
       - The man **whom** I saw is not here.
       - He is a person to **whom** I gave the book.
       - They are people **whom** she said.

c) WHOSE; is used to say exactly which person or thing you mean.

Examples;

- A boy **whose** mother is a doctor is my friend.
- The girl **whose** leg was injured yesterday is coming.
- The house **whose** doors are red is burned.
- The boy **whose** book is lost is crying.

d) WHICH; is used for saying exactly what thing or things you are talking about.

Examples;

- The book **which** I read is very interesting.
- The pen **which** I bought is not writing.
- The book **which** I used is very expensive.

e) WHERE; is used to refer to the place or situation mentioned.

Examples;

- **Where** can I buy a newspaper?
- I asked him **where** he lived.
- She ran to **where** they were standing.

f) WHEN; is used for talking about the time at which something happens or happened.

Examples;

- **When** did she arrive?
- I don't know **when** she arrived.
- Sunday is the day **when** I can relax.
- I last saw her in May, **when** she was in London.

g) WHY; is used for talking about a reason for something.

Examples;

- I wonder **why** they went.
- I'm tired and that's **why** I'm in such a bad mood.
- **Why** was she so late?

h) HOW; is used to refer in what way.

Examples;

- She's gone. **How** strange!
- I can't believe **how** expensive it is!
- **How** do you spell your name?

i) THAT; is used for person and things.

Examples;

- I know the house **that** he lives in.
- This is the boy **that** I told you of.
- All **that** I said had no effect on him.

j) WHAT; refers to things only.

Examples;
- I say **what** I mean.
- He found **what** he was looking for.
- I mean **what** I say.

k) WHICHEVER; is used to refer any person or thing.

Examples;
- You can choose **whichever** book you want.
- **Whichever** way did you come?

CONJUCTIONS;

Are the words that connect other words or group of words e.g. and, or, so, for, yet, but, although, as, because, even if, as if, even though, wherever, neither... nor, either....or, not only... but also, as... as, whether...or.

TYPES OF CONJUCTIONS;

1. **Coordinating conjunctions;** are the conjunctions which connect words or sentences that are grammatically equal or similar in status e.g. and, or, but, so, for, nor, yet.

   Examples;
   - John likes tea, **but** Aisha likes coffee.
   - She is kind **so** she helps people.

2. **Subordinating conjunctions;** are words that connect words or sentences that are not grammatically equal or similar e.g. after, although, as, because, before, how, if, once, than, since, that, though, till, until, when, where, whether, while, except, as though, as if, even if, even though, for, lest.

   Examples;
   - I will go **wherever** you ask me too.
   - Jomo went swimming **although** it was raining.
   - **Unless** you become a hardworking student I won't help you.

3. **Correlative conjunctions;** these are the pairs of conjunctions that work together to link words, phrases, clauses e.g. neither...nor, whether...or, both...and, either...or, not only...but also, as...as.

   Examples;
   - **Both** my mother **and** my brother work here.
   - Asher and **neither** cake **nor** ice cream.
   - Mr. Shamrock is **not only** intelligent **but also** friendly.

<h1 style="text-align:center">USES OF CERTAIN CONJUCTIONS;
AS....AS</h1>

Examples;

- I am **as** strong **as** him.
- No other metal is **as** useful **as** iron.

SO THAT;
Examples;

- I read many books **so that** I can become an author.
- He goes to school **so that** he can help his parents.
- I was **so** tired **that** I couldn't walk any further.

ENOUGH TO;
Examples;

- You are old **enough to** know better.
- She is strong **enough to** carry the box.
- He is tall **enough to** reach the picture.

TOO...TO;
Examples;

- She is **too** weak **to** carry the box.
- I am **too** busy **to** attend the party.
- He talks **too** fast **to** be understood.

DESPITE;
Examples;

- **Despite** his poverty, he went to school.
- **Despite** her beauty, she sold flowers.
- They failed their exam, **despite** of studying.

INSPITE OF;
Examples;

- She did not win the competition **Inspite of** her beauty.
- **Inspite of** running fast, they did not finish the race.
- **Inspite of** calling him bad name, he was not angry.

SELDOM; Means less often.
Examples;

- He often did not think of his responsibilities.

Seldom did he think of responsibilities.

- Up country train is usually late during the rainy season.
  Seldom does the up country train on line during the rainy season.
- I had little time to read novels then.
  Seldom did I have time to read novels then.

PREFER…TO
Examples;

- I **prefer** tea **to** coffee.
- I **prefer** English **to** Kiswahili.
- I **prefer** reading **to** writing.

BETWEEN; is used with two things.
Examples;

- Henry is standing **between** two girls.
- The car is **between** two buses.

AMONG; is used with more than two things.
Examples;

- Johannes is standing **among** four girls.
- Juliana is **among** ten girls who failed the exams.

SO AS TO;
Examples;

- He studies biology **so as to** become a doctor.
- I read many books **so as to** improve English.
- I came to school **so as to** get education.

IN ORDER TO;
Examples;

- I go to school **in order to** meet my friends.
- I eat food **in order to** live.
- I bought a house **in order to** live with my family.

BOTH…AND
Examples;

- Daniel gave you **both** pen **and** note-book.
- **Both** you **and** your friend are right.

THOUGH;
Examples;

- **Though** he has two cars, he walks on foot.
- **Though** she resisted rapper, she was raped.

THE FACT THAT;
Examples;

- Despite **the fact that** he was rich he failed to pay school fees.
- Despite **the fact that** he was tall he ran fast.
- Inspite **the fact that** he was drunk, he saw the snake.

ALTHOUGH;
Examples;

- **Although** he was in our group, he is not same like us.
- **Although** I had a gun, I did not shoot him.
- **Although** Sam has eaten some food he is hungry.

EITHER...OR; is used when you are giving a choice, usually of two things.
Examples;

- **Either** you leave **or** I do.
- You can **either** write **or** phone.
- **Either** he **or** his friend has done it.

NEITHER...NOR; is used to say about two people or things not one and not the other.
Examples;

- **Neither** she **nor** her sister passed.
- **Neither** she **nor** her friend was to blame.
- **Neither** Amir **nor** Salzmann were present.

USED TO;
Examples;

- I **used to** play football when I was young.
- My grandfather **used to** tell folk stories at night.

NOT ONLY...BUT ALSO....
Examples;

- Juba is **not only** rich **but also** kind.
- Anna is **not only** intelligent **but also** wise.

UNLESS = if not

Examples;

- **Unless** he speaks English, he will go to London.
- **Unless** I study hard, I won't be the first.
- **Unless** they come late, they won't find me.

AS SOON AS
Examples;

- **As soon as** I had finished eating a visitor arrived.
- **As soon as** the patient died, the doctor reported.

NO SOONER HAD…THAN…
Examples;

- **No sooner had** the patient died **than** the doctor reported.
- **No sooner had** I finished eating **than** a visitor arrived.

HARDLY HAD…WHEN…
Examples;

- **Hardly had** I finished the work **when** the church bell rang.
- **Hardly had** we planted our seeds **when** it rained.

CONDITIONALS;

TYPE 1 (OPEN CONDITION);
This type tells us that something will happen if a certain condition is fulfilled.
Examples;

- **If** you study hard, you will get first class.
- **If** he runs all the time, he can get there in time.
- **If** her uncle arrives, she may not come with you.

TYPE 2 (IMPROBABLE OR IMAGINARY CONDITION)
Conditionals of this type are used when we talk about something which we don't expect to happen or which is purely imaginary.
Examples;

- **If** you studied hard, you would get first class.
- **If** we started now, we could be in time.
- **If** he stopped smoking, he might get fat.

TYPE 3 (UNFULFILLED CONDITION)
Conditionals of this type say that something did not happen because a certain condition was not fulfilled.

Examples;

- **If** you had studied hard, you would have got a first class.
- **If** I had seen him, I could have saved him from drowning.
- **If** you had left that wasp alone, it might not have stung you.

PREPOSITIONS;

Are the words that placed before a noun or a pronoun to show its relation to another word in the sentence e.g. with, at, below, beyond, out, in front of, outside, inside, up, toward, down.

Examples;

- I killed a lion **with** a gun.
- School begins **at** nine o'clock.

TYPES OF PREPOSITIONS;

1. **Simple prepositions;** are the prepositions that consist of one word only e.g. above, below, beyond, between, against, among, on, at, in, inside, outside, behind, near, beneath, out, up, down, off, over, within, beside, through, for, toward.
2. **Complex prepositions;** are the prepositions that are made by combining two or three words that function together as a single unit e.g. in front of, because of.

KINDS OF PREPOSITIONAL PHRASE;

1. **Prepositions of place;**

   Examples;

   - I went **near the NBC bank.**
   - The cat is sleeping **under the table.**
   - **The book was** on the table.

2. **Prepositions of time;**

   Examples;

   - We were studying **before the exam.**
   - The exam starts **at six o'clock.**
   - We stayed there **for several days.**
   - We go to church **on Sunday.**

3. **Prepositions of direction;**

   Examples;

   - We walked **towards the forest.**
   - Jumna went **into the room.**
   - The dog was looking **at the corner.**

4. **Prepositions of reason or purpose;**

13

Examples;
- She was trembling **with cold.**
- You need to fight **for your rights.**

5. **Prepositions of accompaniment;**
     Examples;
- You need to go **with Arnold.**
- Rice **with beans** is my favorite meal.

6. **Prepositions of similarity or comparison;**
     Examples;
- A boy is **like his father.**
- Chocolate **like ice creams** are sweet.

7. **Prepositions of manner;**
     Examples;
- He passed the exam **by cheating.**
- The work was done **in a lazy manner.**

8. **Prepositions of topics;**
     Examples;
- We were doing homework **on syntax.**
- They were talking **about money.**

9. **Prepositions of possession;**
     Examples;
- I like a girl **with good manners.**
- A girl **of high standards** is normally admired.

10. **Prepositions of means;**
     Examples;
- Upendo goes to school **by bus.**
- He takes the window **with a stone.**

USE OF CERTAIN PREPOSITIONS;

UNDER; in or to position that is below.
     Examples;
- Most of an iceberg is **under** the water.
- We found him hiding **under** the table.

BEHIND;
Example;

- There is a small garden **behind** the house.
- Look **behind** you before you drive off.

IN FRONT OF;
Examples;

- There is a big tree **in front of** his house.
- There is a car **in front of** his shop.

BY;
Examples;

- We travelled **by** train.
- It is two **by** my watch.

ON;
Examples;

- He goes to the office **on** foot.
- Come here **on** 5th May.
- The friends sat **on** the ground.
- He has written books **on** economic.

INTO;
Examples;

- He jumped **into** the river.
- 4 **into** 8 go twice.
- They broke **into** his store.

BESIDE;
Examples;

- Go and sit **beside** Anna.
- The beggar wants shelter **besides** money.

OFF;
Examples;

- He lives 2 miles **off** the main road.
- He jumped **off** the horse.
- Keep **off** the grass.
- Take the curtains **off** their books.

- The child is eating **off** the plate.

OF;
Examples;

- The color **of** her dress is red.
- This house is made **of** brick.
- Give me two kilos **of** mango.
- This is the house **of** my friend.

OVER;
Examples;

- He ruled **over** a large kingdom.
- Donald is **over** forty-five years.
- The sun shines **over** the Earth.
- The match is **over**.
- He spent **over** five thousands rupees for this show.

SINCE;
Examples;

- Henry has been reading a book **since** 6 o'clock.
- Aaron has been sick **since** Monday.
- He was here **since** 1975.

FOR;
Examples;

- I will vote **for** you.
- Angel is clever **for** her age.
- I have studied English **for** 10 years.

FROM;
Examples;

- Examinations begin **from** 7th May.
- Shops will remain open **from** 8 o'clock.
- The mango fell **from** the tree.
- He is coming **from** home.
- Many evils flow **from** fear.
- **From** his appearance, he looks old.

WITH;

Examples;

- The letter was written **with** a pen.
- The soldiers fought **with** courage.
- **With** all his faults, I love him.
- I went to the market **with** my friends.

AT;

Examples;

- I go to bed **at** 10 o'clock.
- Milk sells **at** fourteen rupees a liter.
- She comes here **at** noon.
- She lives **at** Agra.
- I got this job **at** the age of twenty five.

IN;

Examples;

- She came here **in** July.
- He was born **in** 1975.
- My friend lives **in** Mumbai.
- He was born **in** poverty.

INTERJECTIONS;

Are the words which express sudden strong feelings and emotions of the mind. Interjections are always followed by exclamation marks! There are four categories of feelings and emotions which can be expressed by interjections;-

1. **Emotions of desire or aversion;** are the ones that express wishes, expectation of having or possessing something attractive.

   Examples;

   - **Oh!** Only if I were rich.
   - **Mmm!** If I can only pass my exam.

2. **Emotions of pleasure and approval;** are the ones that express the feelings of joy and gladness on a particular thing.

   Examples;

   - Yes, you have done very well!
   - Wow, what a beautiful car!
   - Thank God, I have won the race!
   - Ooh, the milk is delicious!

3. **Emotions of pain or disapproval;** are the emotions that express the sensation of physical hurts which may cause discomfort, distress or agony.

        Examples;
- Ouch, my stomach!
- Wow, it hurts!

4. **Emotions of surprise;** express the feeling of astonishment when something totally unexpected happens.

        Examples;
- Oh, what a lovely car!
- Wow, what a fantastic score!
- Hah, is this what it is!

ARTICLES;

Are the words that precede and specify nouns. They are used to determine the references of nouns by telling whether the noun mentioned refers to the thing in a specific or general sense e.g. a, an, the.

TYPES OF ARTICLES;

1. **The definite article;** is used to refer to the noun which is specific or previously mentioned noun e.g. the

USE OF "THE"

- Before the musical instruments e.g. the trumpet.
- Before the political parties e.g. the Labor Party, The Congress Party.
- Before the name of ships, airplanes, trains, newspapers, magazines, journals and well known buildings e.g. the Times of India.
- Before the name of sacred books e.g. The Bible, The Quran.
- Before the names of rivers, seas, oceans, mountain ranges, group of islands e.g. The Indian Ocean, The Alps, The Arabian Sea and The Bay of Bengal.
- Before nouns which are the name of things of which there is only one e.g. The Earth, The sky, The Moon, The star, The sun.
- Before proper, material and abstract nouns when they are specified e.g. the fish of Bengal, The beauty of the Taj.
- Before the physical position e.g. the top, the back, the side, the front, the outside.
- Before the committee, club and foundation e.g. The Rotary club, The United Nations, The Ford Foundation.
- Before important historical events, empire e.g. The French revolution, The Roman Empire, The middle Ages, The world war.

- Before descriptive geographical names e.g. The Ocean, the United States of America.
- Before names of the branches of government e.g. the executive, the judiciary, the legislative.
- Before the superlative degree e.g. January is the tallest boy in the class.
- Before the ordinals e.g. the first man.
- Before the nationality word e.g. The Indians, The Italians, The Russians, The Americans.
- Before the dates of a month e.g. The 3rd of November, 1975.
- Before any invention e.g. the ratio, the television.
- Before expressed with title e.g. The President of India, The Director, and The Chairman.
- Before the armed forces e.g. The Army, The Air Force, and The Navy.
- Before words indicating number, weight and measure to empress the idea of rate e.g. -Eggs are sold by the dozen.
    -Cloth is sold by the meter.
    -Apple is sold by the kilo.
    -Petrol is sold by the liter.

2. **Indefinite article;** are used to refer to nouns that are not specific to the speaker or hearer e.g. A, An.

USE OF "A"

- Before a word beginning with a consonant having sound e.g. a boy, a woman, a horse, a hole.
- Before a word beginning with 'O' when it has the sound of 'w' e.g. a one-man show, a one-rupee note.
- Before a word beginning with a vowel having a consonant e.g. a university, a European, a uniform, a youth, a UK, a yard.

USE OF "AN"

- Before a word beginning with a vowel e.g. an inkpot, an elephant, an orange, an egg.
- Before a word beginning with a silent 'h' e.g. an honor, an heir, an honest man, an hourly report.
- Before a word beginning with a consonant having a vowel sound e.g. an MP, an S.D.O, an x-ray plant, an S.I, an Msc, an M.A, an F.I.R.

USE OF SOME;

- Some is used in affirmative sentences to express quantity.

Examples;

-There is **some** cheese in refrigerator.

-You have bought **some** books.

- Some may be used in interrogative sentences when these are equivalent to polite request.

    Examples;

-Will you give me **some** money?

-Will you have **some** more milk?

USE OF ANY;

- Any is used in negative sentences.

    Examples;

- I did not give **any** butter.

- Angel did not buy **any** books.

- Any is used in affirmative sentences when it has emphatic meaning.

    Examples;

-**Any** fool can do it.

-She will pay **any** price she is asked for.

- Any can replace some in interrogative sentences.

    Examples;

-Do you have **any** book?

-Did you buy **any** cloth?

- Any is used in sentences which are negative or which have a negative idea.

    Examples;

-I have hardly **any** money with me.

-I didn't see **any** grapes in the market.

USE OF MUCH;

- Much denotes quantity.
- Much is used in negative sentences.
- Much is used in uncountable nouns.
- Much is used in interrogative sentences.

    Examples;

-There isn't **much** sugar in the pot.

-She hasn't **much** money in her pocket.

-Is there **much** difficulty in crossing the road?

USE OF MANY;

- Many denote number.
- Many are used in interrogative sentences.
- Many are used in countable nouns.

Examples;

-Are there **many** houses in this lane?

-I have not seen **many** English films.

USE OF A LOT OF;

- A lot of is used in affirmative sentences.

Examples;

-There are **a lot of** books in the library.

-David has **a lot of** money.

USE OF EACH; means one of two things or one of any number exceeding two

Examples;

- **Each** girl must get her share.
- **Each** member of the family was given money.

EVERY

EVERY; is never used in speaking of one of two but is always used in speaking of some number exceeding two.

Examples;

- **Every** man wishes to be happy.
- Education expects **every** person to be polite.

ALL

USE OF ALL; is used for every.

Examples;

- **All** the students were present in the morning assembly.
- **All** my brothers are at school.

LITTLE, A LITTLE, THE LITTLE

a) **Little;** means hardly any or not much.

   -It has a negative meaning.

Examples;

-There was **little** water in the pot.

-There is **little** hope of his recovery.

b) **A little;** denotes some at least. It has an affirmative meaning.

      Examples;

-He has **a little** money.

-**A little** knowledge is a dangerous thing.

c) **The little;** denotes the small quantity. It has both a positive and a negative meaning.

      Examples;

-He wasted **the little** time he had.

FEW, A FEW, THE FEW;

a) **Few;** means not man. It has a negative meaning.

      Examples;

-**Few** men can keep their words.

-**Few** men are free from faults.

b) **A few;** denotes some at least- a certain number, however few. It has a positive meaning.

Examples;

-**A few** girls attended the class.

-Henry has **a few** friends.

c) **The few;** denotes not many. It has both a positive and negative meaning.

      Examples;

-**The few** are honest, the many are dishonest.

-He lost **the few** friends he had.

CHAPTER 2

TENSES

MEANING OF TENSE;

Is a grammatical device used to show time in which a certain action or event occurred.

TYPES OF TENSES;

1. **Present tense;** it expresses those actions, thoughts or states of being that take place at the present time and those which take place regularly or every day. There are four types of present tense which are;
   - a) Simple present tense.
   - b) Present continuous tense.
   - c) Present perfect tense.
   - d) Present perfect continuous tense.
2. **Past tense;** is used to refer to the actions or events that started and finished in the past time. There are four types of past tense which are;
   - a) Simple past tense.
   - b) Past continuous tense.
   - c) Past perfect tense.
   - d) Past perfect continuous tense.
3. **Future tense;** is used to refer to the actions or events that started and finished in the future time. There are four types of future tense which are;
   - a) Simple future tense.
   - b) Future continuous tense.
   - c) Future perfect tense.
   - d) Future perfect continuous tense.

PRESENT TENSE;

1) **SIMPLE PRESENT TENSE;** is used to express what is taking place at the present moment.

Rules for the formation of simple present tense;

$$\left.\begin{array}{l} \text{I} \\ \text{We} \\ \text{You} \\ \text{They} \end{array}\right\} + \text{verb}^1 + \text{object}$$

$$\left.\begin{array}{l} \text{He} \\ \text{She} \\ \text{It} \end{array}\right\} + \text{verb}^1 + s/es/ies + \text{object}$$

Examples;

- I go to school every day.
- We play football every week.
- You cook rice every time.
- They wait for her every Monday.
- He writes a letter every week.
- She speaks English every day.
- It rains heavily.

Negative sentences;
Examples;

- I don't go to school every day.
- We don't play football every week.
- You don't cook rice every time.
- They don't wait for her every Monday.
- He doesn't write a letter every week.
- She doesn't speak English every day.
- It doesn't rain heavily.

Interrogative sentence/ question form;

Examples;

- Do I go to school every day?
- Do we play football every week?
- Do you cook rice every time?
- Do they wait for her every Monday?
- Does He write a letter every week?
- Does she speak English every day?
- Does it rain heavily?

2) **PRESENT CONTINUOUS TENSE;** is used to show that action is in progress and is incomplete at the moment of speaking or writing.

Rules for the formation of present continuous tense;

I+ am+v^1 +ing+ object

He
She $\}$ + is+ v^1+ing+ object
It

We
You $\}$ + are +v^1+ing+ object
They

Examples;

- I am going to school now.
- He is writing a letter now.
- She is speaking English now.
- It is raining heavily.
- We are playing football now.
- You are cooking rice now.
- They are waiting for her now.

Negative sentences;
Examples;

- I am not going to school now.
- He is not writing a letter now.
- She is not speaking English now.
- It is not raining heavily now.
- We are not playing football now.
- You are not cooking rice now.
- They are not waiting for her now.

Interrogative sentence/question form;
Examples;

- Am I going to school now?
- Is He writing a letter now?
- Is she speaking English now?
- Is it raining heavily?
- Are we playing football now?
- Are you cooking rice now?
- Are they waiting for her now?

3) **PRESENT PERFECT TENSE;** is used to indicate completed activities in the immediate past.

Rules for the formation of present perfect tense;

$$\left.\begin{array}{l}\textbf{I}\\\textbf{We}\\\textbf{You}\\\textbf{They}\end{array}\right\} + \textbf{have}+ \textbf{v}^3+ \textbf{object}$$

$$\left.\begin{array}{l}\textbf{He}\\\textbf{She}\\\textbf{It}\end{array}\right\} + \textbf{has}+ \textbf{v}^3+ \textbf{object}$$

Examples;

- I have gone to school.
- We have played football.
- You have cooked rice.
- They have waited for her.
- She has spoken English.
- It has rained heavily.

Negative sentences;
Examples;

- I have not gone to school.
- We have not played football.
- You have not cooked rice.
- They have not waited for her.
- He has not written a letter.
- She has not spoken English.
- It has not rained heavily.

Interrogative sentence/question form;
Examples;

- Have I gone to school?
- Have we played football?
- Have you cooked rice?
- Have they waited for her?
- Has he written a letter?
- Has she spoken English?
- Has it rained heavily?

4) **PRESENT PERFECT CONTINUOUS TENSE;** is used to express an action which began in the past but is still going on.

    Rules for the formation of present perfect continuous tense;

$$\left.\begin{array}{l} \textbf{I} \\ \textbf{We} \\ \textbf{You} \\ \textbf{They} \end{array}\right\} \textbf{+have been+v}^1\textbf{ +ing + object}$$

$$\left.\begin{array}{l} \textbf{He} \\ \textbf{She} \\ \textbf{It} \end{array}\right\} \textbf{+ has been+ v}^1\textbf{ + ing + object}$$

Examples;

- I have been going to school.
- We have been playing football.
- You have been cooking rice.
- They have been waiting for her.
- He has been writing a letter.
- She has been speaking English.
- It has been raining heavily.

Negative sentences/ question form;
Examples;

- I have not been going to school.
- We have not been playing football.
- You have not been cooking rice.
- They have not been waiting for her.
- He has not been writing a letter.
- She has not been speaking English.
- It has not been raining heavily.

Interrogative sentence/ question form;
Examples;

- Have I been going to school?
- Have we been playing football?
- Have you been cooking rice?
- Have they been waiting for her?
- Has he been writing a letter?
- Has she been speaking English?
- Has it been raining heavily?

PAST TENSE;

1) **SIMPLE PAST TENSE;** is used to express actions that took place sometime in the past. **Rules for the formation of simple past tense;**

$$\left.\begin{array}{l} \textbf{I} \\ \textbf{We} \\ \textbf{You} \\ \textbf{They} \\ \textbf{He} \\ \textbf{She} \\ \textbf{It} \end{array}\right\} + v^2 + \textbf{object}$$

Examples;

- I went to school yesterday.
- We played football last month.
- You cooked rice last week.
- They waited for her.
- He wrote a letter yesterday.
- She spoke English.
- It rained heavily.

Negative sentences/ question form;
Examples;

- I did not go to school yesterday.
- We did not play football last month.
- You did not cook rice last week.
- They did not wait for her.
- He did not write a letter yesterday.
- She did not speak English.
- It did not rain heavily.

Interrogative sentences/ question form;
Examples;

- Did I go to school yesterday?
- Did we play football last month?
- Did you cook rice last week?
- Did they wait for her?
- Did he write a letter yesterday?
- Did she speak English?
- Did it rain heavily?

2) **PAST CONTINUOUS TENSE;** is used to denote an action going on at sometime in the past.

Rules for the formation of past continuous tense;

$$\left.\begin{array}{l} \textbf{I} \\ \textbf{He} \\ \textbf{She} \\ \textbf{It} \end{array}\right\} + \textbf{was+ v}^1 + \textbf{ing+ object}$$

$$\left.\begin{array}{l} \textbf{We} \\ \textbf{You} \\ \textbf{They} \end{array}\right\} + \textbf{were} + \textbf{v}^1 + \textbf{ing} + \textbf{object}$$

Examples;

- I was going to school.
- He was writing a letter.
- She was speaking English.
- It was raining heavily.
- We were playing football.
- You were cooking rice.
- They were waiting for her.

Negative sentences;
Examples;

- I was not going to school.
- He was not writing a letter.
- She was not speaking English.
- It was not raining heavily.
- We were not playing football.
- You were not cooking rice.
- They were not waiting for her.

Interrogative sentences/ question form;
Examples;

- Was I going to school?
- Was he writing a letter?
- Was she speaking English?
- Was it raining heavily?
- Were we playing football?
- Were you cooking rice?
- Were they waiting for her?

3) **PAST PERFECT TENSE;** is used to show an action that had been completed before a given time in the past.

Rules for the formation of past perfect tense:

$$\left.\begin{array}{l} \textbf{I, We, You,} \\ \textbf{They, He, She, It} \end{array}\right\} + \textbf{had} + \textbf{v}^3 + \textbf{object}$$

29

Examples;

- I had gone to school.
- We had played football.
- You had cooked rice.
- They had waited for her.
- He had written a letter.
- She had spoken English.
- It had rained heavily.

Negative sentences;
Examples;

- I had not gone to school.
- We had not played football.
- You had not cooked rice.
- They had not waited for her.
- He had not written a letter.
- She had not spoken English.
- It had not rained heavily.

Interrogative sentences/ question form;
Examples;

- Had I gone to school?
- Had we played football?
- Had you cooked rice?
- Had they waited for her?
- Had he written a letter?
- Had she spoken English?
- Had it rained heavily?

4) **PAST PERFECT CONTINUOUS TENSE;** is used to denote an action which had been going on before another action in the past.

Rules for the formation of past perfect continuous tense;

I We You He She It They	+had been+ v^1+ ing +ing + object

Examples;

- I had been going to school.
- We had been playing football.
- You had been cooking rice.
- They had been waiting for her.
- He had been writing a letter.
- She had been speaking English.
- It had been raining heavily.

Negative sentences;
Examples;

- I had not been going to school.
- We had not been playing football.
- You had not been cooking rice.
- They had not been waiting for her.
- He had not been writing a letter.
- She had not been speaking English.
- It had not been raining heavily.

Interrogative/ question form;
Examples;

- Had I been going to school?
- Had we been playing football?
- Had you been cooking rice?
- Had they been waiting for her?
- Had he been writing a letter?
- Had she been speaking English?
- Had it been raining heavily?

FUTURE TENSE;

1) **SIMPLE FUTURE TENSE;** is used for an action that has still to take place.

Rules for the formation of simple future tense

$$\left.\begin{array}{l} \textbf{I} \\ \textbf{We} \end{array}\right\} + \textbf{shall} + \textbf{v}^1 + \textbf{object}$$

$$\left.\begin{array}{l} \textbf{You} \\ \textbf{He} \\ \textbf{She} \\ \textbf{It} \\ \textbf{They} \end{array}\right\} + \textbf{will} + \textbf{v}^1 + \textbf{object}$$

Examples;

- I shall go to school tomorrow.
- We shall play football next week.
- You will cook rice next Sunday.
- He will write a letter next month.
- She will speak English tomorrow.
- It will rain heavily tomorrow.
- They will wait for her next month.

Negative sentences;
Examples;

- I shall not go to school tomorrow.
- We shall not play football next week.
- You will not cook rice next Sunday.
- He will not write a letter next month.
- She will not speak English tomorrow.
- It will not rain heavily tomorrow.
- They will not wait for her next month.

Interrogative sentences/ question form;
Examples;

- Shall I go to school tomorrow?
- Shall we play football next week?
- Will you cook rice next Sunday?
- Will he write a letter next month?
- Will she speak English tomorrow?
- Will it rain heavily tomorrow?
- Will they wait for her next month?

2) **FUTURE CONTINUOUS TENSE;** is used to show an action as going on at sometime in future time.

Rules for the formation of future continuous tense;

$$\left.\begin{array}{l} \text{I} \\ \text{We} \end{array}\right\} + \textbf{shall be} + \textbf{v}^1 + \textbf{ing} + \textbf{object}$$

$$\left.\begin{array}{l} \text{You} \\ \text{He} \\ \text{She} \\ \text{It} \\ \text{They} \end{array}\right\} + \textbf{will be} + \textbf{v}^1 + \textbf{ing} + \textbf{object}$$

32

Examples;

- I shall be going to school.
- We shall be playing football.
- You will be cooking rice.
- He will be writing a letter.
- She will be speaking English.
- It will be raining heavily.
- They will be waiting for her.

Negative sentences;
Examples;

- I shall not be going to school.
- We shall not be playing football.
- You will not be cooking rice.
- He will not be writing a letter.
- She will not be speaking English.
- It will not be raining heavily.
- They will not be waiting for her.

Interrogative sentences/ question form;
Examples;

- Shall I be going to school?
- Shall we be playing football?
- Will you be cooking rice?
- Will he be writing a letter?
- Will she be speaking English?
- Will it be raining heavily?
- Will they be waiting for her?

3) **FUTURE PERFECT TENSE;** is used to show an action that will have been completed at a future time.

Rules for the formation of future perfect tense;

$$\left.\begin{array}{l} \text{I} \\ \text{We} \end{array}\right\} + \text{shall} + \text{have} + v^3 + \text{object}$$

$$\left.\begin{array}{l} \text{You} \\ \text{He} \\ \text{She} \\ \text{It} \\ \text{They} \end{array}\right\} + \text{will} + \text{have} + v^3 + \text{object}$$

33

Examples;

- I shall have gone to school.
- We shall have played football.
- You will have cooked rice.
- He will have written a letter.
- She will have spoken English.
- It will have rained heavily.
- They will have for her.

Negative sentences;
Examples;

- I shall not have gone to school.
- We shall not have played football.
- You will not have cooked rice.
- He will not have written a letter.
- She will not have spoken English.
- It will not have rained heavily.
- They will not have waited for her.

Interrogative sentences/ question form;
Examples;

- Shall I have gone to London?
- Shall we have played football?
- Will you have cooked rice?
- Will he have written a letter?
- Will she have spoken English?
- Will it have rained heavily?
- Will they have waited for her?

4) FUTURE PERFECT CONTINUOUS TENSE; is used to show an action that will be going on over a period of time and will end in the future.

Rules for the formation of future perfect continuous tense;

I
We $\Big\}$ + shall+ have been+v^1+ ing + object

You
He
She $\Big\}$ +will+have been+ v^1+ ing + object
It
They

Examples;

- I shall have been going to school.
- We shall have been playing football.
- You will have been cooking rice.
- He will have been writing a letter.
- She will have been speaking English.
- It will have been raining heavily.
- They will have been waiting for her.

Negative sentences;
Examples;

- I shall not have been going to school.
- We shall not have been playing football.
- You will not have been cooking rice.
- He will not have been writing a letter.
- She will not have been speaking English.
- It will not have been raining heavily.
- They will not have been waiting for her.

Interrogative sentences/ question form;
Examples;

- Shall I have been going to school?
- Shall we have been playing football?
- Will you have been cooking rice?
- Will he have been writing a letter?
- Will she have been speaking English?
- Will it have been raining heavily?
- Will they have been waiting for her?

QUESTION TAGS AND SHORT ANSWERS

QUESTION TAGS;

Is a statement followed by a little question. It is a common practice in conversion to make a statement and ask for confirmation.

Examples;

In positive statement;

- It is raining, isn't it?
- I am eating, aren't I?
- You are coming, aren't you?

- We shall serve our country, shan't we?
- You will go there, won't you?
- She went there, didn't she?
- She goes to school, doesn't she?
- You have met before, haven't you?
- She can swim well, can't she?
- We must go, mustn't we?

In negative statement;
Examples;
- I am not making noise, am I?
- You did not break the glass, did you?
- They haven't come yet, have they?
- Henry doesn't work hard, does he?
- This is not my book, is it?

SHORT ANSWERS;
Examples;
- Do you help her? Yes, I do.
- Can you speak French? Yes, I can.
- Did she pass in the examination? Yes, she did.
- Is your daughter married? Yes, she is.
- Does he work hard? No, he doesn't.
- Can you swim? No, you can't.
- Did he say anything? No, he didn't.

ACTIVE AND PASSIVE VOICE

VOICE;

Is that form of a verb which tells us whether the subject does something or has something been done to it.

TYPES OF VOICES;

1. **Active voice;** is used when the person or thing denoted by the subject is the doer of the action.
2. **Passive voice;** is used when the person or thing denoted by the subject is the receiver of the action.

Rules for changing the active voice into passive voice;

Pronouns in active voice	Pronouns in passive voice
I	Me
We	Us
They	Them
He	Him
She	Her
Who	Whom
It	It
You	You

Rules for change of verbs;

1. **Simple present tense;** subject+is/am/are+ v^3+by +object

   Examples;
   - Sudha writes a story (active voice)
     A story is written by Sudha (passive voice)
   - The peon rings the bell (active voice)
     The bell is rung by the peon (passive voice)
   - My father helps me (active voice)
     I am helped by my father (passive voice)
   - Do children love flowers? (active voice)
     Are flowers loved by children? (Passive voice)

2. **Present continuous tense;** subject+is/am/are+ being+ v^3+ by+ object

   Examples;
   - They are picking some flowers (active voice)
     Some flowers are being picked by them (passive voice)
   - The doctor is preparing medicine (active voice)
     Medicine is being prepared by the doctor (passive voice)
   - I am reading this book (active voice)
     This book is being read by me (passive voice)
   - Are you writing a book? (active voice)
     Is a book being written by you? (Passive voice)

3. **Present perfect tense;** subject+ has/have been+ v^3+ by+ object

   Examples;
   - I have lost my book (active voice)
     My book has been lost by me (passive voice)
   - She has cleaned the cups (active voice)

The cups have been cleaned by her (passive voice)

- Have you decorated the room? (active voice)
  Has the room been decorated by you? (Passive voice)

4. **Simple past tense;** subject+ was/were+ v^3+ by+ object
   Examples;
   - Columbus discovered America (active voice)
     America was discovered by Columbus (passive voice)
   - Patrick wrote this poem (active voice)
     This poem was written by Patrick (passive voice)
   - I did not take food yesterday (active voice)
     Food was not taken yesterday by me (passive voice)
   - Did you answer all the questions? (active voice)
     Were all the questions answered by you? (Active voice)

5. **Past continuous tense;** subject+ was/were+ being+ v^3+ by+ object
   Examples;
   - Mary was writing a letter to her brother (active voice)
     A letter was being written by Mary to her brother (passive voice)
   - The girls were painting the box (active voice)
     The box was being painted by the girls (passive voice)
   - Were the farmers sowing the seeds? (active voice)
     Were the seeds being sown by the farmers? (Passive voice)

6. **Past perfect tense;** subject+ had been+ v^3+ by + object
   Examples;
   - They had won the match (active voice)
     The match had had been won by them (passive voice)
   - We had defended the country (active voice)
     The country had been defended by us (passive voice)
   - Had you broken the glass? (active voice)
     Had the glass been broken by you? (Passive voice)

7. **Simple future tense;** subject+ shall/will+ be+ v^3+ by+ object
   Examples;
   - Anna will cook the food (active voice)
     The food will be cooked by Anna (passive voice)
   - He will not steal my books (active voice)
     My books will not be stolen by him (passive voice)
   - Will he sell tea? (active voice)

Will tea be sold by him? (Passive voice)

8. Future perfect tense; subject + shall/will+ have+ been+ v³+ by+ object
Examples;

- Henry will have written the letter (active voice)
  The letter will have been written by Henry (passive voice)
- I shall have finished the work (active voice)
  The work will have been finished by by me (passive voice)
- Will she have found her lost book by now? (active voice)
  Will her lost book have been found by her by now? (Passive voice)

9. Passive voice of the modal verbs; subject+modals+be+v³+ by+ object
Examples;

- A doctor should examine him (active voice)
  He should be examined by a doctor (passive voice)
- Ronaldo can win the match (active voice)
  The match can be won by Ronaldo (passive voice)
- I would help him (active voice)
  He would be helped by me (passive voice)
- Even a rat may help a lion (active voice)
  A lion may be helped even by a rat (passive voice)
- Daniel must send a reply (active voice)
  A reply must be sent by Daniel (passive voice)

10. Passive voice of the imperative sentence; let+ subject+ be+ v³+ object
Examples;

- Shut the door (active voice)
  Let the door be shut (passive voice)
- Put out the lamp (active voice)
  Let the lamp be put out (passive voice)
- Help the poor (active voice)
  Let the poor be helped (passive voice)
- Do not let the servant cook the food (active voice)
  Let the food not be cooked by the servant (passive voice)

REPORTED SPEECH; DIRECT AND INDIRECT SPEECH

CHANGE IN PRONOUNS

Person and number	Nominative case	Possessive case	Objective case
1st person singular	I	My, Mine	Me
1st person plural	We	Our, ours	Us
2nd person singular	Thou/you	Thy, Thine	You
2nd person plural	You	Your, Yours	
3rd person singular	He, She, It	His, Her, Hers, Its	Him, Her, It
3rd person plural	They	Their	Them

CHANGE IN WORDS INDICATING NEARNESS IN TIME AND SPACE

Direct speech	Indirect speech
This	That
These	Those
Ago	Before
Last night	The previous night or the night before
Today	That day
Now	Then
Tomorrow	The next day
Yesterday	The previous day, the day before
Tonight	That night
Next week	The following week
Come	Go
Here	There

CHANGE OF TENSES;

1) **Simple present becomes simple past tense;**

   Examples;
   - **Direct;** He said, " My mother cooks our breakfast"
     Indirect; He said that his mother cooked their breakfast.
   - **Direct;** Anna said, "I don't want to go to Iringa."
     Indirect; Anna said that she did not want to go to Iringa.

2) **Present continuous becomes past continuous;**

   Examples;
   - **Direct;** She said, " He is taking his examination"
     Indirect; She said that he was taking his examination.
   - **Direct;** David said, " I am doing work"

Indirect; David said that he was doing work.

3) **Present perfect becomes past perfect;**

Examples;

- o **Direct;** Davis said, " I have finished the work"
  Indirect; Davis said that he had finished the work.
- o **Direct;** Deepak said, " Savita has done her work"
  Indirect; Deepak said that Savita had done her work.

4) **Present perfect continuous becomes past perfect continuous;**

Examples;

- o **Direct;** Ram said, " Graham has been giving us very good milk"
  Indirect; Ram said that Graham had been giving them very good milk.
- o **Direct;** She said, " The teacher has not been teaching for a week"
  Indirect: She said that the teacher had not been teaching for a week.

5) **Simple past becomes past perfect;**

Examples;

- o **Direct;** Mr. Graham said, " I saw the Taj Mahal"
  Indirect; Mr. Graham said that he had seen the Taj Mahal.
- o **Direct;** Daniel said, " The cow died in the morning"
  Indirect; Daniel said that the cow had died in the morning.

6) **Past continuous becomes past perfect continuous;**

Examples;

- o **Direct;** The boys said, "We were watching the game"
  Indirect; The boys said that they had been watching the game.
- o **Direct;** He said, " All were laughing then"
  Indirect; He said that all had been laughing then.

7) **No change in past perfect and past perfect continuous;**

Examples;

- o **Direct;** She said, " I had waited for the bus for an hour"
  Indirect; She said that she had waited for the bus for an hour.
- o **Direct;** Sudha said, " I had been doing work since morning"
  Indirect; Sudha said that she had been doing work since morning.

8) **Shall, will, may are changed into should, would, could, might**

Examples;

- o **Direct;** Varun said, " I will come here again tomorrow"
  Indirect; Varun said that he would go there again the next day.
- o **Direct;** Shailendra said, " Pardeep can stay at home"
  Indirect; Shailendra said that Pardeep could stay at home.
- o **Direct;** The teacher said to me, " The boy shall come"
  Indirect; The teacher said to me that the boy should come.
- o **Direct;** Sudha said, " It may rain any time"

Indirect; Sudha said that it might rain any time.

CHAPTER 3

COMPREHENSION AND SUMMARY

COMPREHENSION;

Refers to the understanding or grasping of ideas or meaning. Comprehension requires the acquisition of a set of skills or habits to aid your understanding of spoken or written substance.

SOME IMPORTANT HINTS TO SOLVE A PASSAGE;

1. Read the passage carefully so as to understand the main idea.
2. Read the questions carefully.
3. Write your answers in your own languages as far as possible.
4. Use complete sentences and write out each answer separately.
5. Answers should be revised.
6. To give the meaning of words or phrases.
7. The title should not be in the form of sentence and be as short as possible.
8. Your title should represent the central idea of the passage.

Example;
AGRICULTURE;

Agriculture is the most commonly activity practiced by human. It involves the cultivation of crops and animal rearing. Agriculture can be done for subsistence or for commercial purposes. Even activities like storage processing and marketing of agricultural products are also regarded as part of agriculture.

Small scale agriculture is practiced on relatively small plots of land to meet both subsistence and commercial needs. It is characterized with the use of elementary tools, family labor and use of organic manure from animals.

However, rapid population growth may affect the small scale agriculture as it leads to the reduction of the sizes of farms.

Small scale agriculture had some advantages including growing of variety of food crops, source of income.

SUMMARY;

Refers to a short description of the main ideas or points of something but without any details.

Example;

Agriculture is the activity of growing crops and keeping animals. Small scale agriculture uses simple tools. Increase in population affect small scale farming. Small scale agriculture helps us to get different varieties of food. It is also the source of income to agriculturalists.

CHAPTER 4

COMPOSITION

MEANING OF COMPOSITION;

Refers to a piece of writing on a particular topic, event or person. It can be expository, narrative, argumentative or descriptive compositions. Composition can be written at collage, school, and university as a part of studies or assignment given on a particular course. In writing composition a student is supposed to generate his/her own ideas and use them to narrate, describe, explain, argue, or persuade a certain thing or event.

Composition involves writing essays, letter, poems, stories, debates, speeches, dialogue, which involve a collection of ideas that are organized in a good manner /pattern on a given topic or subject.

Things to consider when writing a composition

1. **Title:** Start with the title, the title should be written in capital letters. The title should be underlined if hand written and bold if type. The title should relate with the topic or subject given. Think of the number of words if it is given.
2. **Introduction** which relates to the title i.e. defines, explains the key words from the title.
3. **Main body:** This is the main part of the composition. Discuss your ideas in point in relation to the topic or subject given, planned. The main ideas should precede the minor ideas. Consider the logical arrangement of your ideas and points.
4. **Conclusion:** Under this part, you may give suggestions, views, opinions on the topic discussed. It should reflect the whole content discussed in your essay.

There are various types of composition, namely:

1. **Narrative composition/essay;** that account or give stories of events.
2. **Expository composition/essay;** that explain something with facts, as opposed to opinion.
3. **Descriptive composition/essay;** are concerned with describing objects, experience or ideas.
4. **Argumentative/persuasive composition/essay;** are written to present on opinions which either favors or disagrees with a controversial topic.

ESSAY WRITING;

Is generally speaking a written composition containing an expression of one's personal experience, opinions or ideas on a subject.

Main parts of an essay;

1. **Introduction;** in this section you should introduce your view or main theme. It is usually written in the first paragraph.
2. **Body of an essay;** in this section you should describe your view or opinion in your own way, in this way you should prepare the body of an essay.
3. **Conclusion;** in this section you should give your conclusion but not in more than one paragraph. Try to give effective conclusion.

Example;
A RAILWAY JOURNEY

Our school closed for summer vacation on 15th May 2016. My father decided to take us to Nainital. My uncle lives there. We packed our luggage, hired a taxi and reached the station in time. We easily got our seats as we had got them reserved. The train was to start at 7 a.m.

At exact seven the guard blew the whistle. He waved the green flag and the train started. Soon it gathered speed. I amused myself by looking out of the window.

The scenery outside was charming. We were passing over the ponds, tanks and rivers. There were green fields on the way. While passing through fields I was feeling the freshness in the air. All the houses, huts, trees and bushes seemed wheeling back.

The journey from Ihansi to Nainital was very pleasant. The weather was cool and pleasant. After two hours we reached Nainital. Uncle had come to receive us. We stepped down. It had been a pleasant journey. We enjoyed every moment of it.

INVITATION CARDS;

Are those one which people normally send to their friends or relatives to invite them to a certain functions or parties.

Tips for writing a post card;

1. Write day or date at the top.
2. Depending on our relationship you can begin with Dear…. A first name or just initials.
3. Sentences can be short and informal language is appropriate.
4. Write your name at the bottom.

Example;

Mr&Mrs Henry Morton have a great pleasure to invite Mr/Mrs/Mr&Mrs/Hon/Rev/Prof/Miss/Gregoryto the graduation ceremony of their beloved son Stanley Morton which will be held on 3rd May 2016 at Must hall from 4.00 p.m to 10.00p.m.

For those who will not attend
Contacts; 0749097883
07420978483

SPEECH;

Is a formal occasion when someone speaks to an audience. The someone whose job is to write speeches is known as speech writer. It may also denote a formal presentation on a given topic or subject. A speech may also refer to a formal faculty or act of speaking, expressing or describing thoughts, feelings or perceptions through the articulation of words. Speech is written first before presenting. Normally, speech can be presented during seminar, graduation, workshop, political campaigns, report, project presentations, religious speeches, meetings, public meeting, ceremonies and functions.

Structure of a speech;
1. Introduction.
2. Body.
3. Conclusion.

How to write a speech
1. Think on the purpose of the speech- why do you want to prepare a speech?
2. Think on the context and audience whom do you want to write a speech.
3. Plan for the heading/ title of your speech. The title/heading should be taken from the topic or subject given. It should relate with the event that takes place and requires a speech.
4. The title/heading should be very brief, clear and readable. It should be direct to the event/function that takes place.
5. Make a good introduction, starting with, greeting from the superior/guest of honor to the least people. Example; Honorable Guest of Honor,…,Your Excellency……,Secretary General…..Mr. president….., the highness…….., the majority……., etc. It will depend with the title/position of the guest of honor during the event.
6. After introduction/greeting, clarify a little bit about the event, clarify the function taking place.
7. The main body –concentrate on ideas as conveyed in the question/topic given, put each idea in a new paragraph giving examples and evidences. Observe a logical arrangement of ideas with good grammar.
8. If you have a guest of honour, address your speech to him/her, but if there is no a guest of honour and your speaking to general audience use the words'' ladies and gentleman —in every beginning of a new idea.
9. Use appropriate vocabulary.. Do not use contractions example; I'll, I don't, we've, I've, etc.Use link words/connectors such as besides, finally, moreover, despite, on top of that, etc.
10. Give your own suggestion / view opinions on what you have discussed in your speech.

Example;
DRUG ABUSE AND ITS EFFECTS ON NIGERIAN YOUTHS;

The Chairman, Chief, Special Guest of Honor, The President, The Presidents and Representatives of invited social clubs, Distinguished Guests, Ladies and Gentlemen.

I feel highly honored to have been chosen as one of the speakers at the 10th anniversary of this great club. The topic of this year's lecture is also a pointer to the fact that the blood of humanity runs in the veins. You will agree with me that the damage which drug is doing on Nigerian citizens is great. Seven out of every ten Nigerians are guilty of drug abuse one way to another but the youths are most affected.

The reasons given by these youths for taking to drugs are not tenable. Some, if asked, would still tell you that they feel. Some may even tell you that they are always moody if they are normal selves but will work better.

The effects of Drug abuse are limitless. It constitutes a hazard to the human race. Cigarettes and Indian hemp cause lung and kidney cancer. After a prolonged use youths run the risk of becoming thieves and high way robbers because the moment they become addicted.

The government should also be up and doing through the ministry of health in the campaign against drug abuse. The nation's youth will be grateful for a useful future while the old ones will go to their graves with the joy of leaving the world a better place.

Thank you very much indeed for the attention. Good evening.

DEBATE;

Is a formal occasion which consists/involves two parties such as opposer and proposer. Debate may be done in schools, community and other social contexts.

Example;

Imagine that you are in a debate club; argue for the topic "Trafficking of girls from rural to urban areas to be employed as house girls (house maids) should be stopped".

Answer;
TRAFFICKING OF GIRLS SHOULD BE STOPPED.

Mr Chairman, Secretaries, time keeper and the audience at large. Good evening. I feel honored to get this chance to support the motion that says trafficking of girls from rural to urban areas to be employed as house girls should be stopped by the following views;

To begin with, it leads to family separation. These girls who are transported most of them are usually young. The period for them staying in the town is not known. This long stay makes them to forget their homes, neglect their families and hence family separation.

Also, it is against human rights because these girls are obviously young and in town their labor a lot depending on their masters. This is simply termed as child labor which is totally against human rights.

Moreover, it creates an environment for mistreatment. These young girls are sometimes beaten by male members of the family as a situation which leads to mistreatment of these young girls.

Finally, in order to eradicate the trafficking of girls from rural to urban areas; the government should formulate laws which prohibiting the usage of young girls as house girls hence this will facilitate the eradication of child labor.

LETTER WRITING;

FRIENDLY LETTERS;

Refers to the kind of letters which use your thought and feelings to get something done both the content and the form of a letter say something for you and about you.

COMPONENTS OF FRIENDLY LETTER;

1. **The writer's address;** the writer must have an address and this could appear at the top right hand corner.
2. **The date;** it is important in any document including letters and it could be written in several ways e.g. 30th June 2008.
3. **The salutation;** in writing letters to friends, relatives and loved ones, the salutation is usually Dear….
4. **The body of the letter;** after the salutation, you can start the letter with a form of greeting which you know the addressee will be happy with.
5. **Ending of the letter;** you can end the letter by asking about some familiar names or people that you have not asked at the beginning of the letter.

Example;

AZANIA SEC SCHOOL,

P.O.BOX 9074,

DAR ES SALAAM.

12th DECEMBER 2008.

Dear mother,

It is my hope that you are doing well. It's been a long time since I last wrote to you. I am generally fine and continue with my studies. By the way, we will close school for a short holiday this Saturday till early April. I ask that you to send me some money for a bus fare from school.

Please send me the money very soon so that I may pay the transport officers. Greetings to brothers Jorum and Maven and sisters Jacky and Joan, as well as all my friends.

I hope to see you during holiday and pray for you with best wishes.

Your loving son,
Henry Morton.

APPLICATION LETTER

This is an official letter which should always be completed, logically planned, clearly and politely expressed in grammatically correct and accepted English.

COMPONENTS OF APPLICATION LETTER;

1. **Sender's address;** this is placed at the top right hand corner of the sheet of paper in which the letter is written.
2. **Date;** the date of the letter is written normally placed one line after last line of the sender's address.
3. **Recipient's address/receiver's address;** this is placed on the left hand-side of the paper.
4. **Salutation;** begins of the page and is placed one line under the last line of the recipient's address.
5. **Heading;** it is useful to put heading at the top of your letter so that your recipient can see immediately what the letter is about.
6. **The body;** this is the main part of the letter bearing content.
7. **Closing greeting;** this comes after the last paragraph of the body.
8. **Signature of the writer;** this is placed one line after and under the closing greeting.
9. **Name of the writer;** this followed after the signature of the writer.

Example

ZANAKI SEC SCHOOL,
P.O.BOX 123,
DAR ES SALAAM.
22ND JULY 2016

GENERAL MANAGER,
MTWARA WATER AUTHORITY,
P.O.BOX 8877,
MTWARA.

Dear sir/madam
RE; APPLICATION FOR THE POST OF SECRETARY
With reference to the heading above which was advertised recently in the newspaper that I learned about that position and so I write in response.

I am a Diploma holder of Secretarial courses at Mwalimu Nyerere College in Dar es Salaam. I have worked as a secretary in an NGO in Dar es Salaam for two years after receiving my Diploma hence I have an experience on this field. The certificates to prove this plus other qualifications I have indicated in my CV will be attached with letter.

I have considerable working experience which makes me feel confident about the fact.
I will be very pleased to get job with a good and accurate company.

Yours faithfully,
A. Morton
Angela Morton.

Example 2

P.O.BOX 777,
DAR ES SALAAM.
8TH OCTOBER 2014

GENERAL MANAGER,
KARUME KENGE COMPANY LTD,
P.O.BOX 777,
DAR ES SALAAM.

Dear sir/madam

RE; A REQUEST FOR PERMISSION

With reference to the heading above my name is Calvin Donavan; I am an employee in your company at the technology department. I am kindly asking for your permission for two days off work due to the following reason;

My son is very ill and he is admitted at Muhimbili Hospital since he is suffering from ulcer ache. I am kindly asking for this permission so as to provide my support for him during his operation.

It is my hope that my request will be permitted.

Yours faithfully,
C.Donavan
Calvin Donavan.

LETTERS TO THE NEWSPAPER EDITOR;

Theseshould always be addressed to the Editor and they usually end with yours faithfully.

THE FORMAT OF LETTER TO THE EDITOR (COMPONENTS OF LETTER TO THE EDITOR)

1. The name and address of the receiver.
2. Salutation.
3. Subject/ short heading.
4. The main body.
5. The ending.

Example;

Editor,
Mwananchi Newspaper,
P.O.BOX 2020,   22nd July 2016
Tabata-Dar es Salaam

Dear Editor,

WATER PROBLEM AT BUSEGWE VILLAGE

I would like to take this opportunity to appreciate the good work of your Newspaper that has been doing in keeping the public informed and educated on different socio-political and economic matters.

Although I am a regular reader of Mwananchi newspaper, it is my first time to appear in this column to express my deep concerns on the problem of water in our village. Busegwe village is located just a few kilometers from Lake Victoria. Nevertheless, since independence the problem of water has never been solved.

In my opinion, if really the leaders were serious enough about the welfare of their citizens, there is no way that they would fail to supply piped water to the village which is located just few kilometers from the largest lake in Africa.

I would like to advice our MP to stand up for this and see it that water is supplied to our village or else we are not going to re-elect him in the forth coming general election.

Yours faithfully,

Son James

A peasant

P.B.OX 1820,

BUSEGWE-MUSOMA

E-mail; sjames@gmail.com

Contacts; 0768909192

CHAPTER 5

INTERPRETATING OF LITERARY WORK

THE THEORY OF LITERATURE
Meaning of Literature

Here is no single definition that suits the meaning of literature. As a result there have been various attempts to define the term literature. Some of these attempts are;

- **Literature**is the work of art that uses the language creatively to portray the message to the intended audience.
- **Literature**is a work of art that uses the language creatively to express human realities to the society.

IMPORTANT KEY TERMS IN THE DEFINITION OF LITERATURE

- **Imagination**, literature is said to be an imaginative work because what we read is the creation of an artist. It is the result of someone's imagination.
- **Art**, literature is said to be a work of art because it involves creativity in presenting it. The artist may use creative characters and incidence to make his or her work succeeded
- **Language**; is another important term in the definition of literature. There is the creative way of using language through figures of speech to make it different from other works of writing. Literature and language are inseparable.
- **Social reality,** literature does not develop into vacuum; it tells things that happen in our society politically, socially and economically.

CHARACTERISTICS OF LITERATURE

1. It uses language so as to deliver the intended message to the readers.
2. It has form and content.
3. It has its origin and development.
4. It touches the whole sphere of life.
5. It is usually suggestive.
6. It is imaginative.
7. It expresses thoughts and feelings.
8. It reveals hidden facts.

TYPES OF LITERATURE

Literature can be categorized into major two types, which are;
   a) Oral literature.
   b) Written literature.

ORAL LITERATURE

Refers to the type of literature that is delivered by means of mouth. It is presented orally or in spoken form. Oral literature is made by different elements such as *proverbs, recitation, songs, chants, lullabies, myth, folktale, riddle, legend, idioms, fable, anecdote.*

1. **PROVERB;** Is a well known phrase or sentence that gives advice or say something that is generally true. Proverbs are also termed as philosophical statements. Example *Hurry hurry has no blessings. Little by little fills the purse.*

51

2. **SONG;** Refers to the set of words put in music form. Songs are sung on special incidents like wedding ceremony, harvest ceremony, etc.
3. **RECITATION** - Refers to the act of saying a piece of poetry before an audience.
4. **CHANTS** – These are prayer songs sung for religious purposes.
5. **LULLABIES** – are songs to soothe children or babies.
6. **MYTH** – are stories talk about how different things originated example how death came to earth, why animals live the way they do.
7. **FOLKTALE**- is a very old traditional story from a particular place that was original passed on to people in a spoken form.
8. **RIDDLES** – refers to a puzzle that is set in order to make somebody discover the hidden meanings. Example "We are three in our family".
9. **ANECDOTE** –is a brief story about an interesting, amusing or strange event. Writers tell anecdote or include them in a larger work, to entertain the readers or to make a point.
10. **EPIC** –is a long narrative poem, about the adventures of a hero, whose actions reflect the ideals and values of a nation or a group. Epics address universal concerns such as good and evil, life and death, and other serious subjects. One of the famous epics in African literature is "The Epic of Sundiata"
11. **FABLE**- is a brief story or poem usually with animal characters that teaches a lesson or a moral about life. Or is a very brief story in prose or verse that teaches a moral, or a practical lesson about how to get along in life. The moral is usually stated at the end of the fable. E.g. what goes around comes around' or 'do unto others what you would have them do unto you.'
12. **FOLK TALE** – is a story composed orally and then passed from person to person by word of mouth. Or it is a simple story that has been passed down from generation to generation by word of mouth. Folk tales are usually about ordinary people, animals, or occurrences in nature and are usually set in time long past. They originated from people who could neither read nor write. These people entertained one another by telling stories aloud – often dealing with heroes, adventure, magic, or romance. E.g. "why monkeys live in Trees"
13. **LEGEND** – is a widely told story about the past – one that may or may not have a foundation in fact. Or is a story that is handled down from the past and may tell about something that really happened, or someone who really lived. Legends usually mix facts and fictions. Every culture has its own legends that mean its familiar traditional stories.
14. **PARABLE**- a short story that teaches a moral or spiritual lesson, especially one of those told by Jesus as recorded in the Bible. E.g. the 'Prodigal son', 'the sower', 'The Rich man and Lazarus' etc.
15. **BALLAD** – is a song-like narrative poem that tells a story, often one dealing with adventure and romance. Most ballads are written in four – six – line stanzas and have regular rhythms and rhyme scheme. A ballad often features a refrain – a regularly repeated line or group of lines at the end of each stanza as in "A freedom Song by M. O Macgoye". Originally ballads were not written down. They were composed orally and then sung. A person who sings or writes ballads is called a **balladeer**
16. **TALL TALE** -this is an exaggerated far-fetched story that is obviously untrue but is told as though it should be believed. Most tall tells are humorous. As tales are passed on, they often get taller and taller – more and more exaggerated.

17. IDIOMS – a group of words whose meaning is different from the meaning of individual words. Example "Don't let the cat out of the bag" To tell a secret by a mistake.

WRITTEN LITERATURE

This is a type of literature that presents the message through/ in written form. This began with the invention of writings. This has two major forms. Fiction and non-fiction

NON-FICTION LITERATURE

This is a kind of literature that deals with factual materials or events. The people written about in non-fictions are real. Literary non fictions are written to be read just the same way as fictions. These include;

- **Autobiography.** This is an account of someone's life and experiences written by himself/herself. The person may choose to tell about an important event from his/her life or tell the whole life story up to the time when it is written. Forms of autobiography are; personal narratives, journals, memoirs, diaries, letters etc. Autobiographies are almost always written in the first person I. Example; "Gifted Hands" by Ben Carson and "The Narrative of Frederick Douglas: An American Slave. Written by himself.
- **Biography.** This is a story of someone's life and experiences written by another person. In biographies the author may choose to interview the biographical subject and also gather information from other sources. The subjects of Biographies are often famous people. E.g. Lincoln: A Photo biography. A biographer is one who writes, composes or produces a biography.
- **Essay.** This is a short piece of writing in which the writer shares his/her point of view about a certain subject. Or is a short work of non-fiction that usually deals with a single subject. Essays can be classified as formal and informal, personal or impersonal. A formal essay is highly organized, thoroughly researched, and serious in tone. An informal essay is lighter in tone and usually reflects the writer's feelings and personality.
- **Informational articles.** These are articles that present factual materials about a specific subject. They appear in newspapers, magazines, and in reference books like Encyclopedias, almanacs, and atlases.

FORMS OF NON-FICTION

Nonfiction is broken down into four kinds of writing.
- **Exposition.** This is a writing that explains something or gives information about a topic.
- **Persuasion or argumentation.** This is a writing that attempts to convince you of something by showing you that the statement is true or false.
- **Description.** Is a writing that helps you to form a clear mental picture of something. Writers use specific details such as shapes, tastes, sounds and textures to help you form the picture.
- **Narration.** A writing that tells a story of an event or series of events.

ORGANISATION OF NON-FICTION

There are three parts to most nonfiction writing.
1. **Introduction.** It tells you the main ideas of what the piece is about. It may also give background material or state a problem.
2. **The body.** It develops the main idea through the details that support the main idea.

3. **Conclusion.** It shows that the work is ended. The conclusion may restate or summarize the author's main ideas, it may answer the question raised in the work or it may urge the reader to future actions.

FICTION

It is a kind of literature that deals with non factual materials or events. Characters, setting and events are the product of imaginations from the author. It can be inspired by the actual events or completely made up.

The differences between fiction and non-fiction;

1. Fiction uses imaginative language that involves the use of figures of speech while non-fiction does not use figurative language.
2. Fiction describes imaginary events while non-fiction describes real things e.g. Arusha Declaration.
3. Fiction aimed to entertain rather than informing while non-fiction aimed to inform people about what happened.
4. Fiction works of arts do not follow the rules of grammar while non-fiction follows the rules of grammar.
5. Fiction uses imaginary characters while non-fiction involves the use of real characters.
6. Fiction based on the writers' choice while non-fiction writing the writer is not free to write what he/ she wants.

GENRES OF FICTION LITERATURE
PROSE FICTION

A prose is any kind of writing that is not poetry or that is not presented in verse form or stanza. It is a specifically imaginative work that includes short stories, novella and novels.

SHORT STORY

This is a story usually about imaginative characters and events that is short enough to be read from the beginning to the end without stopping. It is also a brief work of fiction that can generally be read in one sitting. It usually focuses on one or two main characters that face a single problem or conflict. E.g. The voter by C. Achebe, Ajaiyi and the Witchdoctor by A. Tutuola, Mabala the Farmer by R. Mabala Etc

ELEMENTS OF A SHORT STORY

There are four basic elements of a short story. These are; Setting, plot, characters and theme. Short stories differ from the novel in its treatment of these four elements. The main difference is partly dictated by length. In short stories characters are usually not fully developed and usually centre on one idea. Other minor elements include conflict, point of view, symbolism, flashbacks, fictitious quality etc.

FEATURES OF SHORT STORIES

1. Like novels, a short story is presented in narration i.e. a narrative work.
2. Short stories can be read in a single setting.
3. In short stories, the number of characters is smaller than in novels.
4. Incidents are fewer than those of novels.

5. Its plot is not complex.

- **NOVELLA**. This is a fiction work that is longer than a short story but shorter than a novel. It is longer than a short story but the characters are not fully developed as in novels. EXAMPLE; Samuel Beckett's novella First Love. In this episode the unnamed narrator, who spends most of the time lying prostrate on a park bench, begins to feel his privacy threatened by the visitations of a woman to the same bench.
- **NOVEL** is a work of fiction that is longer and more complex than a short story. Or it is a fictional prose usually consisting of more than fifty thousand words. (Probst, et al, 2000). In novels, setting, plot characters and theme are fully developed in great details. Like a short story the novel has four main elements, setting, plot characters and theme. A person who writes novels is called a novelist E.g. Passed like a shadow by B. Mapalala. The Interview, by P. Ngugi etc
- **DRAMA/PLAY;** Is a literary genre that tells a story through actions and dialogue and is written to be performed on stage by actors. Drama has the same elements as those in novels and short stories. i.e. setting, plot characters, theme, climax, conflict, symbolism, etc. An element that is unique to drama is

DRAMATIC TECHNIQUE; This includes:

- **Dialogue.** These are the words that the characters speak in a play. It is a conversation between characters. It is the dialogue that reveals the character's qualities, personality traits, and reactions to other characters.
- **Soliloquy/monologue.** This is a speech made by a character when he/she is alone on stage. Or it is a speech in which a character alone on stage, expresses her thoughts and feelings aloud for the benefit of the audience, often in a revealing way.

TYPES OF DRAMA

1. **Tragedy;** It is a serious drama/play with a sad ending especially one in which the main character dies. Theevents in a tragic plot are set in motion by a decision that is often an error in judgment. Succeedingevents are linked in a cause-and-effect relationship and lead inevitably to a disastrous conclusion,usually death. E.g. Oedipus the King, by Sophocles. Julius Caesar by W. Shakespeare, MfalmeJuha by F Topan etc.A person who writes tragedies for the theatre or an actor in a tragedy is called a tragedian. E.g.Sophocles, Shakespeare, etc
2. **Comedy;** It is a dramatic work that is intended to be funny, humorous and usually ends happily with apeaceful resolution of the main conflict. To achieve a comic effect sometimes the playwrights use mistaken identity. Sometimes certain characters are mistaken about their surroundings. They say or do things that would be appropriate in a different social situation but are inappropriate in their surroundings. The resulting confusion results to a silly series of events. The confusion of characters causes a ridiculous conflict. The climax arrives when the characters learn the truth. E.g. Juliette and Oko or Atangana and Abessolo in Three Suitors One Husband. Other examples of comedies are The trials of Brother Jero and The Lion and the Jewel both by W. Soyinka An entertainer who makes people laugh by telling jokes and funny stories is called a comedian/comedienne.

3. **Tragic comedy;** It is a dramatic work that combines the elements of tragedy and comedy but here the hero/heroine does not end in danger or death. A comic relief is a technique used to achieve this effect. This is a humorous scene that is inserted into a serious work of drama to provide relief from the seriousness felt by the audience.
4. **Melodrama;** A play that is full of exciting events and in which the characters and emotions seem tooexaggerated to be true/real. It is accompanied with a melody –hence melody drama (melodrama)
5. **Historical drama;** This is a type of drama that expresses the history of a particular society but usually contains some elements of tragedy and comedy. E.g. Dedan Kimathi by Ngugi, Kinjeketile by E.HusseinOther important terms in drama.
   - **Act.** This is a major unit/part of action in a drama or play.
   - **Scene.** This is a smaller section or a subdivision of one act. So a scene is a section presenting events that occur in one place at one time.
   - **Costume.** The clothes worn by actors in a play or film/movie or worn by somebody to make them look like somebody or something else. E.g. a student, a housemaid, a judge, etc
   - **Prop.** A small object used by actors, during the performance of a play or in a film/movie
   - **Audience.** Is a group of people sitting in a room, auditorium or in the theatre listening to and watching a performance.
   - **Theatre.** This is a special building or an outdoor area where plays/movies/films and other entertainments are performed.

FEATURES THAT DIFFERENTIATE DRAMA FROM OTHER LITERARY GENRES

1. **Drama is meant for stage performance.** Drama is written to be acted or staged by live actors to a live audience. And drama can be performed anywhere at any time. Other literary works like novels are written to be read and poems are written to be sung or recited.
2. **Drama is written in a dialogue form.** Since drama is meant for stage performance it is written / printed in dialogue or conversations form that makes it easier to be acted. However to make it live at some points the playwright may use monologues (soliloquies), poetic language, songs, or mime (dumb show).
3. **Drama is divided into form of Acts and Scenes.** An act is a major unit of action in a play and a scene is a smaller section or a subdivision of one act. Once act may have several scenes each carrying one event. Other works like novels are divided in forms of parts/chapters and paragraphs while poems are divided into verses and stanzas.
4. **Drama has stage direction.** These are the instructions or notes which describe how the work is to be staged/performed. These show areas of the stage where the characters sit, stand, when they leave or enter, how the dress, time of the day, when the curtain rise and fall etc. Other works of literature do not include stage direction because they are not meant to be performed.
5. **Drama has a strong influence to the audience.** Drama allows the audience participation since people are attracted by actions drama has a strong influence than other literary works. People are tempted to live or act imitating the life and actions of the characters. Also the audience can participate by clapping, laughing, screaming, frowning, or responding as the actors involve them.

6. **Drama makes extensive use of 1st person pronoun (I, me, we and us).** Since drama is meant to be acted by actors, most characters speak from the first person point of view. (I, me, we or us). Other works like novels make extensive use of 3rd person (he, she it, they).

7. **Drama uses shorter time in performance than novels.** It takes only two to three hours to what a performance but it takes days or weeks to finish reading one novel. This makes drama more appealing to the audience since it is time considerate.

8. **Drama is characterized by action.** When drama is presented on the stage it involves actions that are carried out by characters. Characters can fight, make love, laugh, cry, etc. all these add effect to the livelihood of drama and make it more appealing to the audience.

9. **Drama has language economy.** Words are not wasted in drama. The playwrights usually choose the suitable words that express their intended meaning. Most plays are very short as compared to novels. For example Soyinka's 'The trials of Brother Jero' and Ngugi's 'This Time Tomorrow' are very short but with strong messages.

10. **Drama involves many people in its production.** For the drama to be staged many people are involved unlike novels and poems which can be produced by the authors only. In production of a drama there should be actors/actresses, the director, floor manager or location manager, production manager, designer (costumes and makeup) etc. on top of that there should be the live audience.

11. **Drama involves imitation of real life events.** Or it reflects the experiences of Human kind like other literary works Drama is a product of the society. Drama imitates the real life events and brings them on stage. This makes drama t be more meaningful to the audience.

12. Drama can be performed anywhere and/or any time.

13. Drama brings the whole world on stage.

FEATURES THAT DIFFERENTIATE NOVELS FROM OTHER GENRES

1. **Novels are written in prose form.** The novels are presented in form of prose narratives applying ordinary grammatical structure and natural flow of speech rather than rhythmic structure as in poetry. Although there may be lines of verses inserted for various effects, when this occurs, it is clear that the verse portion is distinct from the rest of the narrative.

2. **Novels are written to be read.** Novels are not to be acted as in case of plays or to be recited as in case of poems. This is chiefly because novels don't have stage directions showing how it should be staged.

3. **Novels are divided in terms of Parts/Chapters and paragraphs.** Since the novels are meant to be read, their divisions are in form of paragraphs, chapters and/or parts. Other works like plays are divided into acts and scenes while poems are in form of verses and stanzas.

4. **Novels make extensive use of third person point of view.** Since novels are written in prose they mostly use third person point of view because either the author or a character in the story narrates the story. Unlike plays which make extensive use of 1st person point of view.

5. **Novels are longer than other literary genres.** In other words, they have no word economy. The shortest is approximated to contain between 60,000 to 70,000 words and the longest coming in around 200,000. So it can take many days or weeks to finish

reading one novel while it takes minutes or few hours to watch a drama or to listen to a poem.

6. **One novel can tell multiple stories.** Some novels break with tradition and avoid conventional plot structure, either by telling multiple stories that are interwoven involving characters that are not directly related, by utilizing a highly imaginative formula of story within a story.

7. **Another distinguishing feature of a novel is innovation.** Even the name (from Latin Novellus means young and new) of a literary form indicates that its contents should be something on the cutting-edge of literature evolution. Indeed the novel has seen countless adaptations over the years and continues to evolve constantly, unlike some other literary formats that have remained frozen in their development. (i.e haikus, or Shakespearian sonnets)

8. **In novels characters and plot are highly developed.** The length and realistic elements of the novel allow for deeper and broad development of characters and their circumstances. Novels are long enough to support many participants, even group of participants in the actions of the story. Novelists have much more room to fresh-out each individual more fully than other literary artists.

9. **Another distinguishing feature of a novel is publication practices.** Historically, one of the most popular ways to publish one's work has been either to collect it in similar works in anthologies, or to print it in another media (i.e. magazine, newspaper, or other periodicals) as a serial, or sequentially segmented piece distributed over time. But the size and complexity of many novels make it difficult to publish them in any other way than as their own independent, self-contained works.

POETRY

Is the composition that arouses emotion and imagination by using the figurative language to create a specific emotion through its meaning. It involves the use of rhyme, imagery, metaphor, symbols, onomatopoeia, meta and repetition.

TERMS USED IN POETRY.

1. **Poem**– is the piece of writing characterized by strong imagination, significant meaning and appropriate language.
2. **Poet**– is a person who writes or composes a poem.
3. **Verse**– Is a line in a stanza. Several verses make a stanza.
4. **Stanza** – is the group of verses forming part of a poem.
5. **Persona**– is the person who speaks in a poem.
6. **Tone**– refers to the persona's state of mind (attitude) in relation to what is being talked about. There are times when the persona sounds angry, happy, and lovely or friend.
7. **Rhyme**– is the similarity of sounds at the end of consecutive lines or at the same interval in a stanza. Example life/wife, grand/band.
8. **Rhythm**– refers to the pattern of stresses and pauses that link words in a unit. Rhythm is affected by the presence of stressed and unstressed syllable.
9. **Rhyme scheme**– is the specific order of rhymes shown by using letters of alphabets example ab/ab, ef/ef, aa/bb etc.
10. **Poetic license**– is the permission granted to poets to manipulate language to suit the poetic needs example ''Came they to us'' instead of "They came to us."

11. **Refrain**– is a word or stanza or line that is repeated at the end of each stanza in a poem. Example in the poems "I love you my Gentle One" and "A freedom Song", refrain has been employed.
12. **Alliteration** – is the repetition of initial identical consonant at close interval in a poetic line example, "*delicate diplomatic duties*"
13. **Consonance**– refers to the repetition of consonants at the end of words in a poetic line. **Example;** *we don't need any kid*
    Food is not wood.
    Set your foot here.
14. **Assonance** – refers to the repetition of similar vowel sounds in stressed syllables that end with different consonant sounds. Example ' *'I like the dike Mike hide*"
15. **Onomatopoeia** – is the use of words that suggest meaning through the sound contained. Example the use of words like "tick–tock" which suggest the sound of a clock.
16. **Ellipsis** – refers to the intentional omission of some words done by the poet. Normally, functional words such as prepositions, auxiliary verbs, conjunctions as well as determiners are the ones which fall under this category.
17. **Diction**– refers to the choice and arrangement of words in a given literary work.

TYPES OF POEMS

Poems are broadly classified into two types which include the following;
1. Traditional poems.
2. Modern poems

1. **TRADITIONAL POEMS;** Are those which strictly follow ancient poetic principle. These poems are actually the ones that make sure that rules such as balance in the number of words per stanza, rhyming and rhythm are strictly followed.
2. **MODERN POEMS;** Are the poems which follow only some poetic principle and ignore others. Most of modern poems are free verse poems. Free verse poems are a category of poems that do not rhyme.

FURTHER CLASSIFICATION OF POEMS

Apart from the above classification i.e Traditional and Modern poems, there are other ways of classifying poem as a result there are many types of poems.
1. **Narrative poems;** Are long poems used to explain a story about a certainsociety. They are presented like a story, example"MajiMaji" by Yusuph Kassim and Song Of Lawino by Ocol.
2. **Lyric poems;** Are poems which concentrate on the expression ofemotions or feelings. Example of a poem which falls inthis category is "I love You my Gentle One".
3. **Didactic poems;** Are poems designed to give instruction to readers.Poems of this kind tell readers what to do. So, thepoems are intended to move readers so that they mayact in some ways. Example "Your Pain" by ArmandoGuebuza
4. **Epic poems;** Are poems deal with actions of great men and womenor history of a nation. Example, a composed to praisegreat deeds of the first president of Tanzania who ledthe people of Tanganyika in their struggle forindependence will be of epic poem.
5. **Ode;** Are poems that either address a person / thing or celebrate an event. Example a poem composed at one's wedding may fall in this category.

6. **Elegy;** Are lyric poems that express sadness about someonewho has died. When someone dies, people mourn.Poems composed for mourning or praising someonewho has died are called elegy.
7. **Ballad;** Are dialogue like poems, there are two or more people speaking to each other in turns. They are also called dramatic poems because they are presented like drama. Example the poem called "Ballad of the Landlord" by Langstone Hughes.
8. **Sonnet;** Are lyric poems that contain fourteen lines in two stanzas. The first stanza is normally made of eight lines (octet) and the second stanza is made of six lines (sestet).

FEATURES OR CHARACTERISTICS OF POETRY
Poetry differs from other genres of literature, the features include the following.
1. It is arranged in lines and stanza, while other genres are arranged in chapters' example novels, scenes and acts example plays.
2. Poetry is very economical in words in language use. It uses few words but convey a lot of information.
3. Poetry occurs occasionally compare to other prose which are daily used.
4. Poetry is more rhythmical i.e it makes much use of musical devices such as rhyme, rhythm and various types of repetition example refrain, alliteration, assonance, consonance and anaphora.
5. It uses words connotatively more than being denotatively while other forms denotation is more used than connotation.
6. Poetry uses persona while other genres use characters, example in novels and plays.
7. Poetry is very rich in figures of speech such as simile, metaphor and personification compare to other works.

THE DIFFERENCES BETWEEN ORAL AND WRITTEN LITERATURE
1. Oral literature is presented or delivered through the words of mouth while written literature involves writings and it is presented in written document.
2. Oral literature is not selective i.e both literate and illiterate ones are involved and enjoy it. It is the property of the whole society while written literature is selective, only educated ones are involved. It is not the property of the whole society.
3. Oral literature must be done when there is an audience i.e. the speaker and the Hearer while written literature can be done even by one person i.e the writer.
4. Oral literature is older than written literature .Oral literature was there even during the time of ancestors and transmits from generation to generation orally while written literature is not old; it came after the invention of science and technology.
5. Oral literature is flexible i.e it can undergo changes easily in the course of speaking while written literature is not flexible and cannot undergo changes easily.
6. Oral literature is less expensive, it does not need any cost when somebody speaks while written literature is expensive and it is presented by using written documents. One needs to buy things like pens, papers or text books to achieve it.

SIMILARITIES BETWEEN ORAL AND WRITTEN LITERATURE
1. They both use language. In oral literature language is used in spoken form while in written literature language is used in written form.

2. They both use characters. In telling story one can use animals as characters example fable, while in written work an artist can use characters by using human names example Baroka, Sidi and Lakunle.
3. They both criticize bad behavior, Oral literature through fable, myth and folk tales creates moral lesson especially to children while written literature through novels, plays and poetry, the wrongs of the society such as corruption and child labor can be criticized.
4. They both reveal social realities; they say something which comes from the society. They do not develop into vacuum.
5. They both entertain the society. Oral literature through songs and proverbs one can be entertained while in written literature such as poetry one can enjoy the figures of speech.

THE IMPACTS OF SCIENCE AND TECHNOLOGY TOWARDS ORAL LITERATURE
When it comes to technology one should think of technological devices such as Radio, Television, Computer, Tapes Recorder and shooting Video. These devices have big impacts on literature particularly on Oral literature.
1. Technology has changed mode of presentation, before science and technology people used to meet face to face between an artist and the audience. This is not the case today because it can be presented through Television, Radio, DVD AND CD.
2. Before the invention of science and technology, literature was stored by using human head, technology has changed the mode of storage to Tape Recorder, CD and DVD.
3. It is not flexible. This means when oral is recorded; it does not undergo changes easily.
4. The cost has been increased because of recording, shooting and distribution.
5. The ownership has been shifted from the society to individuals like artists and buyers.
6. There is a delay of feedback.
7. It has changed the medium.

ART;
Refers to the way something is done. It involves the use of skill and imagination in the creation of aesthetic objects, environments or experiences that can be shared. Literature is an imaginative work of art that uses language to reflect social realities.

Why is literature said to be an art?
1. **Language use.** The language of literature is different from the language of everyday use (normal language). Literature uses figures of speech and words are assigned an extra meaning than what they ordinarily imply. Some words carry literal meaning and others have symbolic meaning. It is therefore advised not to take words for granted in literature. You need to dig a bit deeper before you settle and say this is what it means.
2. **Characters and characterization.** Literature uses real people or other characters that represent real people in the outside world. Inanimate beings may be personified in a way that they represent human qualities and act accordingly. This adds artistic effect to the literary work. (more details are given in subsequent chapters)
3. **Choice and presentation of incidents.** Literature is not just a collection of facts and stories to be reported. Incidents in literature are presented in artistic way that makes the audience think that they are actually happening. There is the use of skilful narrative technique like point of view, flashbacks, foreshadowing, suspense, etc all these help the

readers to visualize the events as though they are just unfolding before their eyes. (more details are given in subsequent chapters)

4. **The link between the titles and content is an art** because can enable the literary artist to deliver the intended message to the audience.
5. **The use of technique;** like flashbacks and ironies, which all involves the use of skills.
6. **It involves imagination;** because the writers create the story through imagination to reflect what is happening in our society.

The similarity between literature and other works of art;
1. Both involve creation of imagination.
2. Both involve skills.
3. Both create employment.
4. All educating.
5. All express social and physical realities.
6. Both involve the expression of emotions.
7. Both transmit culture from one generation to another.
8. Both involve creation of beauty.

Differences between literature and other works of arts;

1. Literature involves many techniques like narrative technique and symbolism.
2. Literature has many forms such as poetry, drama and novels.
3. Literature is either written or spoken text while other works of arts are neither spoken nor written.
4. Literature uses language as its medium of its representation while works of arts like painting do not use language as its media.
5. Literature is divided into form and content, something which does not exist to other works of arts.
6. The target messages in literature are represented through character while other works of art do not have what we call characterization.
7. Literature carries a lot of message as compared to other works of art.

Why is literature said to reflect social realities?

Social realities are the things that human beings experience in their daily lives. It is not mandatory that all the incidents discussed in one literary work should be found in one society all the time. Some issues become relevant and exist across time and space and later become obsolete. So the themes that were once relevant in one society may be irrelevant in the same society as time passes by. Likewise, the themes that are relevant in one part of the world may be irrelevant at another part of the world. However, there are issues like corruption, classes, humiliation, betrayal, FGM, HIV/AIDS.

- **Aside.** This is a direct address of the audience by a character. The other characters do not hear what is being said.
- **Stage direction.** These are the instructions/notes included in a play/drama which describe how the work is to be performed or staged. They indicate areas of the stage in which actors sit, stand, move, speak, exit, enter, and so on, lighting, music, sound effect,

costumes, emotional state, etc. These are typed in italics and enclosed in the parentheses or brackets.

ELEMENTS OF LITERATURE;

1. **FORM**; It is the artistic technique in which the work of art is made. It is the superstructure or general appearance of the literary work. Form includes elements like setting, title, plot, characterization, style, point of view, suspense and figurative language.
   a) **SETTING;** Refers to the time and place where the events found take place. If the place where events are told is truly geographically located, it gives the type of setting called *real setting*, if the case is otherwise; it gives the type of setting called *imaginary setting*.
   b) **TITLE;** Refers to heading or name of a literary work. If it relates with the content, it is called *direct title.* If the heading does not relate with the content, it is referred to *indirect or ironic title.*
   c) **PLOT;** is the arrangement or organization of events in a novel or play. It might be *chronological plot* if the events are arranged in order or series basing on the way they occur. It might be **non –chronological plot (flashback),**if the events are not arranged chronologically i.e when the events are arranged in such a way the last incident is placed first. **Foreshadowing** – is the technique by which the hint of action which will happen later in a story is given.

ELEMENTS OF PLOT STRUCTRURE OR DRAMATIC STRUCTURE OF PLOT
This was established by Gustav Freytag (1816 - 1895), a German dramatist and novelist. He came up with the structure for the way stories are told in ancient Greek and Shakespearean drama. This analysis is known as **Freytag's analysis**. His analysis consisted of dividing a play Into FIVE parts:
- **Exposition;** This is the introduction of story - background information that one needs to understand it. Thisinformation can include the protagonist, antagonist, the setting and so forth. The **inciting incident** occurs here - the initial event which triggers the rest of the story.
- **Rising Action;** Rising action is what occurs leading up to the climax. It is the part of dramatic action that has todo with complication. This part begins as the opposing ideas or groups come into conflicts andproceeds to the climax. It can also be called the complication.
- **Climax;** The climax is considered the turning point of the action. It is the most exciting part of the story.This is where all the rising action and conflict building up in the story finally reaches the peak. Itis usually the moment of greatest danger or decision-making for the protagonist.
- **Falling Action**; the falling action deals with events which occur right after the climax. These events are usually the after-effects of the climax. It often exhibits the winding down of the climax.
- **Resolution/Denouement**; Here is the end of the falling action and the conclusion to the story. There is usually a release of dramatic tension and anxiety (also known as **catharsis**). It can also be the portion at the end of the plot that reveals the final outcome of its conflicts or the solution of its mysteries.

d) **CHARACTERIZATION**; is the process of giving attributes to characters. The way an artist presents and reveals characters. A character is a person or thing that is given a role to play in a literary work. Characters are imaginary people create and use them to carry message.

TYPES OF CHARACTERS

- **Major or main character** is the character who dominates the literary work; he or she is found from the beginning of the novel to the end of the novel or play.
- **Minor character** is the character that assists the main character to convey the message. A minor character occurs once or occasionally.
- **Static character** is the character that does not change behavior in the work of art. Static character is alternatively known as rigid or conservative character.
- **Dynamic character** is the character that changes behavior very easily. A dynamic character is also called flexible or developing character.
- **Protagonist character** is the main character that the readers admire; when this character gets trouble the readers pity him or her. Sometime a protagonist is called a hero.
- **Antagonist character** is the character that is in opposition with the protagonist. He or she is the character whom the readers hate.
- **Flat character,** is the type of character who is one dimensional, he or she is shallow or thin and he has not got depth. He or she is also called a wooden character.
- **Round character** is the type of character who is a multi – dimensional one, he or she is a complex one given different attributes.

e) **STYLE**; Refers to the way an author presents his or her work in a manner that makes him or her differs from other authors. It is the individuality of the author. Style is achieved through the choice of vocabulary, use of certain figures of speech, oral literary devices such as idioms, proverbs and songs.

f) **LANGUAGE USE/DICTION;** This refers to the writer's or speaker's choice of words. People use different types of words depending on the audience they are addressing, the subject they are discussing and the effect they are trying to produce. Diction is an essential element of a writer's style and has a major effect on the tone of the piece of writing.

- **SUSPENSE;** Is the technique of delaying an incident at the time the reader is eagerly following it. This is done to create enthusiasm.
- **POINT OF VIEW;** Is an angle in which a story is told. It is dived into three parts namely; *First person point of view,* this is when the narrator is identified by the use of pronoun "I" or ''we'', *Third person point of view,* this is when the narration is affected by means of the pronouns "he" "she" and "they" and *Omniscient point of view* which means all knowing. An omniscient narrator is God - like in knowledge because he or she has even the ability to know the thoughts of characters.

2. **CONTENT**; the term content in literature refers to things that are contained in a literary work. The authors write to present themes, messages, conflict and philosophies that lead them to write what they write and influence the way they write.

a) **THEME**; This can be defined as a central or dominant idea in a literary work. A theme can be moral or evil be it social, political, economic, etc. Things such as corruption, true love, sacrifice, disappointment, humiliation, oppression, irresponsibility, patriotism and the like may be the themes in a literary work. Themes are not stated directly but implied by readers.

b) **MESSAGE**; Refers to what an audience or readers learn from the themes. Just like themes, messages are also created by readers themselves revealed through characters; they are not given directly in the text.

c) **PHILOSOPHY OR IDEOLOGY**; This can be defined as a system of principle and idea on which life/society is defined. Ideology is what makes us to analyze literary work and make value judgment on how characters relate with each other.

d) **CONFLICT**; this is misunderstanding between characters. If the conflict happens between one person and another, it is termed as *inter personal conflict* while the one that occurs within the soul of a person, it is referred to as *intra personal conflict*.**OTHER TYPES OF CONFLICTS**.

- Family conflicts.
- Religious conflicts.
- Political conflicts.
- Economic conflicts.

- **RELEVANCE**; this is the comparison of literary work with what is going on in the society. Normally the work of literature does not develop vacuum, it has something to do with our society. This means literature is relevant to our living society because whatever it talks of, we always come across with in life.
- **CRISIS**; brief period of time when a conflict rises to a point where resolution is necessary.
- **CLIMAX**; the movement when the crisis of the play or narrative reaches the highest point and is resolved.

FIGURATIVE LANGUAGE

This is writing or speech that is not meant to be taken literally. One has to dig deeper and uncover the underlying meaning. The many types of figurative language are known as figures of speech.

Why literary artists use figurative language in their works?
1. For explanatory purposes e.g. personification
2. To give emphasis over the message being communicated e.g. the use of repetition.
3. For challenging the minds of the reader.
4. For aesthetic beauty of the work.
5. To arouse readers feelings and imagination e.g. imagery
6. For communicating the message.

What is the importance of using local language in African literature?
1. It is the way of expressing African culture.
2. It is the way of promoting our languages.
3. It is the way of developing our languages.

4. It is comprehensive or easy to understand.
5. It encourages local people to engage in writing.

Functions of language in literature;
1. Language is used to communicate messages in literature.
2. Language creates beauty in a literary work.
3. Language is used to determine characters.
4. Language determines uniqueness of writers.
5. Language distinguishes literary genres.
6. Language expresses culture.

Relationship between literature and language;
1. Language is among of the elements of literature.
2. Language is the medium through which literature is represented.
3. Literature develops language.
4. Literature acts as content or material to be communicated through language.
5. Language makes literary work to be aesthetic.
6. Language makes literary work to be figurative.
7. Language makes literary work to be symbolic.
8. Language makes literary work to be imaginative.
9. Language distinguishes literary genres.
10. Language distinguishes the forms of literature.

How literature is the workshop of language;
1. It makes the language used to be popular.
2. It expands the grammar of a particular language.
3. It teaches people how to use language according to the situation.
4. Sometimes new pronunciation and spellings of words are invented.
5. It expands the vocabulary of a particular language.
6. It creates social classes in language according to the level of understanding.

FIGURES OF SPEECH
Definition:

- **Figure of Speech** is a word or group of words that describes one thing in terms of another and is not meant to be understood as literally true.
- **A figure of speech** is a word or phrase that departs from everyday literal language for the sake of comparison, emphasis, clarity, or freshness.
- Also known as, rhetorical figure, metaphorical language/ literary devices. Used well, figures of speech greatly enhance your fiction, and can be a very economical way of getting an image or a point across, but used incorrectly, they will confuse the reader. The special emphasis is typically accomplished by the user's conscious deviation from the strict literal sense of a word, or from the more commonly used form of word order or sentence construction. From ancient times to the present, such figurative locutions have been extensively employed by orators and writers to strengthen and embellish their styles of speech and composition. A number of the more widely used figures of speech, some of which are also called tropes, follow.

1. **Metaphor** is a figure of speech that makes a direct comparison between two unlike things without using the words "like or as". A metaphor suggests that one thing is another thing, or is equal to another thing. It uses a word or phrase denoting one kind of idea or object in place of another word or phrase for the purpose of suggesting a likeness between the two. Metaphors create vivid descriptions with few words, as the subject of the comparison takes on the qualities of the thing with which it is compared.
   - 'He was a lion in the fight'.
   - In the biblical Book of Psalms, the writer speaks of God's law as "A light to his feet and a lamp to his path."
   - "The LORD is my shepherd"

2. **A simile** is a figure of speech that makes a comparison between two unlike things and uses the words "like," "as," "than" or "resembles". Or Simile is specific comparison by means of the words "like" or "as" between two kinds of ideas or objects. Similes make descriptions vivid by comparing their subjects with known events or things. Effective similes help readers visualize what is being described. Examples,
   - As cool as a cucumber',
   - 'As white as snow',
   - 'Life is just like an ice-cream, enjoy it before it melts',
   - "Christianity shone like a beacon in the black night of paganism"

3. **Irony:** It is the expression of ideas which are exactly opposite to the implied meaning. Or Irony is a disagreement or incongruity between what is said and what is understood, or what is expected and what actually occurs. Irony can be used intentionally or can happen unintentionally. Authors can use irony to make their audience stop and think about what has just been said, or to emphasize a central idea. The audience's role in realizing the difference between what is said and what is normal or expected is essential to the successful use of irony.
   - 'A student of psychology going insane',
   - 'A bank lends you money provided you show that it's not needed'
   - Or the warning found on every cigarette pack, 'Smoking is injurious to health' is an irony!
   - For Example, Ibsen's An Enemy of the People is ironically used since Dr. Stockman who is declared an enemy, is in really sense, and is a friend of the people.
   - The son of the English teacher fails the English Exam.
   - The daughter of a rich merchant is expelled from school for lack of school fees of 20,000/=.

4. **Personification:** It is a representation of abstract ideas or inanimate objects as having human attributes or qualities. Or Personification is the representation of inanimate objects or abstract ideas as living beings. Personification connects readers with the object that is personified. Personification can make descriptions of non-human entities more vivid, or can help readers understand, sympathize with, or react emotionally to non-human characters.
   - 'Death laid its icy hands on kings',
   - "Necessity is the mother of invention

- "The mountains cried, the valleys wept, and the hills wailed all mourning the death of Nyerere.

5. **Apostrophe:** It is a direct address to the dead or an inanimate object creating an emotional surge. In Apostrophe, an actor turns from the audience, or a writer from readers, to address a person who usually is either absent or deceased, an inanimate object, or an abstract idea. As in John Donne's
   - "Death Be Not Proud"
   - 'Caesar, only if you were alive'
   - 'O stone, O might, O heart of man-made God, Thou art the emblem of our hope',

6. **Rhetorical question** is the act of asking questions not to gain information but just for emphasis. No answer, in fact, is expected by the speaker. The device is illustrated in the following series of sentences:
   - "Did you help me when I needed help? Did you once offer to intercede in my behalf? Did you do anything to lessen my load?"

7. **Hyperbole/overstatement** is a figure of speech in which the truth is exaggerated for emphasis or for humorous effect. In exaggeration a person or thing is depicted as being better or worse, or larger or smaller, than is actually the case. It is, used often to ridicule, create humor or any drastic emotional appeal.
   - 'The waves rose as high as the mountains,'
   - 'I am so hungry that I can eat a whole cow'
   - 'She wept and wept until there was a sea of tears'.

8. **Litotes/ understatement:** It is an understated expression when the actual idea to be expressed is quite significant. It is like downplaying an idea when it seems to be the best possible course of action or description. Statements such as,
   - 'I was not feeling unhappy". Meaning I was feeling happy
   - "The English poet Thomas Gray showed no inconsiderable powers as a prose writer, "meaning that Gray was in fact a very good prose writer
   - I am not unmindful- meaning I mind

9. **Euphemism,** this is the substitution of an offensive/unpleasant term or phrase by the one that has pleasant associations, as in the use of "lavatory" or "rest room" for "toilet," and "pass away" for "die."

10. **Metonymy** is a figure of speech that associates the name of one thing with that of something else. This is a word that substitutes for an object, the name of an attribute or concept associated to that object. The use of 'crown' for 'king' or for the government ruled by a king is an example of a metonym.
    - "We waited hopelessly for two sunsets"
    - "Sunsets" here implies two days,
    - "He has a good name in our society." Or,
    - "They spoilt his name." "Name" refers to reputation
    - "A press conference by the "Statehouse". Here, statehouse refers to the officials of the Statehouse who will be holding the press conference.

11. **Synecdoche:** is a figure of speech in which the whole is represented by a part or a part by the whole is called as synecdoche. Example
    - 'He has several mouths to feed'. Here mouths represent people.
    - "50 head of cattle; "head" is used to mean whole animals,

- "The president's administration contained the best "brains" in the country; "brains" is used for intellectually brilliant persons.

12. **Onomatopoeia,** imitation of natural sounds by words. Examples in English are the italicized words in the phrases
    - "The humming bee,"
    - "The cackling hen,"
    - "The whizzing arrow,"
    - "The buzzing saw."
    - The Hissing snake,
    - The Splashing water,
    - The Bang of a door.

13. **Oxymoron:** This is a figure of speech which includes words or ideas opposite in meaning placed one after the other. Oxymoron combines two seemingly contradictory or incongruous words.
    - 'True lies',
    - 'Open secret',
    - 'Pretty ugly face',
    - 'Feeling alone in a crowd',
    - Living deaths,
    - Dear wounds,
    - Fair storms,
    - Silent noise
    - Freezing fires
    - Pain for pleasure
    - Clearly confused
    - Cruel kindness

14. **Paradox,** this is a figure of speech which includes a statement or sentiment that appears contradictory to common sense yet is true in fact. Simply put it is a statement that seems to contradict itself but is, nevertheless, true. These statements or assertions, according to logic, cannot be true, yet the figure links them in a way that creates a new meaning, one that defies logic but works on situation. Example of paradox is found in Martin Luther's speech "I Have a Dream" "..The Negro is still languished in the corners of American society and finds himself an exile in his own land" In the above sentence, logically speaking, one cannot be in exile while he is still in his own land, as the true meaning of the word exile is. But the situation described, is the one that makes us see as if the Negros are in exile, since they have nothing to enjoy in their own land.

15. **Antithesis** is a juxtaposition of two words, phrases, clauses, or sentences contrasted or opposed in meaning in such a way as to give emphasis to contrasting ideas. An example of antithesis is the following line by the English poet Alexander Pope: "To err is human, to forgive divine." "The LORD gave and the LORD has taken away.

16. **Conceit,** it is an elaborate, extended and sometimes surprising comparison between things that, at first sight, do not have much in common. It is also defined as an elaborate, often extravagant metaphor or simile making an analogy between totally dissimilar things. The term originally meant "concept" or "idea." The use of conceits is especially characteristic of 17thcentury English metaphysical poetry. An example occurs in the

poem "A Valediction: Forbidding Mourning," by the English poet John Donne, in which two lovers' souls are compared to the legs of drawing compasses.

17. **Allusion**; is a literary device in which the writer or speaker refers either directly or indirectly to a famous person, event, place or thing in history, religion, mythology, politics, sports, science or to a work of art or literature. Allusion connects the content of a text with the larger world. Allusion calls to mind the ideas and emotions associated with a well-known event or published work. Those ideas and emotions then contribute to what the author conveys. As in Martin Luther's speech "Four score and seven years ago our fathers brought forth on this continent, a new nation, conceived in Liberty, and dedicated to the proposition that all men are created equal."

18. **Parallel structure /parallelism / Parallel construction** is a repetition of the same pattern of words or phrases within a sentence or passage to show that two or more ideas have the same level of importance. Parallel structure helps to organize ideas, making a text or speech easier to understand. Parallel structure can also create a satisfying rhythm in the language an author uses. In this literary device, the idea to be stated is repeated in some other form to emphasize the articulation.
    - 'She cried, she wept but he was unmoved',
    - 'Show me your strength, your stamina, your energy only where it is needed'

19. **Anaphora Also called epanaphora,** the repetition of a word or expression at the beginning of successive phrases for rhetorical or poetic effect, as in Lincoln's
    - "We cannot dedicate-
    - We cannot consecrate-
    - We cannot allow this ground"
    - I am a true Acoli
    - I am not a half-caste
    - I am not a slave girl

20. **Imagery**; this is a figure of speech which creates mental pictures that appeal to readers, five senses. Writers use sensory details to make readers imagine how things look, feel, smell, sound and taste. There are different types of images depending on the five senses. Visual image- this is an image of sight e.g.
    - Greater than the Rift-Valley;
    - Camera film to light, coils of the greatest python
    - Stronger than the blows of the sea
    - When the hurricane is at its height.
    - Organic image -this is an image of feeling
    - Dying in agony
    - More painful than the yell
    - Audio image – this is an image of sound

21. **Anadiplosis**; the repetition in which the last expression of one statement becomes the first expression in the following statement. As in the poem "Africa" by David Diop
    The blood of your sweat
    The sweat of your work
    The work of your slavery
    The slavery of your children

22. **Symbolism;** a literary device that uses one object to stand for something else or to mean something else. Actions can also be symbolic, such as washing hands to indicate noninvolvement. Some symbols are universal, with generally accepted meanings, such as a crown to mean superiority or the color red to mean danger. Symbols, especially specific ones, often mean more than one thing. Sunrise symbolizes the beginning of the struggle and sunset symbolizes the end of the struggle in the poem "Sunrise"

23. **Pun** - It is a humorous play on two or more meanings of the same word or on two different words with the same sound. It is also understood as a play on the multiple meanings of the word or on two words that sound alike but have different meanings. It uses words that have similar or identical sounds but very different meanings. Quite often it is used to pass a witty remark or bring about a sarcastic effect. Examples are,
   - "It is better to have loved a short person and lost, than never to have loved A TALL."
   - 'I KNEAD the dough so that I can eat',

24. **Allegory** is a form of extended metaphor, in which objects, persons, and actions in a narrative, are equated with the meanings that lie outside the narrative itself. The underlying meaning has moral, social, religious, or political significance, and characters are often personifications of abstract ideas as charity, greed, or envy. Thus an allegory is a story with two levels of meanings, a literal meaning and a symbolic meaning. A more modern example of allegory is George Orwell's Animal Farm, which on the surface level is about a group of animals who take over their farm but on the deeper level is an allegory of the Russian Revolution and the shortcomings of the Communism.

25. **Anastrophe:** Also known as inversion, it is a sentence or a poetic expression which reverses or changes the order of words for greater emphasis. The following are examples of anastrophe.
   - 'Ten thousand saw I at a glance' instead of "I saw ten thousand at a glance"
   - 'Forward they go" which is not a normal English structure of SVA. 'They go forward'
   - 'And away they go' instead of 'and they go away'
   - 'While your hive they plunder' instead of 'while they plunder your hive'.

26. **Satire:** is a literary technique which principally ridicules its subject which includes individuals, organization or states often as an intended means of provoking or preventing changes. Satire is any piece of writing that uses devices such as irony. It is a text or performance that uses irony, derision or wit to expose or attack human vice, foolishness or stupidity.

27. **Depersonification;** Is an explanation in which a human being is given non-human characteristics or behavior.Example*He is like the village stone.*

28. **Sarcasm;** Is a statement given for the purpose of hurting or humiliating someone, to make him or herunhappy or angry. It is the use of words that create bitterness. It is like an irony. Example, Ifsomeone goes to the party with hair uncombed, then his friends tells him or her *"Guy, your hairis well combed and you look good"* or if someone scores zero in the class, and his or her friendstell him or her *"Congratulation, you have passed with flying colors".*

29. **Analogy;** is a literary device that helps to establish a relationship based on similarities between two concepts or ideas.
   - In the same way as one cannot have the rainbow without the rain

ROLES /FUNCTIONS OF LITERATURE

Since literature does not develop from a vacuum, but from the society in which it emanates, it has got different roles to play in the society. The following are some of the most important functions of literature in the society.

1. **Literature educates people in the society.** Literary works are used to impart knowledge to the members of the society. It creates awareness on different social political and economic matters taking place in their societies. It educates the young people on how they are expected to behave in accordance with the demands of their societies and the roles they are required to fulfill.

2. **Literature expresses people's culture.** Since literature develops from the society, it automatically expresses the culture of its people. All cultural aspects like traditions, beliefs, customs, norms etc are expressed so that the society may cherish the good ones and carry them over to the next generations, and modify or discard the outdated ones.

3. **Literature is used to entertain people.** Most literary works appeal to the emotions. By reading, listening and watching literary works, we get entertained. Poems and dramas create an enjoyment to the audience different from one we get when we are eating food. Literary enjoyment is called aesthetic pleasure. E.g. comedies and melodrama.

4. **Literature is used to influence people in the society.** More often than not people who are interested in watching, listening and reading literary works are tempted to act like those characters in the respective literary work. During the struggle for independence for example literary works were used to instill revolutionary ideas to the oppressed to take up arms against the oppressor. Consider the poem "Your Pain" by Armando Guebuza.

5. **Literature is used to develop language.** By reading, listening and watching literary works, people improve their language skills such as listening, speaking, reading and writing. People may also improve their vocabulary stock since they will not only come across a number of new words but also know how they are used in real contexts. Authors do also come with new words, phrases, idioms, figures of speech, that help to develop the language.

6. **Literature is used to liberate people mentally and physically.** Literary works present the message that helps to liberate the society mentally as a result they liberate themselves physically. It conscioutized the society about the existence of oppressive systems and suggest ways to get rid of those systems. E.g. United we stand, divided we fall.

7. **Literature is used to criticize the society.** Literature may be used to criticize the society in a sense that it points out the burning issues andrequests the society to resolve them. More often than not literary artists point out the evils done bythe traditional society e.g. perpetuating the outdated customs like FGM, Widow Inheritance,forced marriages etc. and ask the society to discard them. They may also point the wrongs done bythe ruling class and suggest the ways to get rid of these leaders.

PLAYS ANALYSIS

TITLE; THREE SUITORS ONE HUSBAND

PLAYWRIGHT; FERDINAND OYONO MBIA

SETTING; CAMEROON

ACTS SUMMARY

ACT ONE:

Mbia is expected and Juliette arrives on the same day. The scene breaks by Atangana who is complaining about his wife who has delayed to come back from the farm and cook for him. They have a serious discussion in which Abessolo suggests that Atangana and Ondua should beat their wives and daughters. On the same day they are expecting Mbia the civil servant to come in order to marry Juliette who is still studying at Libamba. Unknowingly, Juliette arrives the same day and when she is told the idea of marrying Mbia she rejects it because she claims not to love him.

The whole family is surprised to hear such a response and becomes disappointed by her reaction. The whole family expects to get rich through her, just as Meca's daughter who was married the 12th wife of the Deputy of the Secretary of State and since then she has been helping her family, so they expect Juliette to do the same. We are also told that there is a young farmer called Ndi who has already paid 100,000/= francs for Juliette. Eventually, the Civil Servant arrives and everybody is impressed.

ACT TWO:

The discussion of the Bride price with Mbia. Atangana beats the drum to welcome the whole village to come and meet Mbia. Mbia is pompous and boastful. He introduces himself as a great man who is known personally by the Secretary of State. Additionally, he brings a lot of drinks for villagers to drink. In the middle of the discussion Abessolo asks Mbia's genealogy, and finds out that he is related to Juliette and declares marriage impossible. There is a general tension among the villagers, such that they decide to brush aside the idea of genealogy and continue with the process.

Mbia pays 200,000/= francs as a bride price and Atangana declares marriage settled. On top of the bride price they also mention a lot of things to be brought along before the marriage is registered. They also find out that Mbia has got 8 wives and Juliette is going to be the 9th wife. Women are not involved in this discussion. When it is over, Juliette again refuses to marry Mbia no matter how much he has paid. She tells them that she is engaged to someone else whom she loves. Atangana threatens to beat her and says she will marry Mbia whether she likes or not. Oko appears and they discuss the matter with Juliette. Juliette steals the money paid for her and hands it to Oko and Kouma to be used later as a bride price.

ACT THREE;

Ndi comes from his wife and the theft is discovered. The family is happy because Oyono (Juliette's brother) will now have enough money for which to pay for the wife he wants to marry. Still Juliette refuses and says that money does not prove love. Bella says girls are not allowed to fall in love without the permission of their families. Atangana comes back with Ndi, who has come to take Juliette on hearing that she has come. They tell him the story about the civil servant and Ndi suggests that he would rather have his money back. On hearing this Atangana is impressed and rushes into the house to take the money and finds out that the money is missing.

Meanwhile Abessolo, Mbarga and Mezoe are discussing about young boys - Owono and Belinga – who have eaten a taboo animal – the viper – without the permission of the elders. After noticing the theft they ask Ndi to pay some more 200,000/= francs to marry Juliette but he refuses and threatens to bring the police. They turn to Mbia and ask him to add some more 100,000/= francs and take Juliette right away. He also refuses and demands his money back plus threatening to bring 10 police commissioners while Engulu his servant takes notes of all other claims against the villagers. Atangana is worried about the two police threats and they decide to call the witchdoctor.

ACT FOUR;

Sangatiti – the witch doctor comes to recover the lost money Sangatiti the witchdoctor performs his rituals and in the process he asks them to give him a lot of things like goats, chicken, money, rams etc. He cheats the villagers about evil spirits like chimpanzees and owls that are troubling them and promises to sell them powerful fetishes to protect them from evil spirits. We are also told of Mbarga the village headman who has 12 wives and wants to marry the 13th. Sangatiti continues with his performance but gives false information about the stolen money. He says for instance that Atangana sold 10 sacks of cocoa two days ago and the trader gave him a magic banknote that took the cocoa money plus the bride price back to the cocoa trader two days ago. The fact is, Atangana sold only 3 sacks of cocoa and it was almost a week and he had received the bride price just the same day of the event. They discover that he is a liar, robber, scoundrel and they beat him up and chase him away.

ACT FIVE;

At last OKO marries Juliette. They all blame sending girls to schools because they believe schooling has polluted Juliette. They advise Atangana to take Juliette and move with her around the city to find her a husband there, who can pay 300,000/= francs. Juliette proposes to them that if a man comes who will be able to pay the 300,000/= francs at once she will marry him on a condition that they should not demand anything else on top of the bride price. Unfortunately for her a rich trader called Tchetgen appears and they propose the idea to him. They mention a lot of qualities that Juliette has such as education and the foreign languages she can speak. Hearing this Tchetgen says he can only pay the maximum of 200,000/= francs.

Eventually, Oko arrives with Kouma and a band of musicians, dressed like the really great man they are looking for greater than even the civil servant. They all prefer him to marry Juliette because of the way Kouma introduces him. Oko tells them that he will marry Juliette only if she herself agrees. They are all surprised because women have no choice to decide who they should marry. Lastly Oko pays the 300,000/= francs and marries Juliette.

CHARACTERISATION;

1. **Juliette**;
   - She is Atangana's daughter, Oyono's sister and Oko's fiancée.

- She is educated and struggles to change the traditional values that oppress women.
- She is intelligent.
- She uses her intelligence to fool the villagers by stealing the money paid by other suitors and gives it to Oko who pays it back and the two get married legally.
- She is forced to marry men who are not of her choice but she refuses. These are Ndi, the first suitor, Mbia the second suitor and Tchetgen the third suitor.
- She is a revolutionist who advocates for change.
- She is fighting for freedom of women in aspects like freedom of expression, choice and decision making.
- She is aware of her rights. S
- She wants to show that women are equally important as men and should be consulted on matters affecting them directly.
- She has true love and a stand. Juliette shows an example of true love as she loves Oko for who he knows that he has no money and is still studying.
- She knows that he can't even afford to pay the bride price that's why she helps him to get the bride price.
- She is courageous and liberal. She is not easily swayed by circumstances. Even when the whole family turns against her, she is still determined not to follow their decisions even after being threatened to be beaten by her relatives.
- She does not run away from problems but takes an active role in finding the solution to the problems affecting her.
- She comes from an extended family in which even the issue of marriage is not a personal phenomenon. Many people come together each of them hoping to benefit in one way or another.
- She leaves her family in a desperate situation. After stealing the money, Oko pays back the money which will be used later to refund the previous suitors but the family itself remain with nothing.
- She represents young generation who go against the outdated traditional customs. She is worthy being emulated in the society.

2. **Atangana ;**
   - He is Juliette and Oyono's father and Makrita's husband.
   - He is a traditionalist. He believes in witchdoctors' power. He invites Sangatiti to come and recover his lost money. Also he believes that bride price is still important to settle marriage of the youngsters.
   - He is oppressive to women and hot tempered. He believes in men's superiority and women inferiority. He doesn't want a woman to speak when he is speaking. Also his wife Makrita does the farm work alone but he complains when she delays to come back and cook for him.
   - He is an opportunist. He sends Juliette to school not because it is her right to education but because he knows that someday he will benefit from it. Pg 12" when I sent her to secondary school, I was justly saying to everybody: 'some day, I'll benefit from that" Also he wants to marry Juliette off to Mbia hoping that through him he would be able to easily get a gun permit and medals of honor.

- He is greedy and money monger. He is so greedy for money. He has already received the bride price for Juliette from Ndi, yet he accepts the 200000/= francs paid by Mbia for the same girl. Lastly he receives th 300000/= paid by Oko just for the same girl.
- He desperate and fears the police terribly. He suffers an intrapersonal conflict when he notices that the money is stolen and fears the police who might be brought by Ndi or Mbia.
- He is ignorant, illiterate and does not want changes. He is not worthy being emulated in the society.

3. Kouma;

- Juliette's cousin and educated young man who owns the moped.
- He is intelligent. He uses his intelligence to bring about changes in his society. For example he dares to contradict the witch doctor when he keeps on telling lies about the stolen money while he knows where the money is.
- He is a revolutionist. He also fights for the rights of women like freedom of choice, expression and decision making. For example he says 'she's left free to choose, you see?" pg 68.
- He is literate and so creative. He presents Oko as a great man dressed immaculately and magnificently that everybody suggests him for Juliette. He takes advantage of the ignorance of the villagers and introduces Oko as a great man, greater than the civil servant. Finally all the villagers bless the marriage between Oko and Juliette.
- In collaboration with Oko and Juliette they teach the villagers that women are also valuable human beings with their own feelings, decisions etc. which must be respected.

4. Oko;

- He is an educated young man from Ambam who studies at Lycee Leclere and Juliette's fiancé.
- He is also a revolutionist. He fights for women's rights like; freedom of choice, expression and decision making. He says for instance in pg: 67 "I will marry your daughter if she herself agrees", "if she is to marry me she must do as she wants"
- He is creative. He comes at Atangana's home magnificently dressed and is easily accepted by the whole family not realizing that he is the same schoolboy they have been rejecting.
- He is the one who succeeds to marry Juliette. He pays the 300000/= francs given to him by Juliette and the two get the blessings of the family.
- He advocates for change in the society and is worthy being emulated.

5. Abessolo;

- He is Juliette's grandfather, Atangana and Ondua's father and Bella's Husband.
- He is a traditionalist and conservative. He upholds the traditional values of the society whether good or bad. For example, He believes that bride price is still important. Also women should not be allowed to eat certain taboo animals, and should not be consulted about anything. He traces Mbia's genealogy and declares marriage impossible after discovering that Mbia is related to Juliette.
- He is oppressive to women. He believes that women should be beaten as a way of disciplining them. He suggests that Ondua and Atangana should beat their wives and daughters. Pg. 12

- He is a hypocrite. He is against sending girls to secondary schools but he wants to benefit from it.
- He is against changes in the society thus not worthy being emulated.

6. Sangatiti;
- He is a witch-doctor from Mfouladja who comes to recover Atangana's lost money.
- He is a liar. He lies to the villagers to know about the lost money while in fact he learns from their own words. He says for instance that Atangana sold 10 sacks of cocoa two days ago and the trader gave him a magic banknote that took the cocoa money plus the bride price back to the cocoa trader two days ago. The fact is, Atangana sold only 3 sacks of cocoa and it was almost a week and he had received the bride price just the same day of the event
- He is superstitious. He believes in witchcraft and evil spirits. For instance he threatens to bewitch the whole village. He also promises to sell the villagers powerful fetishes that would protect them from the evil spirits.
- He is a robber. He keeps on robbing the ignorant villagers a lot of things like rams, goats, cockerels, etc by using tricks.
- He is ignorant and illiterate. He doesn't know the ordinary geography that he says north and South is just the same thing.
- He is corrupt. He wants to get rich by using tricks. E.g. He says that if they want to recover their money they must give him; 15 cockerels, 12 goats, 2 rams and 6 pigs.
- He is pompous/ boastful. He boasts of being a competent witch-doctor while he is not. He says "as you couldn't have known about the magic bank note without the help of a powerful witch-doctor like me…" pg 57. He is not worthy to be emulated in the society.

7. Mbarga;
- He is the headman of Mvoutessi village.
- He is a traditionalist. Like Atangana Ondua Mezoe and Abessolo he too upholds the traditional values. He complains about Belinga and Owono who have eaten the viper without the permission of elders. Pg42
- He is a hypocrite. He pretends to praise Ndi in order to soften his mind to add some more 200000/= francs he even pretends to cry mourning the death of Ndi's father who after all isn't dead yet.
- He is a polygamist. He has 12 wives and is proposing to marry the 13th wife from

8. Ngoantet;
- He is superstitious. He believes in superstition because he is the one who suggests the idea of calling the witch-doctor to recover the stolen money.
- He is an irresponsible leader. He is not a responsible leader because he is supposed to take actions to people who distil illegal drinks 'Arki" but he himself does the same illegal business.
- He is pompous. He brags about himself for instance for bringing a competent witch doctor. He also brags about being the headman of the village.
- He is an opportunist. He is opportunist because he also wants to take advantage of Juliette's marriage to Mbia to get a gun permit. He even invites Mbia in his house so as to create a close tie with him.

9. Ndi;

- He is a young hardworking farmer from Awae. He helps Makrita his expected mother-in-law to clear her farm. We are also told that he is an expert in laying monkey traps pg 17.
- He is Juliette's first suitor who pays 100,000/= francs.
- He is betrayed by Atangana's family that takes Mbia's money while knowing that Ndi has already paid for Juliette.
- He threatens to bring the police to arrest Atangana if he fails to pay back his money.

10. Mbia;

- He is a rich civil servant from Sangmelima and Juliette's second suitor.
- He is pompous. He brags about himself being a very important civil servant and that the Secretary of state knows him personally. He also likes to be praised. When Mbarga praises him he becomes pleased and orders drinks for him.
- He is a polygamist. We are told he is married to 8 wives and is now proposing to marry Juliette the 9th wife.
- He has no true love. The fact that he has 8 wives signifies that he has no true love but to him women are objects to satisfy his sexual desires.
- He misuses the government position for private gain. He uses his position and money to attract more wives to himself. He threatens to use his position to send police officers to arrest the villagers for not paying respect to him.
- He is a hypocrite and has no stand. Initially he praises Atangana's family and even drinks an illegal drink "Arki" because he wants them to give him Juliette as his wife. When the deal fails he changes his opinion and threatens to arrest the villagers for distilling arki.
- He is an opportunist. He promises to give the villagers a lot of things on top of the bride price so as to have Juliette.
- He is a drunkard. He is a heavy drunkard as he comes with a lot of strong drinks from Sangmelima and even goes to drink at the headman's house.
- He is not worthy being emulated in the society.

11. Tchetgen;

- He is a trader from Bamileke and Juliette's third suitor.
- He owns two shops in Sangmelima and a bar in Zoetele.
- He agrees to marry Juliette but proposes to pay the maximum of 200000/= francs only.
- He is not interested in marrying Juliette after noticing that she costs too much.

TITLE OF THE PLAY

The title of the play is "Three Suitors One Husband". Tracing through the play we find that it has a close connection with the content of the play. The following are the three suitors and one husband from "Three suitors One Husband";

1. **The first suitor is Ndi,** a young hardworking farmer from Awae who proposes to marry Juliette and pays the sum of 100,000/= francs. Unfortunately for him he does not succeed to marry Juliette. As the second suitor overpowers him.
2. **The second suitor is Mbia,** a rich civil servant from Sangmelima who proposes to marry Juliette and pays the sum of 200,000/= francs plus a lot of things that he has to bring along on top of the bride price to have the marriage settled. He too does not succeed to marry Juliette.

3. **The third suitor is Tchetgen,** a rich trader/businessman from Bamileke who pays the maximum of 200,000/= francs for Juliette. He does not succeed to marry Juliette since the family wants him to pay 300,000/=francs. He is not interested and moves away.
4. **The husband is Oko** a young educated man from Ambam who succeeds to marry Juliette after paying the required amount 300,000/= francs at once. He manages to pay the money after being assisted by Juliette who steals the money her father received from the previous suitors and the two get married legally.

SETTING;

The setting is typically rural. The play is set in Mvoutessi village in the southern part of East Cameroon. A typical Bulu village built along the road. There are sub-settings like kitchen where there are some events taking place and the description of the contents in Makrita's kitchen at the beginning of Act three sums up the rural setting.

STYLE;

The playwright has employed the dialogue style throughout the play. There are few cases of narrative technique especially in stage direction at the beginning of each Act. To enrich his style he has also made use of songs as when Ondua sings in page 23 Aya yam one minga a a ah,
O lig Ondua a nyea'avee? Aya yam one minga a a etc.

LANGUAGE USE/DICTION

Language used is simple and straightforward. Additionally the playwright has made use of;

FIGURES OF SPEECH

1. **Personification;**
   - "When a chameleon dies a grey lizard should inherit his sacks of cola nuts" pg 50
   - …These tiny radio sets which always tell lies" pg 28
2. **Simile;**
   - "Juliette runs to the safety of the kitchen like a frightened antelope" pg 41
   - "…to marry young men as poor as flies.." pg 16
   - You want me to let them sell me like a goat?
3. **Hyperbole/exaggeration;**
   - ''The man we are talking about is the one who rules everybody in Sangmelima." Pg 42
   - "The most obedient girl in the world" pg 63
4. **Under exaggeration;**
   - "Three hundred thousand francs- pocket money". Pg 66
   - "…Who once was the poorest man in Messam" pg 18
   - "Girls are nothing" pg 66
5. **Sarcasm/satire;**
   - "A doctor of Mathematics. That is to say, he can count all the leaves of on a palm tree". Pg 65
   - "He is fluent in French, English, German, Spanish, German English and French". Pg 65
   - "He is also as I'm told the Doctor of the Bachelor." pg 69.
   - "Where in the city? In the market place?"

79

6. **Metaphor;**
   - "A real white man" – pg 13
7. **Rhetorical Questions;**

   - "What? He is a bachelor? Such a great man?" pg 65
   - "Where in the city? In the market place?" pg 61
8. **Barbarism;**
   - "Aa keeaah, Oyono Eto Mekong ya Ngozip aah." Pg 12
   - "Nane Ngok!" Pg 13
9. **Onomatopoeia;**
   - Ooo-oo-ooo-ooo pg 70
10. **Sayings;**
    - "Important rivers can only be recognized by the size of their tributaries" pg 24
    - "When a chameleon dies a grey lizard should inherit his sacks of cola nuts" pg 50
    - "The first day of the marriage is just the beginning of it" pg 26

THEMATIC ANALYSIS;

1. **AFRICAN TRADITIONS AND CUSTOMS;** There are different traditions and customs portrayed in the play. Some of these traditions areworth preserving for the future generation and some are not.

a) **Bride price.** Just like many other African societies, bride price is important and has to be paid before the girl is married. However in this society it is so ridiculous that they are ready to receive whoever pays the highest bride price for the same girl. For example, they receive 100000/=francs from Ndi, then 200000/= from Mbia and lastly 300000/= francs from Oko just for the same girl-Juliette. For them, the girl for whom the largest bride price is paid is respected. However the issue of bride price is seen to be one of the major sources of conflict in African families as manifested in Juliette's family. It is not a good custom thus it should be discarded.

b) **Polygamy.** As it is in most African societies, polygamy is rampart in this society. Men marry many wives to satisfy their sexual desires. Take for example the Deputy of the Secretary of State, has 12 wives, pg 18, Mbarga has 12 wives and is proposing to marry the 13th, pg 52 and Mbia has 8 wives and is proposing to marry Juliette the 9th wife pg 26. However it is revealed by Sanga-titi that polygamy is not safe for men since wives struggle to win the heart of their husbands and beat their rivals and thus bring along powerful fetishes. This is also dangerous in this era of HIV/AIDS thus it should be discouraged.

c) **Superstition.** People of Mvoutessi believe in superstition and witchcraft just like many other societies in Africa. Consider the following cases;
   - When Abessolo collapses they attack Ndi for bringing his witchcraft to kill people there. Pg 46
   - When the money is stolen they send for a witch doctor to recover the lost money. Pg 50
   - Mbarga says he once saw their dead ancestors in a dream and they blessed him. Pg 25.

- Sanga-titi makes them believe that owls and Chimpanzees are not ordinary birds or animals but evil spirits of the past that killed their ancestors.pg 55
- This is not a good custom so it should be discouraged.

d) Taboos. These are customs that restrict certain group of people from doing some things. In this society we see the following taboos;
  - A girl should not speak when her father is speaking. Pg 17
  - Women are not allowed to eat taboo animals like vipers, wild boars, pg 12
  - Young men are not to eat vipers and if they do they must be permitted by elders. Pg42. This is an outdated custom so it should be uprooted.

e) Eating etiquette. Eating manner is also strictly observed as the playwright shows that the elders are heard scolding those children who don't eat properly. Pg 32. This is a good habit that has to be promoted.

f) Spouse battering/wife beating. In this society women are beaten as a way of silencing and disciplining them. Abessolo brags about himself how he could not have tolerated nonsense in his days and advises Ondua and Atangana to beat their wives and daughters. Pg 12 this is not a good habit and it should be discarded.

g) Traditional Religion. Still many villagers keep the traditional local beliefs. They believe in the spirit of their dead ancestors and that owls and chimpanzees are evil spirits of the past. They also believe in the power of witchdoctors like Sanga-titi and that his fetishes can protect them from the evil spirits. This is an outdated custom so it should be discarded.

h) Traditional dances. In this society cerebrations are accompanied by a dance. They celebrate a happy event by beating drums and dancing their traditional dance called "Nyeng'". This is a good custom to be preserved as it promotes African culture.

i) Economy the economy of these people depends mainly on agriculture based on cash crops like; cocoa, cola nuts, peanuts etc. also there are some people like Monica and Mbarga who earn their living by distilling and selling illegal liquor "Arki". Yet others like Tchetgen engage themselves in trade by selling different merchandise to willing buyers.

j) Extended family. In this society there is a spirit of cooperation when it comes to important matters like marriage. Atangana beats the drum to welcome the villagers to witness the marriage of his daughter. Also the decisions are made by collective bargaining among the members of the extended family. For example they decide who should marry Juliette expecting that each member of the extended family will benefit.

k) Forced marriage. Love is important in marriage. However in this society marriage is not defined by love but by money. The whole family forces Juliette to marry Mbia not because she loves him but because he has paid much money. Forced marriage is also one of the major sources of conflict between youngsters and elders. It should be discouraged.

2. POSITION OF WOMEN IN THE SOCIETY; Women are portrayed in different positions and roles both positive and negative. Here are some of the positions women occupy in this society.

a) Women are portrayed as hard workers. In this society women do all the work while men do almost nothing. Most men are portrayed as lazy and keep blaming their wives. Atangana blames his wife for delaying to come back and cook for him. Monica also distills illegal arki and sells it to support the family. Ondua blames her for denying him one bottle. Pg 11

b) **Women are portrayed as revolutionists.** Juliette represents women who are after changes. Despite the inferior position of women in this society, she takes an active role in fighting for women rights like freedom of expression, choice and decision making. Although Abessolo says "Since when do women speak in Mvoutessi" pg 15 she still speaks out her views.

c) **Women are portrayed as caretakers (custodians).** In this society women are the caretakers of the family, and when the children misbehave the women are blamed for it. Take for instance how Makrita is blamed that she is the one who teaches Juliette such a disgraceful behavior. But Makrita says "Juliette haven't I always told you to be obedient to your family?" pg 18

d) **Women are portrayed as courageous.** Juliette presents a positive role women can play in bringing about social change. She is courageous enough to fight for her rights despite men's dominance and superiority. For example she asks "you want me to let them sell me like a goat? After all I'm a valuable human being." Pg18

e) **Women are portrayed as inferior to men.** Women are shown to be weak individuals with no say. They are also beaten as a way of disciplining them. Abessolo suggests that Ondua and Atangana should beat their wives and treat their daughters just the same way. Also girls should not fall in love without the permission of their families. This portrays inferior position of women.

f) **Women are portrayed as tools for pleasure.** In this society women are treated as objects to satisfy men's sexual desires. Most men are polygamous which shows that they have no true love for their wives. E.g. Mbia already has 8 wives yet wants to marry Juliette, Mbarga has 12 wives and he is proposing to marry the 13th. Etc.

g) **Women are portrayed as a source of income.** In this society women are taken as a source of income. Atangana for instance sends Juliette to school not because of respecting her right to education but because he expects to benefit later. Also people want her to marry a rich man-Mbia so that they can get rich through her. Juliette asks "Am I a shop or some other source of income" pg 16

h) **Women are portrayed as people with true love and a firm stand.** Juliette loves Oko for who he is. She does not expect to get anything from Oko apart from love. She asks them "Does money prove love?" pg 39 and she adds "I've told you my fiancé hasn't got any money, and yet I'm sure he loves me." Pg 39

i) **Women are portrayed as superstitious.** In this society women are portrayed as superstitious. Sanga-titi reveals that due to polygamy, some women are given by their mothers some fetishes to "win their husbands heart, bear him many children, and beat all your rivals in beauty, charm and housekeeping" pg 55

j) **Women are despised and segregated.** In this society women are looked down upon. Men do not want to consult women on any matter. For example Abessolo says "consult a woman about her marriage!" pg 12. That's why Juliette and all women are not involved in the meeting discussing about her marriage. Ondua says "women will have their way! No sensible man should waste his time trying to reason with them." Pg11

k) **Traditionally a girl for whom the highest bride price is paid is respected.** In this society the girls for whom the largest bride price is paid is the one to be respected Pg 18. That's why they all propose Mbia for Juliette since he has paid what is considered as high bride price so that she can earn their respect.

3. **CONFLICTS;** This refers to the misunderstanding or collision of ideas, viewpoints or opinions within aperson, between or among groups of people in the society. Like other plays, in this play there are several conflicts as analyzed below;

  a) **INTRAPERSONAL CONFLICT;** This occurs within a person. It is manifested within the following individuals.
  - **Juliette;** She suffers an intrapersonal conflict because of outdated customs in her society that forces girls to marry men who are not of their choice and without consultation. As a result she steals the money paid by the previous suitors and gives it to Oko (whom she loves) and the two get married.
  - **Atangana;** He suffers an intrapersonal conflict after discovering the theft of his money. The conflict grows worse when both Mbia and Ndi threaten to bring the police to arrest him. As a result he calls the witchdoctor to recover the lost money but he fails. Finally, he receives the money from Oko as a solution to his problem.

  b) **FAMILY CONFLICT;**
  - **Juliette with her family;** This occurs when she refuses to marry the rich man they have chosen for her. It intensifies as she argues with the family contrary to their expectation since women do not speak in Mvoutessi. It ends when she marries Oko who pays 300,000/=francs
  - **Mbia and Juliette's family;** This occurs when they tell Mbia to add some more 100,000/= francs for Juliette. He demands his money back and threatens to bring the police.
  - **Ndi and Juliette's family;** This occurs when they tell Ndi to add some more 200,000/= francs for Juliette. He demands his money back and threatens to bring the police.

  c) **CULTURAL CONFLICTS;** There is a conflict between traditional culture and modern culture. Young Generation represented by Juliette, Oko, Kouma, Belinga and Owono embrace modernism by going against the traditional culture that forbids them to do certain things like eating vipers, freedom of choice, decision making and speech. On the contrary there are elders like Mbarga, Atangana, Abessolo, Bella and Ondua who uphold traditionalism. They condemn new ways of life and think that things are falling apart since youngsters no longer listen to elders as they are expected to do.

  d) **SOCIAL CONFLICT;** This occurs between the villagers and the witchdoctor Sanga-titi. It occurs when the villagers discover that Sanga-titi is not only a liar, but also a robber and is not able to recover the lost money. He just keeps on robbing them and threatens to bewitch them. They beat him up and chase him away.

  e) **POLITICAL CONFLICT;** There is a conflict between the Rulers and peasants (villagers). This occurs when the police keep on beating the villagers for not paying the taxes and arresting them for being drunk. They want Mbia to marry Juliette to help them.

4. **AWARENESS;** It is a state of being conscious about what is going on around you. This is a vital tool in so far as the liberation of the oppressed is concerned. Awareness is manifested in the following aspects.

  a) **Kouma is aware of Sanga-titi's lies.** He knows where the money is but Sanga-titi keeps on telling lies. Kouma contradicts him on spot and helps all the other villagers to discover that Sanga-titi is a liar and a robber.

b) **Juliette is aware of her rights** like freedom of speech, decision making and choice. She doesn't want to be considered inferior that's why she says "but I'm a free person. Pg 31

c) **Kouma and Oko are aware of the fact that women are important people in the society and should be respected.** They teach the villagers a lesson by giving Juliette a chance to choose her own suitable suitor who becomes her husband.

5. **THE INFLUENCE OF MONEY AND POWER;** In this society everybody thinks that money is a solution to every problem and is the sourceof happiness. As a result most people engage in different legal and illegal activities to getmoney. The following scenarios are just few cases in point.

- They cultivate cash crops like cocoa in order to get money.
- Some distill illegal liquor (Arki) to get money. Examples are Mbarga and Monica Ondua's wife.
- Marriage has also become a business. Parents want their daughters to marry rich men so that they can get money. E.g. everybody wants Juliette to marry Mbia since he brings a lot of money.
- Love is based on money. In this society the girl for whom the highest bride price is paid is considered to be loved and is respected. Matalina says to Juliette "How could a girl refuse a man who loves her enough to pay 200,000/= francs for her?
- Sanga-titi is corrupt and wants to get rich easily through people's ignorance. He uses tricks and lies to get more money.
- Money leads girls into polygamy. Some people use money to marry as many women as they please. Mbia has 8 wives and wants to use his power and money to win Juliette's love. The deputy of the secretary of state also has 12 wives.
- Mbia is opportunistic. He treats people dearly (giving them drinks and money) to influence them to give him Juliette. When it fails he uses his power to threaten them that he will bring the police to arrest them.
- Money and power make people arrogant and boastful. Mbia is arrogant because of his money and power. He accuses the villagers that the roads are poorly kept and the houses have not been whitewashed in expectation of the honour of his visit. Mbarga is also arrogant because of his power as a village headman. He dictates respect from people by using his authority.

6. **NEPOTISM/FAVOURITISM;** This is a common phenomenon in Africa now. People are treated on the basis of whom you-know and not what-you-know. For example in this society everybody is in favor ofthe Civil Servant because on top of the bride price they expect to be favored in otherspheres as well, such as;

- To get medals and gun permits. They say it is so difficult to get it when you do not know the right people in the government.
- To avoid frequent beatings from police. For example Mbia discovers that the people of the village are distilling illegal Arki but takes no action since he wants to become their in-law.

7. **INFLUENCE OF EDUCATION;** Education is a necessary tool for social change. If used positively it acts as a medium fortransforming a traditional society into a modern one. In this society education has beenused positively to bring about social changes in the following ways:

- **It has brought awareness to young people who acquired it.** Unlike Matalina who has not gone to school Juliette knows her rights as a girl. She demands her freedom of expression, choice and decision making.
- **Oko and Kouma are also aware of women rights.** Although they come from the same male dominated society, they don't like the way women are mistreated. They use their education to bring changes.
- **Education increases the value of an individual.** Most people who are educated are considered valuable compared to uneducated ones. Villagers believe that since Juliette is educated they should demand high bride price for her.
- **Education has brought about cultural change.** Young people who have acquired education have begun to question certain traditional values. Even elders believe that it is due to schools that these changes occur though they put it in a negative way by complaining that" schools have corrupted everything"

8. **CLASSES IN THE SOCIETY;** The play depicts different classes of people in his society. There are several classes that can be classified in the following categories.

- **Educated vs. uneducated;** There is a class of educated people represented by people like Juliette, Oko and Kouma and that of uneducated represented by people like Mbarga, Matalina Abessolo, Atangana etc. Their differences are manifested even in the way they look at things.
- **Traditionalists vs. modernists;** There is also a class of those who wish to see the traditional values of the societywhether good or bad upheld at any cost and those who see no need to continue withoutdated customs. People like Mbarga, Abessolo Atangana Ondua etc uphold traditionalism while people like Belinga, Owono, Juliette, Oko and Kouma embrace modernism.
- **Rich vs. poor;** There is also a class of rich people (the ruling class) like Mbia who enjoy the nationalcake and traders like Tchetgen while the majority like the villagers (peasants) are suffering from poverty expecting to get rich when rich men come to marry their daughters.
- **Town dwellers (townies) vs. Village dwellers (villagers.);** The life of the people in town is different from those in the villages. Mbia despises thevillagers. We are told that even Engulu a mere driver despises the villagers since hecomes from town. Also people in the village even distil and drink illegal drinks like"Arki" while those from the city enjoy strong bottled drinks.

9. **HYPOCRISY;** Many people in this society seem to be affected by hypocrisy. They do or say whatevermight earn them a favor from somebody. They even contradict their own statements forthe same reason.Mbia is a hypocrite. When he wants to marry Juliette he praises the villagers and evendoesn't take action when he discovers that they conduct illegal business by distilling Arki.When his plans finally fail he changes his opinion and accuses them of the same. This is high level of hypocrisy. Mbarga is a hypocrite. At first he praises Mbia and favours him for Juliette and they kick out Ndi. When the money is stolen he praises Ndi to soften him to add 200000/= francs so as to cover up the loss. He even pretends to weep, mourning the death of Ndi's father who after all isn't dead yet. This is hypocrisy. Elders like Abessolo are hypocrites. They condemn secondary schools for polluting girls yet when it comes to the issue of marriage they want to benefit from the same education by demanding high bride price because Juliette is educated.

10. STRUGGLE FOR CHANGE; The play tries to show the areas that need reformation and urges the society to makethe necessary social changes. There are outdated customs which need to be reformed like: forced marriage, bride price, women beating, taboos, superstitious beliefs and polygamy. There are also good ones that we may cherish such as traditional dances and eating etiquette. Also education seems to be a great agent of change that needs to be embraced. Men should change their mentality by sending girls to school since they are capable of contributing to societal development.

MESSAGE;

1. Bride price, polygamy, superstition, forced marriage and spouse battering are outdated traditions they needs to be discouraged.
2. People should use their education positively to bring about social change.
3. Hypocrisy is not good in any ideal society.
4. Witch doctors are liars and robbers.
5. Love and not money should be the determinant of true marriage.
6. Illiteracy is an obstacle to development.
7. Both boys and girls should be given equal right to education.
8. Food taboos should be discouraged as they deprive women and children of required nutrients.

RELEVANCE;

The play is relevant in a number of ways.

1. Polygamy is still a problem in most African societies and among the Moslems.
2. Bride price is still a common custom in many African societies and is a source of conflicts in marriage among the youngsters and elders.
3. People still believe in witchcraft and superstition as a solution to their problems.
4. There are people who earn a living by conducting illegal business like distilling "gongo".
5. Many people misuse their money and power for private gain.

TITLE; THE BLACK HERMIT
PLAYWRIGHT; NGUGI WA THIONG'O
SETTING; KENYA

ACTS SUMMARY

ACT ONE - THE COUNTRY
Scene I – In the Hut

Thoni and Nyobi are in a hut when Nyobi notices that Thoni has been crying. She (Nyobi) complains since Remi does not reply the letters she sends to him. She advises Thoni to find another husband but she refuses. Thoni believes that Remi hates her. She wonders why men do not rest in her hands. Then Nyobi gets an idea of asking the pastor to go the city to look for Remi since he was once a God-fearing child. The elder comes to ask Nyobi to give them a mother's blessing to their traditional medicine that will make Remi come back. Being a Christian she hesitates a bit but later overwhelmed by a mother's desire to see her son back, she betrays her heart, giving the required blessings.

Scene II – A meeting ground;

In the Open. The elders of the tribe meet to discuss the return of Remi. They discuss how the situation is worse to them even after independence. Poor social services, taxation are just a few. They believe that Remi's mind was spoilt by the evil eyes of their neighbors. Then they turn to the mountain to say a prayer. Then the leader cautions that when Remi comes back he must not fall under the influence of his mother nor the pastor.

Scene III –The Same

The pastor meets Nyobi and she confesses that she has betrayed her faith. The pastor believes Remi was polluted when at the university by engaging in politics. Then Nyobi asks the pastor to go and look for Remi in the city. The pastor agrees.

ACT TWO –THE CITY
Scene I – In Remi's room

Remi is with his white girlfriend in his room. In their conversation Jane discovers that there is something that has been disturbing Remi for so long. Jane requests Remi to tell her about his background and she suggests that Remi should take her to his parents but Remi puts it aside and suggests that they go to the night club instead.

Scene II – the same room

Remi is visited by his friend Omange and the two discuss a lot about the political situation in the country. They discuss the dangers of tribalism, religious factions, and racism. Remi narrates his background to Omange; how he loved Thoni who got married to his brother and how his brother died. He shows that according to their custom his father asked him to inherit Thoni and that is the reasons why he ran to the city. Omange advises him to go back home.

The elders come to persuade Remi to go and save them. They explain to him the troubles they get just because of his absence. They leave the room dropping a bundle of medicine at the door way. The pastor comes to see Remi for the same reason. Eventually Remi promises that he will go back home. The pastor goes and leaves the bible behind.

Scene III – the same room (a few days later)

Jane visits Remi again and Remi is determined to go home. She insists to go with Remi but he refuses. She believes may be it is due to their differences in races that Remi is denying her so she promises to be faithful to him and his people. She insists that Remi should tell her about his history. Lastly Remi tells her that he is married. She is disappointed and the two come into a conflict. Finally Jane runs out.

ACT THREE – THE RETURN OF THE HERMIT
Scene I –Nyobi and Thoni in the hut

Nyobi and Thoni discuss the return of Remi and Thoni is happy. The pastor joins them and insists it is the work of Christ. The 1st neighbour rushes into the hut announcing the meeting of so many people who have come to meet Remi. The pastor narrates how Remi addressed the meeting with a roar. How he came with a man from another tribe and said he is his brother and theirs. How he blamed the elders for preaching tribalism etc. Remi attacks the pastor for dividing people and his mother for making him marry Thoni. On hearing this Thoni disappears.

Scene II – the same Thoni foretells her death

Thoni begins thinking of going where no one can find her. She talks to the woman about her death in a figurative way. The woman advices her to go and stay with her since Remi is not the only tree under whose shadow she can rest. She says; goodbye mother, goodbye father, goodbye my village and goes out.

Scene III –the death of Thoni

Omange and Remi talk about their success in the meeting. They discuss their future strategies. Omange suggests the state to lead the way and the Africanist part to give back the settlers land to the people. Then Remi receives a letter from a woman who blames him for what he did to his tribe. Omange reads the letter and notices how Thoni expresses her love for Remi. They begin searching for her and hope that she will be found. Remi regrets for what he has done. Then four men enter carrying Thoni's body on a stretcher. Remi becomes remorseful for what he did to her. His final words are "oh, what have I done? I wish you sent the letter earlier. But I never gave you a chance, nor even tried to understand you. I came back to break tribe and custom, instead, I've broken you and me"

CHARACTERIZATION

1. REMI;

- He is the son of Ngome and Nyobi.
- He is educated. We are told that he is the only one in his Marua tribe who has had a chance to go to the university.
- He is a betrayer. He betrays Jane by refusing to marry her as he promised. He also betrays his tribe for not using his education to help them solve their social problems instead he runs away to the city to enjoy the city pleasures leaving his people in a bad situation.
- He has a changing behavior. At first we are told he is God-fearing, but when he later goes to the university he abandons religion and becomes an active politician. Also at first he is shy with girls but later he becomes bold with ladies. Jane confirms this when she says "you! Shy with girls! And you almost ate me the very day you met me in the club!" pg20
- He is an active member of Africanist Party which is in power. He has a strong convincing power. He convinces his people to join the party and they obey him.
- He is a revolutionist but uses wrong approaches. He is against tribalism, racism, and religion factions but wants to bring changes overnight without giving the villagers enough time to adjust. This makes his strategies to prove a failure.
- He is arrogant because of his education. Because of his education he despises the elders including his own mother. He addresses them without respect and by attacking rather than educating, something that makes him fail to reach his goals. He says "there is no time for soft hearts" pg 53 in pg 48 he says "everything will give way to my leadership"
- He is a victim of outdated customs. He is forced to inherit the widow of his late brother without his consent. He believes the lady does not love him so he runs away.

- He is remorseful (regretful). He seems genuinely remorseful for what he had done to Thoni. He says "I came back to break Tribe and custom, instead I've broken you and me." Pg 58

2. OMANGE;

- He is Remi's friend from Njobe tribe.
- He is very wise and aware of the effects of tribalism, racialism, and religion factions after independence.
- He is a good advisor. He advises Remi on different matters including going back to his wife and giving her a chance to express her love to him.
- He is after changes and believes that education is necessary for changes.

3. THONI;

- She is a very obedient village girl who gets married to Remi's brother.
- She is a widow. She lives alone after her husband's death. She is inherited by Remi according to the custom but he runs ways leaving her alone.
- She has true love. Thoni is portrayed as a person with true love to Remi. Despite the fact that Remi runs away from her, she is determined to wait even for 20 years. She does not want to take the third husband as Nyobi advises her.
- She is patient and optimistic. Despite the terrible loneliness she is experiencing she still hopes that one day Remi will come back to her and is determined to wait for him.
- She suffers from intrapersonal conflict. This happens since her husband is dead and now she faces loneliness. Then her next husband Remi has disappeared. Something that she might translate that he does not love her. Expressing her situation she says "why do men not rest in my hands? Death took away my first husband. Now the next, his brother has left me. The hut's gloom and loneliness has started eating into me." pg 4.
- She uses a wrong approach to solve her problem. When Remi comes back and degrades her in public she decides to commit suicide. This is one of her weakness.

4. NYOBI;

- She is the wife of Ngome and Remi's mother.
- She is a sympathetic and caring mother. She takes care of Thoni like her own biological child. She wishes to see Thoni having happiness and she is deeply hurt when she sees the loneliness that Thoni is experiencing.
- She is a good advisor. She advises Thoni to take a husband who will restore her happiness. She also advises Remi to be careful by the way he deals with villagers. She says to him "My son, don't be dazzled by the blaze which will burn for the night and tomorrow it is out." Pg 48
- She suffers intrapersonal conflict. She suffers an intrapersonal conflict after the death of her son, followed by her husband and the later disappearance of Remi.
- She is a Christian. She is a very devoted Christian but at some times because of a mother's desire to see her lost son, she blesses the traditional medicine that may help to bring Remi back. She admits this by telling he pastor; "And I, overwhelmed by a mother's desire to see her son back, betrayed my heart, giving the required blessings" pg 14

- She is disappointed by Remi's changes. She becomes disappointed by the way Remi who was once God-fearing has changed. She even wonders how Remi talks to her in a rude way. "You talk to me so? You talk to me so? Pg 48

5. PASTOR;

- He is a strong Christian who mentors Remi to be the future leader of the Church. He even goes to the city to find Remi for the same reason.
- He is against traditional beliefs although he also takes part in advising Remi to inherit Thoni.
- He is blamed for causing disunity in the society.
- He too is optimistic. He believes that Remi who was once a God-fearing child will change and lead the church after he has retired.

6. JANE;

- She's Remi's girl friend in the city working in the office as a typist.
- She is anti-racism. She believes that color differences should not create barriers between people. She tells Remi "What matters is not race, creed, or custom, but whether individuals can meet and understand one another" pg 36
- She is betrayed by Remi. Jane is betrayed by Remi when the time comes for Remi to go back home he refuses to go with her.
- Finally she runs away leaving Remi alone.

TITLE OF THE PLAY

The title of the play is "THE BLACK HERMIT." A hermit is a person who, (usually for religious reasons), lives a very simple life alone and does not meet or talk to other people. The word black here may simply imply an African. That is to say the hermit in this play is an African man who decides to run away from his society to be alone (hermit) avoiding some circumstances in his African society. Tracing through the play we can see the main character REMI running away from problems in his Marua tribe to become a hermit in the city as he says himself speaking to Jane "…to be a hermit means escaping from what is around you. My tribe was around me" Pg 35. Among the reasons that make the main character to arrive at this decision include the following;

1. **Remi becomes a hermit because of outdated customs like widow inheritance.** Remi runs to the city to become a hermit because of being forced to inherit the widow of his late brother. This can be revealed in his conversation with Jane.
   JANE: "you call yourself a hermit! A black hermit? You are not a hermit. A hermit looks for truth. You ran away from the truth of your position. Tell me why did you run away from your wife?
   REMI: It wasn't a really marriage
   JANE: Why not?
   REMI: She was my brother's widow. I had to marry her. It is a sacred custom of Marua tribe…." pg 39

2. **Also Remi becomes a hermit because of Tribalism.** The tribe wants Remi to rule them because he is the only one who has university education. They do so because they want someone from their tribe to represent them in the government, something that Remi is protesting against. This can also be revealed in his conversation with Jane.

REMI: "…to you tribalism and colonialism, the tyranny of the tribe and the settler are abstraction. To me they are real. I have felt their shaft here. Yes, they have made a wound here, a wound that made me run to the city." Pg 36

3. **Remi runs to the city to look for White collar jobs;** Additionally, he ran to the city to get a job in the office and earn a living and stay thereforever but later he is fed up of the city as he says "I hate working for these oil-companiesthat have invaded our country. "Files, files, files all day long" pg 21.

SETTING

1. The setting of the play is Kenya after independence. Additionally, the play has employed the urban and rural settings.

2. Urban setting is portrayed by incidents like, night clubs, white collar jobs (like Remi is working in Oil-Company-), people of different races; these are common features in towns/cities. On the part of the rural setting there are practices like traditional customs such as widow inheritance, traditional religion, tribalism, living in a hut and the like are common in the villages.

STYLE

1. The playwright has employed the **dialogue** style throughout the play. There are few cases of flashback technique especially when Remi narrates his Brother's death and back when he was at the college.

2. Also we see the middle of the story is found at the beginning and the beginning is in the middle of the story. The scene begins by showing Nyobi comforting Thoni who has been crying, but we do not know why until later when we are told that her husband died and Remi who was to inherit her has run away. There are also some cases of foreshadowing. People try to **foreshadow** the return of the hermit (Remi) and how he will lead them to victory.

3. To enrich his style he has also made use of songs as in page 47 when the villagers sing the national anthem welcoming the hermit back home. Pg 47

       Mungu ibariki Afrika
       Ili ipate Kuamka
       Maombi yetu yasikize
       Uje
       Utubariki
       Uje roho
       Uje roho
       Takatifu
       Uje roho utubariki

LANGUAGE USE;

- The language used is simple and straight forward. The choice of words is also perfect since there are words that help the reader to get the message across easily. Words like tribalism, racism, taxation, forced community works; bribes etc help us to know the kind of life these people experience.

- There is also frequent use of religious language especially by the pastor and Nyobi e.g. "Salvation is not achieved through the flesh" pg 16. Let us pray, God of Abraham, God of Isaac," Pg 16
- Moreover the play is full of figures of speech. Some of them are:

FIGURES OF SPEECH

1. **Reiteration;**
   - "Files, files, files all day long" pg 21
   - "Depends, depends, depends on the kind of kind of what!" pg 23
   - "Oh promises, promises. I should have known what promises mean to you" pg 39
2. **Onomatopoeia;**
   - "Cha cha cha" pg 22 (imitating the sound of music)
   - "Ha, ha, ha,-!" Pg 8 (sound of laughter)
3. **Simile;**
   - "A trade union without the right to strike is like a lion without claws and teeth". Pg 23
   - "He became lost to us like a seed which falling on the wayside lacked nourishment of the rich earth,..." pg 16
   - "To be like an unwanted maize plant" pg 50
   - "Falling into bits like a cloth long hung in the sun" pg 3
4. **Metaphor;**
   - "My wound is a woman" pg 25
   - "She is a seedling whose eventual fruit will be a blessing to us all" pg 16
5. **Personification**
   - "Your silence touches my heart" pg 29
   - "Our tribe wails under the new government." Pg 29
   - "The tribe waits for you" pg 30
   - "The world will not wait for you" pg 3
   - "The bite of the cold wind" pg 38
   - "The best woman the village has ever borne" pg 54
   - "It's all darkness, swallowing you wholly" pg 50
   - "And now I must go for darkness calls." Pg 52
6. **Exaggeration;**
   - "Remi your son and ours is the only educated man in all the land, exceeding in knowledge all the people, black and white put together" pg 7
   - "Couldn't they read my heat?" Pg 26
   - "The only educated man in the country" pg11
7. **Parallelism;**
   - "To be laughed at, to be flouted, to be driven out, and by him, my husband." Pg 50
   - "Goodbye mother, goodbye father, goodbye my village." Pg 52
8. **Allusion;**
   - "Remi refused to go to Nineveh, he fled to the city of idolatry" pg 17 (reference to the Jonah saga in the Bible"

- "He became lost to us like a seed which falling on the wayside lacked nourishment of the rich earth, He dried up." pg 16 (reference to the Parable of the sower in the bible)

9. **Euphemism;**
   - "Though your husband was called and also your first son..." pg 16 (to express that they died.)
   - "You shy with girls! And you almost ate me the very day you met me in the club!" pg 20 (referring to the act of making love)

10. **Oxymoron;**
    - "These eyes have seen rain come and go."
    - "Have seen sunrise and sunset."
    - "Birth and death alternating" pg 3

11. **Saying;**
    - "A man's public life is given meaning only by the stability of his private life." Pg 32
    - 'A woman's joy is scolding her children" pg 3
    - "A woman without a child is not a woman" pg 3

THEMES IN THE PLAY

1. **AFRICAN TRADITIONS AND CUSTOMS;** There are different traditions and customs portrayed in this play. Some of these traditionsgive us an impression of cherishing and preserving them for the future generation and somedo not.

   a) **Spouse inheritance (Widow Inheritance);** It is a common custom among African societies and Marua tribe is no exception. According to Marua tribe, it is possible to inherit the wife of a brother who is dead. Remi finds himself faced by this fact when his brother dies of a motor accident and his father and elders tell him to inherit the wife of his late brother according to the custom. Speaking to Omange he says, "he called me to his bed and said: 'Remi you know our custom. Your brother's wife is now your wife'". This is one of the reasons why Remi runs to the city. This custom is dangerous especially in this era of HIV/AIDS because more often than not in some cases it is not possible to know whether the person who died was HIV positive or not. So it should be discouraged.

   b) **Superstition and witchcraft;** In this play it is shown that the Marua elders believe in the power of Marua medicine.They believe it has power to work on Remi's mind and change his attitude anddecide to go back home. As they go to look for Remi in the city one of the elderscarries a bundle of medicine well-wrapped with dry banana leaves. On leaving thehouse he drops it at the door way. Pg 31. Moreover the Marua people believe that the neighboring communities are jealousyof them. They even attribute Remi's disappearance to black magic that might have been used by their neighbors to turn his mind against the tribe. Pg 7. Also in page 12 the leader says; "who can doubt that Remi's mind was spoilt by the evil eyes of our neighbors?" This custom is not good as it may lead to hatred and unnecessary conflicts among communities just because of false speculations. So it should be discarded.

   c) **Traditional religion;** In this society some people are still traditionalists who believe in traditional religionwhile others have followed Christianity. For example when the elder talks to Nyobi toconvince her to bless their medicine he says"Last month our diviner had a message from God. He had vision andthere, he saw the tribe expand, becoming powerful, dominating the wholecountry" pg 8. This shows that they believe in their traditional god who decides their future. Before the elders leave for the city they go to the mountain to say their prayers. This is also bad since the mountain cannot hear nor answer their prayers.

d) **Tribalism and racialism;** Some African societies perpetuate the spirit of tribalism and racialism. This isvery bad custom that has to be stopped. For example Remi hates this and istrying his level best to stop it. He says "even at college I hated many smallpolitical and social organizations based on tribe and race" pg 24. He also comeswith Omange, a man from Njobe tribe and introduces him as his brother andtheirs too.Also racism is shown in two ways: Africans don't want people from other races;the elder says "and married this woman a daughter of the tribe, instead of goingto a white-skinned woman. We were happy." page 6. That's the reason whyRemi refuses to take Jane home because she is different. Asians ostracize people who cooperate with Africans. In page 22 Omange says "This affair of an Asian girl who has been ostracised by her community because she was seen going around with an African is not an isolated case."

e) **Respect to elders/parents;** in this society or family the young are supposed to respect the elders or parents. Remiaccepts to inherit his brother's wife at first as a way of showing respect for elders.Talking to Omange Remi says: "…here were people I was leading. I had asked them to be true and faithful to the Africanist Party. They had obeyed me. Now they were asking me to show similar obedience. Finally I agreed to live with her" P. g 28. Later when he stays in the city, without answering his mother's letters, she considers this as lack of respect. She says "this world is really bad, not the same as the old when sons still gave respect to parents…- many letters have we now sent to him, but no reply. Not a word from him. A child I bore" pg 1. Respect to elders when the cause is right can be cherished.

f) **Christianity;** Ever since the coming of the Whiteman, African societies were divided into two major beliefs. There are those who remained traditionalists following the religion of their ancestors and those who were converted to Christianity. In this play both cases are portrayed. The elders represent those who have decided to uphold their traditional religion while people like Ngome, Nyobi, Remi and Pastor chose to become Christians. However, in this play the division is obvious, since religious differences have brought more conflicts and disunity and have split the country apart.

g) **Spouse beating;** Although it appears in a nutshell, it cannot be ignored. It seems that there is spousebeating in this society. Nyobi admits this in page 3 when she says: "I have tasted thepains of beating, the pangs of birth and death's blow"

2. **POSITION OF WOMEN IN THE SOCIETY;**
   a) **Women are portrayed as tools for pleasure by men.** In this play we see Jane being used by Remi just to satisfy his sexual desires, but when it comes to the issue of marrying her Remi refuses. It is then that Jane realizes that she was used as a tool for pleasure. Jane complains "Ah, Remi, cant you remember all the sweet hours we had together? Please take me with you don't leave me here alone." Pg 35
   b) **Women are portrayed as weak individuals.** In this society women are undermined and reduced to properties that can be inherited when the first owner passes away. This Marua custom does not give a woman a chance to decide who will be her husband or whether she loves him or not. Rather she has to conform

to the wishes of the elders by marrying the brother of her husband. However, this custom seems to be one of the major causes of conflicts since Remi runs away from Thoni believing that she does not love him. On coming back he gives degrading words that make Thoni commit suicide. It is also revealed to us by Nyobi that women are beaten ""I have tasted the pains of beating, the pangs of birth and death's blow"

c) **Women are portrayed as care takers/custodians.** Nyobi is portrayed as a mother who takes a good care of the children. Also she wonders what has become of Remi, her own son since he does not reply the letters she sends him. She becomes unhappy for this. She even agrees to bless Marua medicine so that her son may come back. The elders mock her by saying "Her son is dearer to her than her Christianity." pg 12

d) **Women are portrayed as people with true love.** Thoni is portrayed as a person with true love to Remi. Despite the fact that Remi runs away from her she is determined to wait even for 20 years. She does not want to take the third husband. She says "I cannot go to a third husband" pg 2 and she adds in pg 4 "no, no, no, I will not go with another, but him I call my husband, even if I wait for twenty years and more I shall bear all" pg 4 When Remi abuses her in public she takes her life showing that she had a true commitment to Remi.

e) **Women are portrayed as sympathetic people.** Nyobi sympathizes with Thoni due to her state of loneliness and even advices Thoni to take another husband to conquer her world of loneliness. Also the woman advices Thoni not to think of killing herself. She even invites Thoni to go and live with her.

3. **CONFLICTS;** This refers to the misunderstanding or collision of ideas, viewpoints or opinions within aperson, between or among groups of people in the society. Or it is a situation in which thereare opposing ideas, opinions, feelings or wishes. Like other plays, in this play there areseveral conflicts as analyzed below;

a) **INTRAPERSONAL CONFLICT;** Due to some circumstances, there are different intrapersonal conflicts among the following people.

- **Thoni.** She suffers intrapersonal conflict since her husband is dead and now she faces loneliness. Then her next husband Remi has disappeared something that she might translate that he does not love her. Expressing her situation she says "why do men not rest in my hands? Death took away my first husband. Now the next, his brother has left me. The hut's gloom and loneliness has started eating into me." pg 4.

- **Nyobi;** she suffers intrapersonal conflict first, due to the sudden death of her son, followed by her husband and the later disappearance of Remi. She expresses this by saying "My heart is still heavy with grief…, my first son, so big and strong was taken from me just like that,…, our tears had hardly dried before my man follows, and now Remi, …"pg 6 Second, it is with the way Thoni lives in loneliness, thinking of Remi. She advises her to get another husband but Thoni refuses to move from one husband to another like a common whore.

- **Remi;** he suffers intrapersonal conflict because of the circumstances taking place in the country and his tribe in particular. That is why he runs awayto find peace in the city but the problems follow him there. The whole country is suffering from tribalism, racialism, and religious factions. All Remi is doing, is to not only expose the cantankerous effects of tribalism, racialism and religious factions but also to root them out with both hands.

b) **INTERPERSONAL CONFLICT;** These are conflicts or misunderstanding between two people.

- **There is a conflict between Remi and Jane.** This occurs when Remi wants to go back home and refuses to take Jane with him. It grows bigger when Remi tells her that he is already married and Jane becomes angry since Remi has wasted her time lying to her that he would marry her. She says to Remi "do you honestly believe that race matters, that the colour of my skin or yours should form a barrier between people?" Pg 36

- **There is a conflict/misunderstanding between Remi and Omange.** Remi wants the government in the new independent country to be strict. E.g. People have no right to oppose the government; workers have no right to strike for higher wages. Omange opposes this idea by saying that trade union must have the right to strike and demand for their rights. For him "a trade union without the right to strike is like a lion without claws and teeth" pg23

- **There is also a contradiction on the question of marrying Thoni.** Remi believes that she does not love him or else she wouldn't have married his brother. Omange tells him to give her a chance to express her love to him since one cannot read someone's heart or feelings merely by appearance.

c) **FAMILY CONFLICT;** There is a family conflict between Remi and his mother. This occurs when Remi runsaway and leaves Thoni in loneliness and on coming back he attacks his mother inpublic. Remi says "And you mother. I turn to you. What did you do to me? You harpedon my weakness and made me marry a woman whose love and loyalty will ever lie withthose in the grave". NYOBI replies "you talk to me so? You talk to me so?" pg 48

d) **CULTURAL CONFLICT;** There is an obvious conflict between traditionalists who follow traditional ways of life and Christians. When discussing the coming of Remi, the elders want Remi to be on their side, and lead them as a tribe to victory and want him to stay away from his mother and the pastor. On the other hand the pastor wants Remi to be the future leader of the church. He sees politics as something bad and urges that he should stay away from the tribal influence. This causes segregation and disunity among the people.

e) **POLITICAL CONFLICT;** There is a conflict between the new government and the citizens. The conflict arises from the fact that they fought for independence thinking that things will change when they get independence. But to the common people life is still hard as they have no land, taxation is a burden to them while the ministers and their Permanent secretaries fatten on bribes and inflated salaries. Independence has not reduced the amount of racial tension. Omange says "since independence tribalism and tribal loyalties seem to have increased. And even the leaders who were the supporters of the Africanist Party are the very ones who are encouraging these feelings" pg 23. Also the government has enacted legislation against strikes. That is why even Marua people want Remi to represent them in the government so that they can also enjoy the national cake.

f) SOCIAL CONFLICT; There is a conflict between Remi and his society. This results from the approach in which Remi addresses the people without respect. He attacks them for perpetuating tribalism, religious differences and shackles of custom. He says "I will no longer be led by a woman, priest or tribe. I will crush tribalism, beneath my feet, and all the shackles of custom." Pg 49. They all wonder how he could be so rude to them. The pastor narrates how he addresses the people with anger that some elders go away in guilt and shame. Pg 47

4. **DISUNITY;** This implies a lack of agreement between people. Disunity has become a major barrier to the struggle for change in the country. This problem is caused by tribalism, racialism and religious factions. This has become a real obstacle in fighting for their rights. Remi is used by the playwright as his mouthpiece to condemn racialism, tribalism and religious factions in this society. To show that he hates this division and wants to inculcate the spirit of nationalism he says: "we must help ourselves....Turn hearts and minds to create a nation, then will tribe and race disappear. And man shall live free.." pg 48. Then he advises the pastor. "Even you, Pastor. You and other Christians must not live isolated. We must join hands..." pg 48 to show his hatred for tribalism he comes with a friend from another tribe (Njobe tribe) and introduces him as their brother. He tells the people to build more schools as education is the key to success.

5. **BUILDING THE FUTURE;** Remi is struggling to build a better future for his society. He wants people to develop and befree. They suggest some of the ways through which they can bring changes.

- People must be united and work cooperatively.
- Tribalism, racism and religious differences must be crushed down.
- Education should be insisted as an instrument of change in the country.
- The state must play its part by leading the way. Omange suggests for instance that "the Africanist Party must first give back the settler's land to the people. Illiteracy ought to be abolished within a year otherwise they'll revert to tribalism and religion as a cure for their ills" pg 53

    However, changes must go step by step. Remi is too fast in his approaches. He attacks the leaders and other people instead of educating them first, the cantankerous effects of Racism, tribalism and religious differences. As a result he jeopardizes his relationship with other members including his own family members. He admits by saying "I came back to break tribe and custom, instead I've broken you and me". This is to say his intention was right but he used a wrong approach.

6. **PROTEST;** This is the expression of strong disagreement with or opposition to something. People in theplay show protest against unfair new Blackman's government in the country which practices the colonial regime.

- **They protest against exploitation** through heavy taxation. They say that independence has brought them "heavier and heavier taxation" pg 11
- **They protest against land alienation.** It is shown that the land has been taken by the settlers and the people who fought for independence have no land. They ask "look at our country since independence. Where is the land" pg 11
- **They protest against poor social services** like schools, hospitals etc. they ask; "where are the schools for our children?" pg 11

- **They protest against oppression.** They are made to work for long hours without pay.
- **They protest against poor living condition.** They condemn the government for telling them about roads while they are hungry. "we are told about roads, about hospitals; but which hungry man wants a road?" pg 11
- **Remi protests against tribalism** by the leaders, religion isolation by the pastor and other Christians and racism.
- **Remi also protests against some tribe customs** like widow inheritance. He decides to run away from home to avoid such outdated customs.

7. **THE INFLUENCE OF EDUCATION;**
- In this play education has been portrayed as an important tool in bringing awareness. Remi is aware of many political and social affairs because he is educated. He joins the Africanist Party and becomes an active politician. He realizes the dangers of tribalism, racism and religion factions in the building of a nation.
- Also through his education he gets a job in the Oil-Company but later realizes that it is exploiting the country.
- Education has given confidence to Remi to attack any challenging situation and he is even no longer shy to face girls. He also boldly attacks the elders and the pastor simply because he is more educated than anybody else in his tribe.
- Nevertheless, his education has made him proud and boastful, feeling superior to the villagers. He wants to abolish all tribe customs at once and introduce new lifestyles without giving the people enough time to adjust themselves. He speaks harshly to the elders and to his mother and rejects Thoni in public. This is arrogance as a result of negative influence of education.

8. **TRIBALISM;**
- This society seems to be affected by tribalism to a large extent. The elders especially are more affected. They do not view things as a nation but as a tribe. That is one reason why Remi decides to act against them. They want him to be in the government to represent their tribe interest. For example the leader says; "not one of our skin and blood is in the new government" pg 30.
- Moreover when they go to persuade Remi to come back to the village, this is all they have got to tell him "We want a tribal political party" another adds; "A Prime Minister from the tribe". Pg 31. This is one of the dangerous enemies to nation building which must be discarded if we want to create a spirit of nationalism.

9. **CORRUPTION;** Though it does not appear throughout Remi points it out in his conversation with Jane.He shows that the government officials enjoy good life just because they take corruption(bribe) while workers like teachers starve. In page 21 when Jane suggests that he shouldgo back home and become a teacher he says "And starve – while ministers and theirpermanent secretaries fatten on bribes and inflated salaries"

10. **CLASSES**; Just like most societies, in this country also there are classes. There are classes based on economic status and those based on faith (religious differences).
- **The rich and the poor;** There is the class of the rich people comprising the leaders, settlers and othercompany owners who enjoy the national resources by paying themselves highsalaries and engaging in corruption. On the other hand

is the class of the poorcitizens who are exploited through, forced community work, low wages, taxation,land alienation and have generally poor living conditions and inadequate socialservices like schools, hospitals and the like.

- **Christians and traditionalists;** Another class division in this society is between the Christians being represented by the pastor, Nyobi, and other converts, and the non-Christians (traditionalists) being represented by elders. The playwright shows that the division is so severe and intense to the extent that the Christians isolate themselves from other people. Their division is even seen in the way they want to influence Remi when he comes back. Christians do not want him to fall under the influence of elders while elders also do not want him to fall under the influence of Christians. So generally we learn that class division is not healthy in any society that wants to get sustainable development since they become their own enemies instead of becoming the authors of their own destiny.

11. BETRAYAL; There are also cases of betrayal in this play.

- **First, Remi betrays Jane** by refusing to marry her as he promised. Remi promises Jane to marry her when the time is ripe and the two spend time together as lovers. When the time comes for Remi to go back home he tells Jane that he is already married and cannot go with her. She complains; "Just now you are betraying the ideals you used to mirror before my eyes" pg 36
- **Second, Remi also betrays his tribe** for not using his education to help them solve their social problems instead he runs away to the city to enjoy the city pleasures leaving his people in a bad situation.
- **Third, the government has betrayed the citizens.** During the struggle for independence the people were asked to join the nationalistic movements and they agreed, later on their situation remains unchanged after independence. For example they complain, "Look at our country since independence. Where is the land? Where is the food? Where are the schools for our children? pg 11. This is to say the promises for which they fought have been betrayed.
- **Forth, Nyobi betrays her Christian faith** by blessing traditional medicine. When the elders tell her that they want to bring Remi back but they want a mother's blessings to attend them on that difficult journey, she says "with all my heart, go in peace, and success attend you" having discovered her fault she regrets "I know Christo hates our medicine. Suppose God punishes me so that Remi does not come back?" Finally they mock her by saying "Her son is dearer to her than her Christianity" pg 12+

MESSAGES

1. Running away from problems is not a way of solving them.
2. We do not solve problems by committing suicide.
3. Outdated customs like widow inheritance and superstitious beliefs bring more problems to the society so they should be discarded.
4. Bringing about changes is not an overnight process. It needs time, determination, focus and patience.
5. Tribalism, racialism, disunity and religious conflicts are obstacles to development.
6. Betrayal is not good as it causes unnecessary conflicts.

7. We should use our education positively to bring about changes.
8. Classes should be discouraged as they bring disunity in the society.

RELEVANCE
The play is relevant in a number of ways:
1. There are people who run away from problems as a way of avoiding them but finally they find themselves haunted by the same problems.
2. There are people who commit suicide as a way of solving their problems.
3. Betrayal is common among African countries particularly Tanzania. The leaders do not fulfill their promises to the citizens.
4. Widow inheritance is still a common custom among many Tanzanian tribes like the Kuryans of Lake Zone.
5. There are people who still believe in superstition and witch craft as a way of solving their social problems.
6. Racism and tribalism are still common phenomena in some African countries like South Africa, Kenya, Rwanda, Nigeria, etc.
7. The newly post-independent governments in Africa have not solved the people problems yet. Only those in power are enjoying life while the common people are suffering.

TITLE; THIS TIME TOMORROW
PLAYWRIGHT; NGUGI WA THIONG'O
SETTING; KENYA- UHURU MARKET

PLOT SUMMARY
The whole play is organized in only one act. The scene breaks by the conversation between a journalist and the editor who are typing an article. The journalist finishes typing and re-reads it. He explains how the whole incident took place, where the city council warriors demolished slums at the shanty-town near the country Bus Terminal. The place is usually a busy place but on that day nobody was seen. This was a Clean –The City Campaign.

* * * *

We are told of Njango's shelter made of Cardboard and rotting tins. Njango and Wanjiro share the floor as a bed just beside the small wall. Njango tries to wake up Wanjiro who is still snoring so that she may help her with the morning chores. She has to prepare the soup for the morning customers like Githua, Macharia, Gitina and others. Wanjiro wakes up and tells her mother the dream she had. She had seen in her dream the shacks being carried away by the floods. Wanjiro begins sweeping and wonders why the city is so quite. She expresses how she is tired of the familiar scenes and sounds around. She says that she never saw these things before she heard the stranger speak. She remembers Asinjo the man she loves and wonders why her mother drove him away.

* * * *

The journalist continues with his narration as people begin waking up. He was recording his news. Wanjiro says that the village is waking up but the birds are hardly awake. That statement annoys her mother. She speaks to Wanjiro in a serious tone that birds do not have to kill themselves in order to live, they don't need money to buy food, they don't buy clothes neither do they pay school fees. Wanjiro is also annoyed by her mother's statement since she (Wanjiro) does not have good clothes neither does she go to school. She considers her mother's words as a mockery to her since her brother was taken to school but she was not. Additionally she is angry due to the fact that she is not given good clothes like other girls around to the point that she is ashamed to walk in the streets.

Njango is annoyed even more and wonders why Wanjiro talks to her in such a manner. She reminds her how she had trouble rising her up. Wanjiro calms down and wishes she had better gone away with Asinjo. Njango warns her that a man from another tribe cannot protect her. She also warns her not to trust men from the city because they mistreat their mistresses even kill them. Wanjiro wished Asinjo would come for her. Njango threatens her never to mention him again- a man from another tribe. Wanjiro describes how she wishes to have nice dresses like the one she saw in the city and almost stole it. She says that the stranger had told them that the city belongs to them; the shops, the factories and everything. Her mother says it's only for a chosen few. They talk of how the stranger had led the delegation to the city Council, since they were given only few days to move away. She wonders why her mother would call such a man as a cheat and a loafer.

Wanjiro asks her mother whether they are going to pull down their house but Njango says that she is not going to move. Njango tells Wanjiro not to talk about the stranger because her father used to talk like that and it cost him his life. They were captured and he was shot dead by the Whiteman.

******

The journalist continues his narrative that as the day broke people began engaging in their daily activities. Tinsmiths beating their tins, and the buses vomited a lot of people. He followed them and joined the populace for a cup of soup. Shortly the customers were at Njango's hut for soup. As usual she keeps on shouting calling more customers while others are already taking their soup. Inspector Kiongo enters speaking from a loudspeaker telling the people who dwell in Uhuru Market that a month given to them is over and by 12:00 that day all the shacks had to be demolished.

The journalist comes in and takes some photos and begins to interview people to get their views on the story. The tinsmith explains how he had had hard time making a living before and after independence. Njango complains why Kiongo has changed while he used to be her good customer but now he sees himself as a king. The journalist interviews the shoemaker who also complains on how they have been betrayed because he was also an active member of the Party and they fought for freedom having taken an oath and sung patriotic songs.
"Even if they deride me, and beat me and kill me,
    "They shall never make me forget
    "This is a black man's country.

He was even sent to Manyani concentration camp and came back home after the emergency but no jobs and no land for him. After a brief chat they decide to hold a meeting with the stranger who is believed to have magic power to blind the eyes of the City Council Members. They all leave but Wanjiro is left alone. In her opinion she would like the stranger not to work his magic so that they can move from those slums. She remembers Asinjo who she says is the only man who told her she was beautiful and used to touch her breasts.

Suddenly Asinjo comes and Wanjiro welcomes him warmly. He gives out a 10/= shillings note and she is so surprised and impressed. He says that he is no longer without a job; he is now a taxi-driver. He complains on how Njango used to mistreat him just because he was jobless and from another tribe. He invites Wanjiro to go and live with him in Old Jerusalem where he has got a house. He promises her also to buy her nice dresses and shoes. She asks him to hold on until her mother comes back.

* * * * * * * *

The crowd enters with posters and the stranger addresses them. He says that Uhuru has brought the people who love driving Mercedes Benz and long American cars while the majority starves in the slums. He also tells them that he cannot work magic as they expect. He says the only magic that can work for them is unity. The police appear and all the people run away while the stranger unsuccessfully tries to call them back. The police arrest the stranger for inciting a crowd to violence and civil disobedience. Njango comes back with the memory of her own husband as the sight of the stranger reminded her how her husband was arrested.

Kiongo announces that people must hurry up taking their things from their houses. Wanjiro reports to her mother that she wants to go away with Asinjo but her mother refuses that she cannot marry a man from another tribe and without a job. Wanjiro assures her mother that Asinjo is different, he now has a job and a house and tells her mother that she is old and doesn't know the ways of the world and the needs of a young woman. She says goodbye to her mother and leaves. Njango is left desperate and Kiongo tells her to hurry up and leave. Njango's final words are "They are herding us out like cattle. Where shall I go now, tonight? Where shall I be this time tomorrow? If only we had stood up against them! If only we could stand together." Pg56

CHARACTERIZATION

1. NJANGO;

- She is a Tribalist. Njango is a tribalist because she is against inter-tribal marriages. She is still conservative and does not want to welcome changes. When Wanjiro says that she is going away to live with Asinjo, She says to Wanjiro; "With that man? A man from another tribe?"pg 55
- She is a poor slum dweller. She is among the poor people who are dwelling in the slums at Uhuru market. She sleeps on the floor with her daughter.
- She is a Widow. We are told that her husband was captured and shot like a dog by the Whiteman.
- She is a Hot-tempered and strict mother. She often treats Wanjiro harshly. E.g. in page 37 she says "Other girls rise up before the sun to help with morning chores. This one snores like a pig. I will truly pinch your fat nose or drench your face with cold water". Also she threatens Wanjiro every time she mentions Asinjo. E.g. in page 56 she says "No child of mine, from my own flesh, will sell her body. I'll break her bones, else she break mine first".
- She is a Petty businesswoman. She earns a living by selling soup to slum dwellers. As one of her customers comments, "Give me another mug of soup. You got to be taught to live in this market city". Pg 45
- She is a Hardworking mother. She wakes up early in the morning daily and prepares the soup to sell to the morning customers.

- She is a Traditionalist. This can be proved from the way she denies Wanjiro to marry a man from another tribe, she believes that a man from a different tribe cannot protect her daughter. Also she sent her son to his uncle to attend school but retained Wanjiro because she is a girl. This is an outdated tradition.

2. WANJIRO;

- She is lazy and stubborn. Unlike other girls who wake up early to help their mothers, Wanjiro is so lazy and always stubborn to her mother. She likes good life but doesn't want to work hard. Njango complains "What a heavy load of flesh, this brat will surely kill me. Other girls rise up before the sun to help with morning chores. This one snores like a pig".
- She is so inquisitive. She asks her mother many questions for knowledge to a point where Njago is annoyed. In page 43 Njago exclaims "You never give me a moment's peace, do you? What do you want to ask? Not about your city Council I hope?"
- She is an avid admirer of western lifestyle. She admires living like Europeans. She wants to marry Asinjo so that she may go to live European-like life in the city. She says "I long for the pleasures of this glittering city. I want a frock. And shoes – high heels – so that I can walk like a European lady. A bag hanging from my left elbow – fingering a cigarette in my right hand." pg 52
- She has true love. Despite the threats and warning from her mother that she should stay away from Asinjo because she cannot marry a man from another tribe, she eloped with Asinjo nevertheless. For her what matters is love and not tribes.
- She runs away from problems. Wanjiro believes that running away from problems is a way of solving them. She runs away with Asinjo as a way of avoiding the poor condition at home. She says to her mother "I am going with him! You are old. You don't know the ways of the world or the needs of a young woman" pg 55
- She is less obedient to her mother. Wanjiro is not obedient to her mother as she likes arguing with her. She doesn't listen to what her mother is telling her. That's why she elopes with Asinjo despite her mother's warnings.
- She is a Victim of women discrimination. She is not sent to school just because she is a girl but her brother was sent to their uncle to attend school. She complains "Where is my brother? You sent him to my uncle in the country so that he might attend school. Me, you kept here to work for you" pg 39
- She lives a poor life. Wanjiro lives in an impoverished neighbourhood where they share a floor as a bed with her mother. She even desires good dresses but due to poverty she is unable to get one. She is even tempted to steal. In her own words she says "Two days ago I saw a dress in the city. I wanted it, so much, I almost stole it". Pg 41
- She is not educated. Wanjiro is not sent to school unlike her brother.
- She is beautiful but not smart. She is a beautiful lady but due to poor living condition at her home she appears not smart. That is one reason she loves Asinjo because he is the only one who acknowledges her beauty despite the fact that she has no nice dresses. She says "Asinjo was different though. Used to touch my breasts. He even said I was beautiful. I felt such a joy – the first time" pg 50

3. ASINJO;

- He is a taxi driver. He drives a tax in Nairobi city. He says "I am no longer without a job. I am a tax-driver" pg. 50

- He is westernised. He too believes that tribal differences should not form barriers in marriage. He comments that Njango is only an old woman who doesn't know the ways of the world or the needs of a young woman.
- He leaves with Wanjiro. Finally Wanjiro leaves her lonely mother and goes to live with Asinjo.
- He has true love for Wanjiro. Despite being threatened by Wanjiro's mother he kept on visiting her. Moreover, after getting the job many girls want him but his love is still with Wanjiro. He says "I have now got a good job, and many girls want me. If I did not love you would I have come back after all these names your mother called me?"
- He is an agent for change. He is anti-tribalism as he tried to show that tribal differences should not be an obstacle in modern relationships. What matters is whether the two parties love each other.

4. STRANGER;

- He is an activist. He makes a speech which conscioutized people about their rights and the importance of unity if they want to get their rights.
- He is sympathetic. At first he was reluctant to lead the delegation to the city council. But when men showed him the notice that they had been given only a few days to move away and women wept in front of him he agreed to lead the delegation.
- He is against oppression, humiliation and exploitation. He is using his intellect to help the slum dwellers get their rights by acting as their representative.
- He is betrayed by the slum dwellers. When the police appear at the meeting ground all the slum dwellers run away leaving him alone to be arrested by the police as he tries unsuccessfully to call them back.
- He believes in unity and not in magic power. The slum dwellers believed that he can use the magic powers to blind the eyes of the City Council, but he assures them that the only magic that can work on their favor is unity.
- He is courageous and agent for change. He is among the freedom fighters that fought the white men in the forests. He is still determined to fight for the rights of poor citizen. Even when all the slum dwellers run away he does not run away.
- He is arrested by the police and charged of inciting a crowd to violence and civil disobedience.

5. INSPECTOR KIONGO;

- He is a City Council officer. He works in the City council in the Health Department. Pg 46
- He is in charge of the Clean the City Campaign. He says that the city has to be cleaned by demolishing the slums since they are a great shame on the city and the tourists from America, Britain and West Germany are disgusted with the dirty of the city. Pg 46
- He is a betrayer. Initially he was a member of the Youth Wing, and a good customer of Njango's soup. But when he becomes a City Council officer he betrays them and drives them away. Njango says "Is that not Kiongo? He used to come here – every lunch time. A bowl of soup and a fleshy bone, and he would go away all thanks and gratitude....Now he is a king – a king!" pg47-48
- He has no mercy. He conducts the Clean-The -City Campaign by mercilessly demolishing the slums but does not allocate an alternative settlement for the slum

dwellers. That is why Njango keeps wondering "They are herding us out like cattle, where shall I go now, tonight? Where shall I be, this time tomorrow?" pg 56

6. **SHOEMAKER;**
   - He is a slum dweller. He is among the poor people who are living in the slums because when he came back from the detention camp their land was taken and he had no job.
   - He is illiterate. He is unable to tell his age.
   - He is an ex-freedom fighter and active member of the ruling Party. He went to fight for freedom and was arrested and sent to Manyani Concentration Camp.
   - He is a shoemaker. He earns a living by mending shoes.
   - He is willing to move but the government should first show him a place to go.

7. **TINSMITH;**
   - He works as a tinsmith. He earns his daily bread by making and selling watertins, pangas, jembes, braziers etc
   - He is illiterate. He doesn't even know his age or the year he came to live at Uhuru market. The journalist asks him his age; he answers "Age? Fifty, sixty, I cannot say. Pg 46. When he is asked about the year he came to Uhuru market, he says "When? Let me count – one, two, three, oh, many years ago. Pg 47
   - He has done many jobs during the war of independence and after it. He has worked as a, cook; cooking, washing and sweeping. He worked as a porter with the Railway and Harbor.
   - He is among the poor slum dwellers. Because of the terrible experiences he went through including sleeping on the shop-verandas, in trenches, public latrines etc, being moved from place to place by the police and hunger, he finally found a place in Uhuru market and started his trade there.

INTRODUCTION/TITLE OF THE BOOK

This book is entitled "This Time tomorrow". The title is a reflection of the future life of the people who live at Uhuru Market.
1. Njango is asking herself, 'Where Shall I Be This Time Tomorrow?' This shows her state of disappointment when the city council decides to demolish their slums. She has nowhere to go.
2. Njago's voice represents all slum dwellers whose slums were demolished. They are all wondering where they are going to spend their future lives because the slums have been their only home. Their land was taken when they were fighting for independence. E.g. The shoemaker says "It is not that I don't want to move. But the government should give me a place to go" pg 48

SETTING

The setting is Kenya after independence. The specific setting is Uhuru Market in Nairobi city. However, the setting can represent many African countries because; Demolition of slums is a common phenomenon in most unplanned African cities.

STYLE

The playwright has employed a number of techniques in his play. The play is largely presented in a dialogue although there are few cases of monologue/narration where the journalist narrates the events. Also the playwright used a flashback when a tinsmith narrates his past life before independence.

1. **He has used the language of journalism** where the journalist writes his article and tries to read it. But also the journalist interviews people to get their views on the story of demolition of the slums.
2. Moreover **he has made use of a song** which the freedom fighters sang;
    "Even if they deride me, and beat me and kill me,
    "They shall never make me forget
    "This is a black man's country.
3. To further enrich his style, **he has used the language of advertisement.** This occurs in two ways; one it is used when making public announcement for a meeting. o "A meeting! A meeting! Everybody – to the meeting at once. Long live Uhuru Market Long live Uhuru Market." Pg 49.But also when Inspector Kiongo announces "This is inspector Kiongo of the City Council Health Department. I remind all those that dwell in these places that today was the date I gave your last delegation....p g 46
4. Additionally, it is used to advertise a business.
    Soup for twenty cents. Soup for twenty cents.
    Soup to build your bones.
    Soup is cheap here today.

LANGUAGE USE;

The playwright has used simple language with full of figures of speech. Some of them are outlined below.

1. **Symbolism;**
    - Filthy mushrooms symbolises the poor houses/slums. Pg 35
2. **Allusion;**
    - Suddenly one was back in the days of Joshua when the legendary walls of Jericho came tumbling down pg 36.(referring to Jericho in the Bible)
    - And forgive us our sins. We are late for our morning soup. Pg 45 (referring to the Lord's Prayer in the Bible)
3. **Synecdoche;**
    - Not a human soul was in sight. Pg 36 (Meaning no any human being was present)
4. **Simile**
    - The terminus normally full of beehive activities was now as quiet as the Kalahari or Sahara desert. Pg 36
    - Njango and Wanjiro share the floor as a bed. Pg 36
    - This one snores like a pig pg 36
    - Asinjo has eyes like the stranger. Pg 39
    - And such thick lips as big as a mountain. pg 41
    - They shot him dead like a dog. Pg 43
    - People who streamed away in every direction like disturbed safari ants. Pg 44
    - They are herding us out like cattle. Pg 56
5. **Metaphor**
    - (Wanjiro) What a heavy load of flesh. Pg 36
    - (Human voices) It was another house of Babel. Pg 44

- (soup) Our daily bread. Pg 45

6. Alliteration
- What...what water? Pg 37
- Cocks crow, babies cry, and tins clash. Pg 39

7. Imagery
- Image of sight
- Bones, decaying meat, white maggots, tins, paper, broken pots etc. Pg 37
- Tactile image. (Image of touch)
- A smooth skin pg 41
- Olfactory image (image of smell)
- The tantalizing smell of meat. Pg 45
- Once or twice I slept in public latrines: Phew! The smell, Pg 47

8. Saying;
- You sleep God's sleep Pg 37 (sleeping as though you are dead)
- Njango you old whore, you know how to milk your men. pg 45

9. Personification;
- Dawn found us there. Pg 37
- Just now noise is dead in the city. Pg 38
- The village was waking up. Pg 39
- Fleets of buses from the country vomited out people ... who streamed away in every direction like disturbed safari ants. Pg 44
- Long live Uhuru Market Long live Uhuru Market. Pg49

10. Rhetorical questions;
- You speak to me like that? Do you know who I am? Do you? Pg 40.

11. Exaggeration;
- And such thick lips as big as a mountain. pg 41
- So black – blacker than the soot on that pot. Pg 41

12. Onomatopoeia;
- Phew! The smell, Pg 47
- Puuu! His voice makes me spit Pg 47
- Cock crowing; chicken cackling. Pg 44

13. Reiteration;
- Run! Run! Run! quickly. Pg 53
- Police! The police are coming pg 53
- Hurry up! Hurry up! Pg 55,56

THEMES IN THE PLAY

There are many themes in the play "This Time Tomorrow" that it's so hard to exhaust them all. In this book, we are going to discuss the following themes among others; Land Alienation, Poverty, Position Of Women, Ignorance And Illiteracy, Classes, Superstition, Disillusion, Tribalism, Betrayal, Colonial legacy, Conflicts, Disunity etc.

1. **LAND ALIENATION;** Land alienation is discussed in two levels in this play. There is Land alienation during colonialism and Land alienation after independence. The Kenyans are complaining and protesting against land alienation in the following ways.

- During colonial occupation of Kenya, people's land was taken by the colonialists and the Kenyans remained landless. So the Kenyans had to fight for their land in which case most of them had to go into the forest to fight for their soil as the Shoemaker narrates: "We were fighting for freedom, we were fighting for our soil" pg 48. The Stranger says "We fought for land! But where is the land? Pg 53.
- After independence, people are still facing the same problem. The new government officials have taken the land of the poor people who more often than not are those who went into the forest to fight for the land. When they came back after independence their land was gone and it was not returned to them. The Shoemaker says "I came back home after the Emergency. The white man had gone. No job for me, no land either". This shows that the freedom fighters labored for freedom in vain.

2. **POVERTY;** Many people are extremely poor in this society. Not only do they find it hard to afford the daily meals, but they also live in an impoverished neighbourhood (slums). The Shoemaker, tinsmith, Njango, Wanjiro, customers are just few cases in point. The issue of poverty is discussed in the following scenarios;
   - Njango's family is poor. Njango is living a poor life with her daughter Wanjiro. The playwright says even their shelter was made of cardboards and rotting tins. Also "Njango and Wanjiro share the floor as a bed". This is a proof of the highest level of poverty. Moreover, Wanjiro desires good dresses but due to poverty she is unable to get one. She is even tempted to steal. In her own words she says "Two days ago I saw a dress in the city. I wanted it, so much, I almost stole it". Pg 41. It's this reason that makes her elope with Asinjo to try a better life in the city.
   - The Slum dwellers are poor. Most slum dwellers are living in slums because that is what they can afford. They have no jobs, no houses and no money to buy expensive land in the city and build decent houses. That is why they fought for Uhuru believing that their lives would be improved once a black man was in power. The stranger says "We fought for Uhuru, because we were told it would mean decent houses, and decent jobs! But where are the jobs? Where are the houses?"pg 53

3. **CLASSES;** There are two major classes in this society; the lower class (poor people) and the Highclass (rich people). The rich class becomes richer by exploiting the efforts of the poor people majority of who are those who fought for independence.
   - **The lower class.** This is represented by the slum dwellers who live miserably because their land has been taken by those in power. As though that is not enough, they are evicted from the only place where they are living; At Uhuru Market. Most of them earn their living by engaging in petty businesses. They are working as shoemakers, tinsmith, selling soup, etc. So driving them away from this place is just adding salt to the wound. Njango is so desperate and she wonders "Where will Wanjiro and I go when they drive us from here? Where to set up a new trade to earn us bread and water?" pg 54
   - **High Class.** The high class comprises the petty bourgeoisie class that took power from the colonialists and simply ideally replaced the colonizer. The rich Africans are enjoying life, driving expensive cars and living in residential areas for the high class people just as it was during colonialism. Speaking to Wanjiro, Asinjo says "Now I know every part of the city. From Kolo where Europeans live, to Westlands and Kabete where rich Africans have bought stone houses". pg 50. To show how worse

class division can be, the stranger speaks in dissatisfaction, "It (Uhuru) has brought us people who love driving Mercedes Benz and long American cars! While we starve in the slums! Let the city council leave us alone in our slums and our misery" pg 52

4. **DISILLUSION;**
   - This is a state of disappointment because the person you admired or the idea you believed to be good and true now seems without value. Many Africans joined the freedom movements because they believed once they drove the White man away and gained their independence then their living standards would be improved as well. But this is not what happened. The poor people remained poor and those who took power are the only ones enjoying the national cake. As a result the majority are disillusioned. They say; "We fought for Uhuru, because we were told it would mean, decent houses, and decent jobs! But where are the jobs? Where are the houses? "pg 53
   - People believe that Uhuru has brought them practically nothing. But the stranger corrects them by saying "It has brought us people who love driving Mercedes Benz and long American cars! While we starve in the slums" pg 52. This is the highest level of disappointment. The majority believe that good life is now entitled to the chosen few. Wanjiro tells her mother that the stranger said "The city belongs to us, the shops, the factories, everything". And Njango responds desperately "Alas, only to the chosen few." Pg 41. This shows that they have nothing to share in the fruits of independence.

5. **CONFLICT;** A conflict is a situation in which people, groups or countries are involved in a serious disagreement or argument. It can also be understood as a situation in which there are opposing ideas, opinions, feelings or wishes; a situation in which it is difficult to choose. In this play there are several conflicts.

   a) Intrapersonal conflict. This is shown in the following ways:
   - **Njango** faces a serious intrapersonal conflict when she is forced to move to the unknown place and wonders where she is going to spend the rest of her life. To express this conflict she says, "Where will Wanjiro and I go when they drive us from here? Where to set up a new trade to earn us bread and water?" pg 54. It is this same conflict that gives us the title of the play when she says "They are herding us out like cattle. Where shall I go now, tonight? Where shall I be this time tomorrow? Pg 56
   - **Wanjiro** suffers an intrapersonal conflict because of the poor condition at home. While she is a grown up girl and very beautiful, she is poorly dressed unlike other girls of her age. This makes her less smart and uncomfortable. She even desires good dresses to the point that she almost stole a dress in the city. To show her dissatisfaction with the poor life at home she says "Look at me. I have no clothes like other girls. I am now a woman. Yet no man dares glance in my direction. Well, maybe once or twice but only to ask: who is that thing in rags? Pg50. As a solution she runs away with Asinjo who loves her.

   b) Family conflict. This occurs between Wanjiro and her mother (Njango). This conflict arises from the lazy and stubborn behaviour of Wanjiro towards her mother. She does not wake up on time to help her mother with domestic chores like other girls do. So Njango keeps complaining and Wanjiro argues back. As a result Wanjiro decides to run away from home as a solution to her problems.

   c) Political conflict. This conflict occurs between the government officers and the slum dwellers. It results from the fact that the government (police) and the City Council want to demolish the shelters of the slum dwellers. The slum dwellers hold a meeting in protest but it is suppressed by the government through the police. The stranger is arrested for inciting a crowd to violence and civil disobedience! These conflicts are common in many African countries.

d) Cultural conflict. There is **a conflict between modern European culture and traditional African culture.** In other words it is a conflict between modernity against conservatism. The young generation being represented by Asinjo and Wanjiro has got their own ways of looking at things different from that of old generation being represented by Njango. In this play we see Wanjiro admiring not only to have better life like that of well-to-do African ladies, but more importantly to live like a European lady. She is an avid admirer of western lifestyle. She wants to marry Asinjo so that she may go to live a European-like life in the city. She says "I long for the pleasures of this glittering city. I want a frock. And shoes – high heels– so that I can walk like a European lady. A bag hanging from my left elbow – fingering a cigarette in my right hand." pg 52

- As if that is not enough, she goes out of her way and says to her mother, "I am going with him! You are old. You don't know the ways of the world or the needs of a young woman" pg 55 they also believe in intertribal marriages. For them what matters is love.
- On the other hand, are those with conservative ideas like Njango who believe that intertribal marriage is impossible. These people believe that a man from another tribe and without a job cannot protect the girl. When these two sides meet with differing perspectives there is obviously a natural conflict.

6. **TRIBALISM;** This is a behavior, attitude, etc. that is based on being loyal to a tribe or other social group. Although it appears in a small part, it is significant that we discuss it. Tribalism is a problem in most African countries. It is also one of the reasons that account for the many civil wars and political instability in African countries. In this play, Njango shows an open involvement in tribal loyalties. She denies Wanjiro to marry Asinjo due to the fact that Asinjo is from a different tribe. Njango is still conservative and doesn't believe that people who are from different tribes can love and protect each other. To Wanjiro she says, "Protected you? A man from another tribe? Tribalism has to be stopped.

7. **IGNORANCE AND ILLITERACY;** Ignorance and illiteracy have been common enemies in developing countries. Manypeople are not only ignorant of important information about their lives but they are alsoilliterate and thus they perpetuate outdated customs and hinder their development. Thistheme is discussed by the playwright in the following ways:

- Njago is ignorant of the cultural dynamics. She still holds tribalistic ideas, believing that people from different tribes cannot intermarry and still be committed to each other. That's why she rejects Wanjiro's proposal to marry Asinjo.
- The slum dwellers are ignorant of the better ways to fight for their rights. They believe in outdated superstations to work in their favor. They want the stranger to work magic by blinding the eyes of the City council. The stranger being aware of their ignorance he tells them that the only magic that can work for them is their unity.

- The tinsmith and shoemaker are illiterate. They don't even know their age nor the year the tinsmith came to live at Uhuru market. The journalist asks the tinsmith his age; he answers "Age? Fifty, sixty, I cannot say. Pg 46. When he is asked about the year he came to Uhuru market, he says "When? Let me count – one, two, three, oh, many years ago. Pg 47. With such kind of people in the society it is hard to develop because more often than not they are the ones who become an obstacle to their own development. Recall how the stranger struggled unsuccessfully to call them back when the police appeared at the meeting square "Brothers and sisters! I beseech you not to run away! Your cause is just! Your homes are dear to you!"pg 54. They all ran away.

8. **SUPERSTITION;** Superstition is the belief that particular events happen in a way that cannot beexplained by reason or science; or the belief that particular events bring good or bad luck. This is a common problem among many African societies. This society also believes in the power of magic to help them in times of trouble. They believe that the stranger has the magic power that can blind the eyes of the City Council officers not to evacuate them from their slums. The 1st customer says "Why don't we hold a meeting with the stranger? He works in magic. Will he not blind their eyes? Pg 49 When he tells them that he cannot work magic and that he has no the power of the witchdoctor to blind the eyes of the determined City council, they are so disappointed. The crowd wonders "What is he saying? Why does he say this? He can help us! He must help us! Pg 52

9. **BETRAYAL;** To betray is to hurt somebody who trusts you, especially by not being loyal or faithful tothem. It also means to ignore your principles or beliefs in order to achieve something orgain an advantage for yourself. Betrayal is another common enemy to development indeveloping countries. Betrayal appears from individual to national levels. Theplaywright has portrayed betrayal in the following cases:
    - **Many Africans freedom fighters were betrayed by those who took power from colonialists.** People believe that Uhuru has brought them practically nothing. But the stranger corrects them by saying "It has brought us people who love driving Mercedes Benz and long American cars! While we starve in the slums" pg 52. This shows that the majority have been betrayed by the minority. The majority believe that good life is now entitled to the chosen few. Wanjiro tells her mother that the stranger said "the city belongs to us, the shops, the factories, everything". And Njango responds desperately "Alas, only to the chosen few." Pg 41. This is to say they have nothing to share in the fruits of independence.
    - **Inspector Kiongo has betrayed the slum dwellers.** Initially he was a member of the Youth Wing, and a good customer of Njango's soup. But when he becomes a City Council officer he betrays them and drives them away. Njango says "Is that not Kiongo? He used to come here – every lunch time. A bowl of soup and a fleshy bone, and he would go away all thanks and gratitude....Now he is a king – a king!" pg47-48
    - **Wanjiro betrays her mother** by running away and leaving her desperate. Wanjiro leaves her mother alone in a demolished homestead and goes to live in the city with Asinjo. Njango calls her unsuccessfully "Wanjiro! Wanjiro! Don't go away. Don't leave me alone! What shall I do without you? I am a useless old woman". Wanjiro ignores all these and leaves. This is betrayal to her mother.

- **The stranger is betrayed by the slum dwellers.** They are the ones who asked him to address them but when the police appear at the meeting ground all the slum dwellers run away leaving him alone to be arrested by the police as he tries unsuccessfully to call them back.

10. UNITY and DISUNITY;

- **Unity is very important in any struggle.** If people want to achieve their goals especially when struggling against oppressive ruling class, unity is a basic requirement. Unfortunately enough this is not the case in this society. At first they joined hands together and requested the stranger to lead a delegation to the city council. Men showed him the notice that they had been given only a few days to move away and women wept in front of him he agreed to lead the delegation to ask for the extension of the time they were given to move and it worked. They were given a grace period of one month.

- In the final round, they ask him to address them in a meeting where they should express their grievances towards the government for evicting them from their homes without showing them where to go. While they believe in magic power, the stranger tells them that the only magic that can help them is unity. He says "Let us stand together. Let us with one voice tell the new government: we want our homes, we love them. Unless the City Council shows us another place to go, where we can earn our bread, we shall not lift a finger to demolish our homes! We must defend our own". Pg 53

- As if he was talking to himself, they didn't understand him. When the police appear all run away while he calls them back unsuccessfully. Finally, Njango wonders what different it could have made if they had stood together "If only we had stood up together! If only we could stand together". Pg 56

- The message we get here is that United we stand, divided we fall.

11. POSITION OF WOMEN; A woman is portrayed in various positions in this play.

a) **A woman is portrayed as a caretaker.** Njango tries her level best to provide for the family and takes care of Wanjiro. She often tries to mould her daughter to be a responsible girl. E.g. in page 37 she says "Other girls rise up before the sun to help with morning chores. This one snores like a pig. I will truly pinch your fat nose or drench your face with cold water". This is an attempt to make her responsible.

b) **A woman is portrayed as a victim of gender discrimination.** Wanjiro is not sent to school just because she is a girl but her brother was sent to their uncle to attend school. She complains "Where is my brother? You sent him to my uncle in the country so that he might attend school. Me, you kept here to work for you" pg 39

c) **A woman is portrayed as a hardworking person and a bread earner.** Njango wakes up early in the morning daily and prepares the soup to sell to the morning customers. She earns a living by selling soup to slum dwellers. As one of her customers comments, "Give me another mug of soup. You got to be taught to live in this market city". Pg 45

d) **A woman is portrayed as a person with true love.** Wanjiro is a case in point here. Despite the threats and warnings from her mother that she should stay away from Asinjo because she cannot marry a man from another tribe, she eloped with Asinjo nevertheless. For her what matters is love and not tribes.

e) **A woman is portrayed as an avid admirer of western lifestyle.** Wanjiro admires living like Europeans. She wants to marry Asinjo so that she may go to live European-like life in the city. She says "I long for the pleasures of this glittering city. I want a frock. And shoes – high heels – so that I can walk like a European lady. A bag hanging from my left elbow – fingering a cigarette in my right hand." pg 52

f) **A woman is portrayed as a Traditionalist.** This can be proved from the way Njango denies Wanjiro to marry a man from another tribe, she believes that a man from a different tribe cannot protect her daughter. Also she sent her son to his uncle to attend school but retained Wanjiro because she is a girl. This is an outdated tradition.

12. **COLONIAL LEGACY;** Colonialism and western life style in African countries have produced people who aresuffering from colonial hangovers. African countries are now politically independent butthey are still mentally colonised. There are people who still admire western lifestyle andways of living.

- **Wanjiro admires living like Europeans.** She wants to marry Asinjo so that she may go to live European-like life in the city. She says "I long for the pleasures of this glittering city. I want a frock. And shoes – high heels – so that I can walk like a European lady. A bag hanging from my left elbow – fingering a cigarette in my right hand." pg 52

- **The high/ruling class that took power from the colonialist is enjoying life**, driving expensive cars and living in residential areas for the high class people just as it was during colonialism. Speaking to Wanjiro, Asinjo says "Now I know every part of the city. From Kolo where Europeans live, to Westlands and Kabete where rich Africans have bought stone houses". pg 50. To show how the high class is mentally colonised, the stranger speaks in dissatisfaction, "It (Uhuru) has brought us people who love driving Mercedes Benz and long American cars! While we starve in the slums! Let the city council leave us alone in our slums and our misery" pg 52.

- **The slums are also demolished to please the American and European tourists.** Listen to Insp. Kiongo speaking. "They are a great shame on the city. Touristsfrom America, Britain and West Germany are disgusted with the dirty of the city.Pg 46. All these are the effects of colonialism in Africa.

MESSAGES

1. Unity is very important in any struggle. United we stand divided we fall.
2. The government officers should allocate alternative settlement for the citizens before they give them eviction orders (notice).
3. Tribalism is an outdated custom so it should be stopped.
4. Both boys and girls should be give equal rights to education.
5. The ruling class should consider the welfare of the masses. (the majority)
6. Betrayal is not good in any society that wants to develop.
7. Illiteracy and ignorance are obstacles and enemies to development. We should fight against these enemies.
8. Classes in the society create unnecessary conflicts and hinder development of the oppressed.
9. We should not believe in superstitions and magic power because it is an outdated custom.
10. People must be aware of their rights and the practical ways to fight for their rights.

11. Youths should listen to the advice given to them by their parents.
12. Youths should not be fooled by the pleasures of the city, but they should fight for their future.
13. You cannot succeed if you are not working hard.

RELEVANCE;

The book is relevant to most African countries as shown below;

1. **Land alienation and Demolition of the unplanned settlements is a common phenomenon in expanding African Cities.** This is seen even in Dar-es-Salaam City where demolition is done on regular basis to improve infrastructure like roads and railways, to provide room for city planning, to set up social services like water pipes, high voltage electric lines, building hospitals, schools, industries, or giving land to the investors.
2. **Tribalismis also prevalent in countries like Kenya** where even the General election is held on the basis of the candidates' tribes. Voters vote for someone from their own tribes.
3. **Illiteracy rate is very high in developing countries.** Most people don't know how to read and write so it is very hard to understand the development plans that are in papers.
4. **In some societies the girl-child is still denied the access to education** because of her gender. Only boys are sent to school because they are believed to be the ones to take over the family responsibilities when the parents are old or gone.
5. **There are classes in all societies.** The ruling class comprising of those in power (Chosen few) in most countries is enjoying the national cake, while the majority are suffering and starving in slums.
6. **There are many people in Africa who are suffering from colonial hangovers.** They admire western lifestyle, dresses, foods, music, cars, and the general western life.

TITLE; THE LION AND THE JEWEL
PLAYWRIGHT; WOLE SOYINKA
SETTING; NIGERIA

PLOT

The play is divided into three acts each one related to the incidents that take place. A further analysis reveals that;

- The story unfolds through a straightforward narration with the play divided into **morning** suggesting the events that are taking place here. Here it is the exposition or introduction of everything that will be developed later in the plot. Introduction of the characters, setting, and the basic conflict. **At noon** the events are in the rising action as the conflict involving the main characters rises to the climax. Finally at **night** things come to a falling of actions that leads inevitably to a resolution whereby Sidi marries Baroka and the conflict ends.
- Furthermore, to enrich his plot the playwright has employed **a flashback plot**. In pages 24-25 Lakunle narrates how Baroka bribed the surveyor in order to divert the railway track that was to pass through Ilujinle.

PLOT SUMMARY

Morning

This is the introduction of the play and which sets the play in motion. The act breaks by showing the beautiful slim girl named Sidi carrying a pail of water. She is strongly admired by the school teacher named Lakunle. Lakunle abandons his students the moment he casts his eyes on Sidi. He tries to educate her that it is not good to carry heavy things on the head. He also insists on the dress code of Sidi by telling her that a grown up girl must cover her shoulders. However, Sidi objects by saying that she has already tried to her level best. By the way she says because of what Lakunle has been saying around the villagers consider him a mad man of Ilujinle.

Lakunle raises sexist claims that Sidi is hard to understand because women have smaller brains than men and that is the reason they are called a weaker sex. Lakunle suggests that in a year or two they will have machines to help them do some of the works. Sidi wonders whether Lakunle goes mad and begins dreaming of the future. Lakunle asks Sidi to marry him because he loves her wholeheartedly. Sidi insists that she is ready to marry him, any day he can name but Lakunle must first pay the bride price in full. Sidi says so because in this society it is believed that if a girl is married without bride price then she wasn't a virgin. Lakunle educates her that Paying Bride price is an out-dated custom because it means buying a woman as a property. He insists that a woman needs equal treatment with a man. He suggests that they will be enjoying life just as the Lagos couples are doing and they will be spending their weekends in night clubs in Ibadan.

Lakunle Kisses Sidi by mouthing but Sidi considers it unhealthy. Sidi sees Lakunle as a mad man and wonders how they allow him to run a school. The crowd of youths entre to bring the news of a stranger who has come with a motorcycle with a camera and a magazine. The magazine features Sidi's picture on the front page and makes her famous in her village and beyond. She boasts herself that she is now a celebrity and can no longer marry Lakunle a mere school teacher. They also say that Baroka's image is in a little corner in that book and even in that corner he shares with a village latrine. On hearing this, Sidi praises herself and sees herself as more important than even the Bale.

They hold a dance to celebrate the event. Meanwhile, Baroka enters and the dance stops. He accuses Lakunle for trying to steal the village maidenhead and orders Lakunle to be slapped. This was a mechanism to make him stay away from Sidi. Finally he says it has been five full months since he last took a wife.

Noon

The act breaks with Sidi still engrossed in the pictures of herself in the magazine. Sadiku meets her to bring the news that Baroka has sent her not only to give Sidi his well-wishes but also to deliver the message that he wants her for a wife. Lakunle overhears the message and reacts by calling Baroka a greedy dog and infidel. He asks Sidi to reject the proposal. Sadiku wants to know what answer to give the Bale and convinces Sidi that Baroka has promised to take no other wife after her. Furthermore Sadiku says that when a woman becomes the last wife of the Bale, when the Bale dies, she gets the honor of becoming a senior wife of the new Bale.

Sidi says she is now famous and cannot marry Baroka since he waited until she became a celebrity. She sees Baroka's proposal as a way he wants to brag about himself and say that he has possessed the Jewel of Ilujinle. Sadiku wonders how in the world a girl can turn down the Chief's proposal to marry her. She thinks that all that was because of Lakunle. Sidi insists that she is still young and beautiful to marry an old man like Baroka who is spent.

Sadiku changes the tactic and says that Baroka said if she doesn't want to be his wife she can just go to supper with him as he has prepared a small feast in her honor. Sidi knows that it is Baroka's trick to get to bed with her since all women who have supped with him one night ended up becoming ether his wives or his concubines.

Lakunle narrates how Baroka foiled the Public Works attempt to build a railway through Ilujinle. Baroka bribed the white surveyor by giving him, money, cola nuts, a coop of hens and a goat. The surveyor pretends that he had made a mistake in reading his map so the railway should be much further away. He also says that the soil cannot support the weight of a railway engine. Lakunle suggest that Baroka does all these because he doesn't want Civilization to come to Ilujinle since it will interfere his traditional life.

The scene shows Baroka in his bedroom with his favorite wife plucking his armpit hair. Unfortunately she plucks him painfully and he chases her away. At the same time Sadiku enters bringing the sad news of refusal from Sidi. Baroka becomes angry at hearing that but he quickly he devises an idea. He makes a trick by telling Sadiku that his manhood has ended for almost a week. While he warns Sadiku not to tell anyone, in his heart he knows she will tell it to Sidi and that is exactly what happens.

Night

Sadiku rejoices because of the wrong information he got from Baroka. She thinks that Baroka is really impotent. She comes with a figure of the Bale and addresses it. Sadiku says she did the same to Baroka's father The Great Okiki when she became his youngest wife. Sadiku celebrates their victory and Sidi wonders what babble she has won. Sadiku insists that it is a victory to every woman. She then tells Sid what the celebration is all about. They both celebrate the victory of womankind.

Lakunle appears and tries t make sense of what is going on. Sidi gets an idea that she should go to the palace and sup with the Bale so that she can get an opportunity to mock him. Lakunle warns her not to go but she ignores him and goes. Lakunle quarrels with Sadiku who reminds him of paying the bride price for Sidi.

Lakunle suggests the transformations that should be done to the village in a year or two. For example abolition of bride price, construction of a motor road, use saucepans instead of clay pots, no polygamy since it leads to impotence, cars for rulers, cut trees and burn the forests to plant a modern park for lovers, print newspapers every day, hold beauty contests, a school of ballroom dancing, and reject the palm wine habit and take tea with milk and sugar instead. He insists that even Sadiku should start attending his school since she is old but uninformed as she doesn't know how to read and write.

The scene changes to Baroka's bedroom. Baroka is having a friendly wrestling with his opponent. Sidi enters in the middle of the wrestling. She pretends that she has come to repent for what she said. Then Sidi begins to mock Baroka in riddles. Baroka says that he changes his wrestlers when he learns to throw them and he changes his wives when he has learnt to tire them.

As Sidi continues mocking him he discovers that she has been told by Sadiku the secret. Then Baroka says that the town dwellers have made tales of the backwardness of Ilujinle until it hurts him since he holds the welfare of his people deep at heart. Baroka keeps on seducing Sidi using the sayings and proverbs like "the truth is that old wine thrives best within a new bottle." Finally Sidi falls under Baroka's control. Lakunle and Sadiku are waiting for Sidi to return. Lakunle senses that something bad has happened to her. He promises to go and rescue. Sidi comes and throws herself in the ground crying. Lakunle thinks that she has been beaten. Sidi tells Sadiku that Baroka lied to her ant that it was a trick to get her. Lakunle later learns that Sidi has slept with Baroka but he promises to marry her nevertheless.

Sidi exits and Lakunle and Sadiku wonder what has become of her. Lakunle thinks she has gone to prepare for the marriage but he says that he also needs time to prepare. The musicians come but Lakunle chases them away thinking they came to celebrate his marriage. Sidi appears and accompanies the musicians to Baroka's house inviting Lakunle to attend if he wishes. She says that she cannot go to another man after testing the strength of Baroka.

The title of the book
"***The Lion and the Jewel***" is a symbolic title of a comedy drama that presents the conflict that exists between Africans who are influenced by western ways and those who are loyal to African traditions.
- The **Lion** represents Baroka the chief (Bale) in his sixties who hunts the village belle (beautiful girl named Sidi)
- The word '***The Lion***' is used because of Baroka's behavior of hunting the *jewel* by using every possible means even oppressing his competitor (Lakunle –the teacher) as a lion does in the forest as the king of the jungle.
- The "*Jewel*" represents the beautiful and true village belle – Sidi. Sidi becomes a "jewel" of Ilujinle especially when the photographer puts her picture on the front page of the magazine and makes her known throughout the village and beyond. Sidi's words in page 23 sums up the meaning of the title *"I am the twinkle of a jewel but he is the hind-quarters of a lion"*

Setting
The setting of the play is Yoruba Village of Ilujinle in Nigeria. However it can generally be applied to any African community that practices these traditional practices. There are also some minor settings like the classroom, Baroka's bedroom, etc.

Style
The playwright has employed different literary techniques to keep the play in motion. The following are some of the techniques employed.
1. **Dialogue**- the play is largely written in a dialogue that reveals the characters personality traits, moods and reactions toward other characters. **Aside;** this is a direct address to the

audience by a character on stage. The playwright employs this style when he says *"SIDI: If Baroka were my father {aside} –which many would take him to be- {makes a rude sign} would he pay mydowry to this man and give his blessings?"* Page 43. This message is intended for the audience and not others on the stage.

2. **Songs, music and drums.** Here and there he has made use of traditional songs, music and dances to bring the events to life. In page 45-46 Sidi, Lakunle and the girls who bring the news about the stranger and the magazine join in a dance to celebrate the event. Everything comes to a sudden stop when Baroka arrives.

3. **Poetic language/style.** The play is largely written in a poetic style. There are short verses that begin with capital letters even when it is still the continuation of the same sentence – a typical feature in poetry. But there are more specific lines that are written distinctively as poems. For example in page 14 Sidi talking to Lakunle she says

> *You are dressed like him*
> *You look like him*
> *You speak his tongue*
> *You think like him*
> *You are just as clumsy*
> *In your Lagos ways –*
> *You'll do for him.*

Characters & characterization

1. **Baroka;**
   - **He is an old village chief (Bale) aged 62**. He inherited the chiefdom from his late father Chief Okiki.
   - **He is infidel and womanizer**. He marries many women just to satisfy his sexual desires. Sidi confirms this when she says "Can you deny that every woman who has supped with him one night becomes his wife or concubine the next" page23.
   - **He is tricky.** He uses tricks to get women. He invites them for supper at the palace and ends up sleeping with them. When Sidi discovers his trick he changes it by says he is no longer sexually powerful and his trick works.
   - **He is a polygamist.** He has many wives but he is not satisfied. He hunts for Sid till he manages to add her to their number.
   - **He is a corrupt and irresponsible leader.** He bribes the surveyor who was to build a railway track through his village to stop and divert the project. He is supposed to be the one attracting these projects to his village for his people.
   - **He is illiterate and primitive.** This can be proved by the following scenarios. He doesn't know the importance of civilization so he works hard to prevent it. He doesn't even know how to say good morning he says "guru morin. He uses his wives to pluck the hair of his armpit instead of shaving.
   - **He is a hypocrite.** He orders his attendants to beat Lakunle but later he pretends to show sympathy to him and orders dry clothes for him. Pg 17
   - **He is jealous.** The third girl says that the bale is jealousy of Sidi when her photo appears on the front page but he pretends to be proud of Sidi.
   - **He is a traditionalist**. He holds African traditions whether good or bad and works hard to prevent western ways. He supports widow in heritance as he inherits his father's youngest wife. (Sadiku)

- **He is oppressive.** He oppresses Lakunle as a way to make him stay away from Sidi by charging him falsely that he tried to steal the village maidenhead.
- **He is selfish and opportunistic.** He only cares about his selfish interest and not that of his village. He for instance diverts the railway project from his village because it will force civilization to his village and interfere his traditional life. Also he does all it takes to marry Sidi despite the fact that he had many wives already.

2. **Sidi;**
   - **She is a slim beautiful girl (the belle).** Sidi becomes aware of her beauty when the photographer features her on the magazine. She brags "I'm beautiful" page 13
   - **She is boastful and pompous.** Sidi boasts when her fame grows beyond the village of Ilujinle. She even rejects Lakunle since she is now a celebrity. She says *"Known as I am to the whole wide world, I would demean my worth to wed a mere school teacher."* Also she adds *"Sidi is more important even than the Bale"* page 12
   - **She becomes a local celebrity.** Sidi becomes a local celebrity after appearing on the magazine. This is one reason why Baroka wants to take her for a wife.
   - **She is a traditionalist and primitive.** Sidi is a young girl but she still observes traditional customs. She insists that Lakunle must pay her bride price before she marries him. Also she follows the traditional culture that, when a virgin girl sleeps with a man she has to marry that man. That's why she marries Baroka despite all the rejections she had mad at first that he is too old and spent.
   - **She has a stand.** She has a firm stand on what she believes. She refuses to marry Lakunle until he pays the bride price despite all the efforts made by Lakunle to educate her. She rejects Baroka's proposal for marriage despite the fact that he is the Chief because she says he is too old until he uses a trick to get her.
   - **She is abusive.** Sidi uses abusive language every now and then when she addresses Lakunle. For example she tells him *"the village is on holiday you fool"* page 14 but also she calls him the madman of Ilujinle.
   - **She loves hearsays.** When Lakunle narrates the story how Baroka diverged the railway project Sadiku says it was just hearsay. Sidi admits that Lakunle should continue narrating since she loves hearsays. Page 24
   - **She finally becomes Baroka's wife.** Sidi finally becomes Baroka's wife because he used a trick to sleep with her and according to the tradition a girl has to marry the man who sleeps with her for the first time.

3. **Lakunle;**
   - **He is an educated school teacher.** Lakunle is a teacher who runs a school at Ilujinle.
   - **He is an irresponsible teacher.** Lakunle is an irresponsible teacher because he allows his love affairs to interfere his commitment to work. He abandons his students and chases after Sidi.
   - **He is an agent for social change.** Lakunle proposes the transformations that have to be done to build a better future in his village – Ilujinle. For example abolition of bride price, construction of a motor road, use saucepans instead of clay pots, no polygamy since it leads to impotence, cars for rulers etc. this will help Ilujinle to be a modern village.
   - **He is westernized. Lakunle is obsessed with European/western culture.** Some of the things he suggests to be part of the transformation are completely European and

that is the reason the Africans don't understand him but they end up calling him mad. For example cutting down trees and burning forests to plant a garden for lovers, having beauty contests, a school for ballroom dancing etc.

- **He is a feminist**. This is a person who fights for women rights and gender equality. Lakunle tries his level best to educate Sidi about her rights and the dignity of a woman. He says that bride price degrades a woman to a level of a property.
- **He is against the custom of paying bride price.** Lakunle fights against the payment of bride price since he believes it lowers the dignity of a woman for whom it is paid. However the traditional society does not understand him because in this society bride price is a symbol of virginity to a girl for whom it is paid.
- **He has true love.** Despite the fact that he discovers that Sidi has slept with Baroka and he still promises to marry her. He suggests that they will have to forget the past.

4. **Sadiku;**
   - **She is Baroka's eldest wife inherited from his late father Okiki**. In this society when the chief dies his last wife becomes the senior wife of the new king. So did Sadiku.
   - **She acts as a go-between for Baroka**. Sadiku is rather a strange woman because she is the one who keeps on seducing girls for Baroka. Lakunle laments "*You spend your days as a senior wife collecting brides for Baroka*" page 38.
   - **She is a traditionalist and primitive**. Sadiku is still primitive and follows the traditional customs even those that seem to undermine the woman dignity like polygamy, and bride price. She too insists that Lakunle has to pay the bride price for Sidi if he wishes to marry her.
   - **She is a betrayer as she doesn't keep secrets**. Baroka uses a trick to get Sidi by telling Sadiku that his manhood has ended for almost a week before. He warns Sadiku not to tell anyone but in his heart he knows that Sadiku won't keep that secret to herself but she will tell it to Sidi and that is exactly what happens.
   - **She is a hypocrite**. She pretends to sympathize when Baroka says he has lost his manhood but later she goes to celebrate for the same.

LANGUAGE USE

The playwright has used a good and profound command of the English language full of figures of speech and sayings that give the flavor of African literature.

1. **Personification;**
   - I thought the world was mad. Pg 28
   - My armpit still weeps blood. pg 39
   - My beard tells me you have been a pupil… pg 47
   - Sidi, my love will open your mind. pg 6
   - Can the stones bear to listen to this? Pg 6
   - The village is on holiday, you fool. Pg 14
   - And my images have taught me all the rest. pg 21
   - Our thoughts fly crisply through the air. Pg 53
   - It is only the hair upon his back which still deceives the world. Pg 54
   - The words refuse to form. pg 59
   - Earth open up and swallow Lakunle. Pg 60

2. **Simile;**
   - Like a snake he came at me, like a rag he went back. Pg32
   - Must every word leak out of you as surely as the final drops of mother's milk pg 35.
   - Sulking like a slighted cockroach. Pg 39.
   - But you are as stubborn as an illiterate goat. Pg 2
   - And you must chirrup like a cockatoo pg 7
   - And her hair is stretched like a magazine photo. Pg 9
   - The thought itself would knock you down as sure as wine. Pg 13
   - He seeks to have me as his property. Pg 21
   - His face is like a leather piece. Pg 22
   - I'll come and see you whipped like a dog pg 55
   - She took off suddenly like a hunted buck. Pg 61

3. **Metaphor;**
   - Sadiku my faithful lizard. Pg 47
   - Sidi will not make herself a cheap bowl for the village spit. Pg 7
   - Romance is the sweetening of the soul. Pg 10
   - You'd be my chattel, my mere property. Pg 8
   - The jewel of Ilujinle. pg 21
   - I am the twinkle of a jewel while he is the hind quarters of a lion. Pg 23
   - Hence parasites, you've made a big mistake. Pg 62
   - Baroka is a creature of the wilds pg. 58

4. **Sayings;**
   - If the snail finds splinters in his shell he changes house. Why do you stay? Pg 6
   - Shame belongs only to the ignorant. Pg 5
   - The woman gets lost in the woods one day and every wood deity dies the next. pg 42
   - If the tortoise cannot tumble it does not mean that he can stand. pg 42
   - When the child if full of riddles, the mother has one water-pot the less. pg 42
   - Charity begins at home. pg 52 (proverb)
   - A man must live or fall by his true principles pg 61
   - Until the finger nails have scraped the dust, no one can tell which insect released his bowls. Pge 43
   - Old wine thrives within a new bottle p 54

5. **Symbolism;**
   - Lion – the king (the Bale -Baroka)
   - Jewel – beautiful girl (the Belle - Sidi)
   - Honey tongue (Sadiku of the honey tongue pg 20)
   - Sadiku's unopened treasure-house –virginity. Pg32
   - Okiki came withhis rusted key- an old male sexual organ Pg32
   - Devil's own horse – motorbike.
   - One-eyed box – camera.
   - Baroka's picture next to the village latrine – he is corrupt and filthy.

6. **Oxymoron;**
   - Inside out. pg 5
   - Upside down. pg 5

7. **Exaggeration;**
   - When the whole world knows the madman of Ilujinle. Pg 3
   - You really mean to turn the whole world upside down. Pg 5
8. **Allusion**
   - A prophet has honor except in his own home. Pg 5 (Referring to the biblical words of Jesus)
   - And the man shall take the woman and the two shall be together, as one flesh. Pg 8 (Referring to the words in the bible)
   - My Ruth, my Rachel, Ester, Bethsheba, thou sum of fabled perfections From Genesis to revelations. Pg 20 (Biblical names)
9. **Parallelism;**
   - Sidi I do not seek a wife to fetch and carry, to cock and scrub, to bring forth children… Pg 7-8
10. **Rhetorical question;**
    - Do any of my wives report a failing in my manliness?
11. **Onomatopoeia;**
    - B-r-r-r-r (sound of a motorcycle) pg 10
    - Ha-ha (sound of laughter) pg 20

THEMES

1. **AFRICAN TRADITIONS AND CUSTOMS**

   a) **Polygamy.** This is a traditional practice in which a man marries many wives. In most African societies this practice is very common. In the book polygamy in portrayed in the following scenarios;
   - Chief Okiki (Baroka's father) had many wives including Sadiku who was the youngest of the wives.
   - Baroka has many wives and concubines but he is not satisfied. Sidi says *"can you deny that every woman who has supped with him one night becomes his wife or concubine the next"* page 23. He is now 62 years old but he marries Sidi.

   b) **Widow inheritance.** This is a traditional practice in which a man inherits the wife or wives of a late relative (a brother or a father). In this society it is possible for the son to inherit the youngest wife of his late father. For example Sadiku was the youngest wife of Chief Okiki (Baroka's father) but she was inherited by Baroka and became the senior wife of Baroka after the death of Okiki. Sadiku says *"Iwas there when it happened to your father, the great Okiki. I did for him, I the youngest of and the freshest of the wives. Ikilled him with my strength."* Page 32.
   Furthermore, Sadiku convinces Sidi to marry Baroka since she will enjoy the privilege of being the youngest and favorite wife of Baroka but since Baroka is too old when he dies she will become the senior wife of the new bale (chief). Sadiku says *"Do youknow what it is to be the Bale's last wife? I'll tell you. When he dies – and that should not be long even the lion has to die sometimes – it means that you will have the honor of being the senior wife of the new bale"* page 20

   c) **Bride price.** Bride price is also a tradition that is in many African societies. However there are different views attached to bride price indifferent societies. While in other societies it is used as a symbol of commitment and seriousness towards marriage, in thissociety is it connected to virginity of a girl. If a girl is married without the bride price it is believed that she was not a virgin andshe did so to sell her shame. This is the reason why Sidi insists that her bride price must be paid in full before she agrees tomarry Lakunle. She says "I shall marry you today, next week or any day you name but my bride price must first be paid." Alsoshe adds "they will say I was no virgin, that I was forced to sell my shame and marry you without a price' page. This causescomplications in marriage question especially among the youngsters who believe in mutual love between the two and not the dowry payment.

d) **Traditional beliefs.** There are also different cases of traditional beliefs in this society; swearing: to confirm whether someone is telling the truth that person has to swear by the name of their god Ogun. Sidi forces the second girl to swear and ask Ogun strike her dead if she is not telling the truth that Baroka's picture is sharing a page with the village latrine in the magazine. They also believe that some traditional gods can take possession of someone and Sango can restore his/her wits Sadiku says to Sidi *"May Sango restore your wits. For most surely some angry god has taken possession of you"* page 23

e) **Traditional dances.** Villagers beat drums and hold dances when there are happy events to celebrate. For example a dance is held celebrating the return of the stranger with a magazine. Also when Sidi marries Baroka a dance is held and people celebrate the marriage ceremony.

2. **FEMINISM AND WOMEN EMANCIPATION;** Feminism is an ideology of fighting for the rights of women. Lakunle in this play acts as a feminist as he tries to educate Sidi about her value as a woman.

   - He educates her that paying the bride price for a woman degrades her dignity and lowers her value to the level of a property. He says *"To pay the price would be to buy a heifer off the market stall. You would be my chattel, my mere property"* page 8

   - He fights against polygamy and advocates for monogamy. He wants to marry Sidi as his only wife and among the transformation he wishes to see in the future he says *"No man shall take more wives than one"* page 37.

   - He believes that a woman should be an equal partner of a man in a race of life. Talking to Sidi he says *"Sidi I seek a friend in need. An equal partner in my race of life"* page 8

   - Sadiku also seems to aspire for the world in which women win and men lose. When she is tricked by Baroka about his state of impotence she celebrates the victory of women over men. She says *"This is the world of women. At this moment our star sits in the centre of the sky. We are supreme."* Page 34

   - The presence of primitive villagers and politically powerful and corrupt people like Baroka makes the movement so complicated and unsuccessful since they use their political power to suppress the supposed changes.

3. **POSITION OF WOMEN IN THE SOCIETY;**
   a) **Women are portrayed as tools for pleasure**. Women are used by men to satisfy their sexual pleasures. In a way, Baroka's father married many wives for the same reason. Baroka has many wives and concubines but he is not satisfied as he wants to marry Sidi for the same. Lakunle wonders how Baroka manages to satisfy them all and says that maybe he keeps a timetable as he does at school. In her own words

Sadiku convinces Sidi to marry Baroka on the ground that *"will you be his sweetest princess, soothing him on weary nights?"*

b) **Women are portrayed as people who cannot keep secret.** A woman is portrayed as a person who cannot keep secrets. Knowing this Baroka uses a trick by telling Sadiku that his manhood has ended for almost a week before. He believes that Sadiku won't keep it to herself but will leak the information to Sidi and that is exactly what happens.

c) **Women are portrayed as betrayers.** Sadiku betrays Baroka by revealing the secret she was told to keep to herself. Baroker warns her not to parade her shame before the world. Page 30. Notwithstanding the warning, she tells the secret to Sidi and admits her betrayal by saying *"Baroka is no child you know, he will know I have betrayed him"* page 35

d) **Women are portrayed as hypocrites.** Both Sadiku and Sidi are hypocrites. Sadiku pretends to sympathise with Baroka when she learns that he has lost his manhood and exclaims *"the gods forbid"*, *"the Gods must have mercy yet."* However the same woman goes to celebrate the victory of women over men and asks Sidi to go and pretend to be repentant and mock the old man. She says *"Use your bashful looks and be truly repentant. Goad him my child; torment him until he weeps for shame."* 35

e) **Women are portrayed as primitive and illiterate.** Despite the fact that Bride price is a custom that undermines women dignity and robs them the opportunity to marry men of their choices, Sadiku and Sidi still support it strongly. Moreover, Women are seen as primitive when Sadiku is used by Baroka to seduce girls for him even those she addresses as "my child".

f) **Women are portrayed as traditionalists.** Not only do women believe in some outdated traditions like bride price, but they are lso confortable living in a polygamous family and being inherited as widows from one chief to another. Sadiku convinces Sidi to marry Baroka since being the last wife when Baroka dies she will have the privilege of being inherited by the new bale. They also support a custom that a girl must marry a man who sleeps with her for the first time even if it was not willingly as did Baroka.

g) **Women are portrayed as people with no true love.** Both Sadiku and Sidi are portrayed as people with no true love in different levels. Sidi has no sincere love to Lakunle despite all the love and affections that Lakunle tried to show her. She still places importance on the bride price and not on mutual love. Sadiku has no sincere love to Baroka that's why she feels free to seduce girls for him. Furthermore when she hears the tragedy that has befallen her husband she celebrates instead of mourning with him.

h) **Women are portrayed as people with no stand.** Baroka believes that it is just a pattern for women to refuse men's proposal at first but later they agree. So he believes that Sidi's refusal is just following the same pattern. And that is exactly what happens. Baroka says *"It follows the pattern – a firm refusal at the start. Why will she not?"* page 27. Finally Sidi goes to Baroka's bedroom, sleeps with him and finally marries him despite all the bad things she had spoken about him.

4. **IRRESPONSIBILITY;** Irresponsibility is shown in two ways:

- One, Lakunle is an irresponsible teacher because he allows his love affairs and affection toward Sidi to interfere his commitment to work. He abandons his students and goes to seduce Sidi for marriage.
- Baroka is an irresponsible leader. He is a corrupt and irresponsible leader because he bribes the surveyor who was to build a railway track through his village to stop and divert the project. He is supposed to be the one attracting these projects to his village for his people. Lakunle says *"Did you never hear of how he foiled the Public Works attempt to build the railway through Ilujinle"* page 24

5. BUILDING THE FUTURE;

- The playwright uses Lakunle as his mouthpiece to communicate the theme of building the future. Being an educated man – who even Baroka admits that he is needed in the society – has a duty to guide this traditional society to progress. Lakunle is educated and westernized so some of the things he suggests reflect his western mentality. He says for example;
- Bride price should be forgotten, polygamy should be abolished, construction of motor roads, replacing clay pots with sauce pans, the rulers should use cars or at least bicycles instead of horses, cut trees and burn the forests to plant a garden (park) for lovers, print newspapers daily with pictures of seductive girls, conduct the beauty contests, and have a school for ballroom dancing.

Lakunle has a point but his mission fails because of four major reasons among other things;

- ***One***, some of the things he suggests are irrelevant to Africans and are not indicators of development. So he uses a wrong approach when he suggests things like having a school for ballroom dancing, cut trees and burn the forests to plant a garden (park) for lovers, print newspapers daily with pictures of seductive girls, conduct the beauty contests.
- ***Two,*** he wants the changes to take place overnight. Lakunle is so quick not realizing that changes usually take time. Villagers must be given enough time to adjust themselves to the new culture he is trying to introduce. He says "within a year or two" this is too short a time for the transformations he suggests.
- ***Three,*** the presence of corrupt and selfish leaders like Baroka and ignorant and primitive villagers like Sadiku and Sidi become obstacles to building the future. Lakunle has intellectual power but lacks political power to act on what he believes. Baroka uses his political power to block the development projects.
- ***Four***, Lakunle's selfish interest to marry Sidi. Lakunle becomes so committed more to his competition for Sidi against Baroka and forgets his role as educated elite to educate the pupils in his school who will later be instrumental in helping him to win his cause. Finally Lakunle fails to build the ideal future he aspired and ends up heartbroken for losing Sidi altogether.

6. BETRAYAL; Betrayal is portrayed in different scenarios;

- ***One***, Lakunle has betrayed his culture by adapting and conforming to western culture. He even forces his own people to abandon their culture and adopt European culture. He suggests for example having a school for ballroom dancing, wearing high-heeled shoes and red paints on the lips, going to night clubs at Ibadan and kissing by mouthing which Sidi considers unhealthy. Page 9. These among other things make the villagers consider him a madman of Ilujinle.

- *Two,* Sadiku betrays Baroka by revealing his secret despite being warned that she is the only one who knows about it.
- *Three,* Baroka betrays his people by diverting the development projects away from his village instead attracting those projects to his village.
- *Four*, Sidi betrays Lakunle when she refuses to marry him. First when she becomes a celebrity she says she is now famous that she cannot marry a mere school teacher and finally when she sleeps with Baroka and leaves Lakunle notwithstanding his willingness to marry her ignoring what had happened.

7. **CONFLICTS;** There are different conflicts in this book.

  a) **Cultural conflict between European culture and African Culture.** Western culture is portrayed by Lakunle who suggests the transformations he wishes to see in his society to make it a modern village. These things bring a conflict because they contradict African culture as a result they see him as a madman. Issues like abolition of bride price, polygamy, and kissing by mouthing cause the conflicts in this society.

  b) **Personal conflicts: these are conflicts involving two individuals.**

    - **The conflict between Sidi and Lakunle;** This occurs when he tries to educate her on the uselessness of some traditional practices like payment of bride price. For Sidi bride price is very important since it carries a sense of respect signifying that a girl is virgin. Furthermore their conflict intensifies when Lakunle forces Sidi to kiss him by mouthing, which she considers unhygienic.

    - **The conflict between Baroka and Lakunle;** This occurs because of their completion for Sidi. Both Baroka and Lakunle are in love with Sidi but Baroka uses his political power to oppress Lakunle and win love from Sidi and Lakunle becomes the loser. Also Baroka sees that the society is better without some of the things that Lakunle suggests while Lakunle sees Baroka as an obstacle to Ilujinle's development.

    - **The conflict between Sadiku and Lakunle;** This occurs when Lakunle accuses Sadiku for seducing brides for Baroka. He sees her as a primitive woman and suggests that she too must attend his school. Sadiku also accuses Lakunle that Sidi's rejection of the Bale's proposal is a direct consequence of his teaching.

  c) **Social conflict between Old generation and Young generation.** There is a conflict between the young being represented by Sidi and Lakunle against the old being represented by Baroka and Sadiku. The youngsters have their own ways of looking at things. Sidi refuses to marry Baroka because he is too old and she is young. Lakunle also accuses Sadiku for convincing Sidi to marry an old man like Baroka.

  d) **Family conflict between Baroka and his wife Ailatu (the favorite).** This occurs due to Baroka's primitive behavior of using his wives to pluck his armpit hair. Unfortunately Ailatu pulls the hair painfully and makes Baroka go mad. He believes that she did it purposely as a kind of revenge for he told her that he was to take a new wife that evening and chases her away from the room calling her an enemy.

8. **MISUSE OF POWER;** Many African leaders misuse the power entrusted to them for their own selfish interests.

- Baroka uses his power to win love from Sidi. First he orders his men to beat Lakunle and accuse him falsely that he tried to steal the village maidenhead.
- Baroka uses his power and position to marry as many wives as he wishes. He says *"it is five full months since last I took a five..."* page. From that time he starts hunting Sidi by using invitation for supper and tricks but it is revealed that whenever a woman accepts his invitation for supper he ends up becoming either his wife or concubine. This is misuse of power and authority.
- Baroka uses his power to humiliate his wives. He uses Sadiku to seduce brides for him. He also humiliates his youngest wife Ailatu by ordering her to pluck his armpit hair. Unfortunately she pulls the hair painfully and Baroka expels her from the house. This is also the misuse of power.

Other minor themes include;

1. **Illiteracy**. Many members of this society are illiterate. This gives a chance for leaders like Baroka to exploit them using their ignorance.
2. **Corruption**. Both Baroka and the surveyor are corrupt. Baroka bribes the surveyor to divert the railway projects and the surveyor accepts the bribe. He then pretends that he had made a mistake in reading his map so the railway track should be further away. Also he claims that the soil cannot support the weight of a railway engine.
3. **Selfishness**. Both Baroka and Lakunle put first their interests instead of those of the society. Baroka diverts the project for his own selfish interest. He also marries many wives for the same reason. Lakunle on the other hand abandons his pupils because of his personal interest to marry Sidi.
4. **Hypocrisy**. Sadiku is a hypocrite. She pretends to sympathise with Baroka on hearing that he has lost his manhood but later she celebrates. Baroka pretends to love his people but he diverts development projects that would help his people.
5. **Infidelity and promiscuity**. Baroka is infidel, womanizer and sex maniac as he marries many wives to satisfy his sexual desires. Sidi confirms this when she says *"Can you deny that every woman who has supped with him one night becomes his wife or concubine the next"* page23.

MESSAGES

There are several lessons that can be learnt from this play.

1. **Corrupt, selfish, and irresponsible leaders like Baroka are obstacles to development.** It is very hard for any society to develop if there are leaders like Baroka who instead of attracting development projects he diverts them away from his village.
2. **Ignorance and illiteracy of the masses also become obstacles to development.** The common people also become obstacles to the efforts to build the future because they don't see the need to change the outdated customs.
3. **Outdated customs like Polygamy, widow inheritance and bride price should be discouraged.** These are the main causes of conflicts in our societies.
4. **Bringing about changes is a gradual process it cannot occur overnight.** People must be given time to adjust and learn the new culture rather that forcing them to abandon their culture in favor of the foreign one.
5. We should fight against betrayal, hypocrisy, and humiliation.

6. **Educated people should use their education to bring about social changes in the society.** It is good to separate love affairs from our commitment to jobs and responsibilities.

RELEVANCE

The play is relevant to our society's especially Tanzanian rural communities in a number of ways.

1. Polygamy, Bride price, infidelity and Widow Inheritance are common practices in rural communities in Tanzania and Africa at large.
2. Betrayal, irresponsibility, corruption, misuse of power, and selfishness are also common phenomena among the leaders and common people in our country.
3. Women emancipation and Feminism are now common slogans. Feminists are now campaigning for women rights and equality advocating for 50/50 chances for both men and women.

TITLE; PASSED LIKE A SHADOW
AUTHOR; BENARD MAPALALA
SETTING; UGANDA

PLOT SUMMARY

Chapter 1
Introduction of Adyeri's family

Daddy comes back home very drunk, wet and dirty and the whole atmosphere changes. He orders his food and as Abooki carries it to him, Atwoki unfortunately crashes into her, sending the meal down. It was a hell of a mistake. Daddy laments and fumes. Both Atwoki and Abooki are frustrated and frightened because they know a cane will soon follow. He calls Atwoki twice and gives him a classic slap in the face. Amoti appears from Virika hospital where she had gone to fetch water. She attacks Adyeri for beating her son a man-sized beating. She regrets for marrying him and calls him a pig. Amoti was good at a war of words since she believed they hurt her husband deeply. Adyeri gives her a sound beating. Atwoki goes to help her but he receives a furious kick in the stomach. At last Adyeri leaves the house not to come back that night.

Chapter 2
Vicky comes with a fiancé.

Vicky, who had gone to Kitangwenda several months ago, comes back with a stranger (Munyamahanga). Vicky was a daughter of Adyeri's late sister. She was forced to move from home due to harsh treatment from both her uncle and aunt –Amoti. She met a rich man who owned a garage at Kamwenge and wanted to marry her. He was called Akena. They receive a cold welcome from Amoti who reports their arrival to Adyeri. Adyeri doesn't react rudely, instead he welcomes Vicky politely. On hearing that Akena owns a garage Amoti becomes jealous and complicates the matter that Vicky cannot marry a Munyamahanga. For Adyeri, as long as the bride price is settled it doesn't matter who/what marries Vicky whether it is a person, a cow or a donkey. He meets with his drinking pals and they put a proper breakdown on the bride price as follows.

> *15 heads of cattle. 8 goats*
> *50,000/= shillings for buying back cloth.*
> *15,000/= shillings for buying Daddy's walking stick and*
> *2 jerry cans of beer.*

At the end, the meeting ends without a consensus between the two parties. (Adyeri's side and Akena's side)

Chapter 3
Uncle Araali pays the visit.

We are told of Atwoki who is very intelligent and good footballer when young, who suggests that he would be a good footballer in the future. He makes prophesies with his fellow children about their future. We are also told of Abooki (Atwoki's sister who is in the same class with him). One day their uncle (Araali) comes to visit them and brings them sweets and biscuits. He finds the children very hungry and they have no firewood in the house. He gives them money to buy all the needs in the kitchen. Then Daddy comes staggering and singing his favorite song. He is told that uncle Araali has come and is the one who bought the domestic needs. He feels ashamed to see the visitor footing the food bills in his house.

Chapter 4
Vicky is introduced to a bad company.

Vicky is back from Bundibugyo where she went to pluck tea in a neighbor's plantation. She is now chatting with Tusiime and Kunihira (Lacking any comfort and guidance at home, she had increasingly felt drawn closer to the two.pg 16). They advice Vicky a lot of things including running away with Akena or getting involved in commercial sex because they are doing it. These two friends of hers were both the worst by-products of Fort Portal education system. Tusiime led others in the burning of the mattresses at Maria Goretti Secondary School and was discontinued. Kunihira was expelled in the third year from Kyebambe Girls Secondary School. She spends a lot of time with them and takes many of her meals at their place. Vicky changes and becomes a polished lady and men begin chasing her. She begins footing the food bills and brings drinks (beer) for her uncle. That silenced both Amoti and Adyeri. She then elopes with a man from Kasese and leaves the house.

Chapter 5
Adyeri's background (flashback)

One day Adyeri was invited at Kinyamasika Primary School as one of the pioneer teachers of the school. The children of class five sang the song that struck deep in his heart strumming painful memories of his whole life. It is this song that bears the title of the book. It needs people to reflect on their lives when they are still alive and think of what will be left behind when they are gone, lest they pass like a shadow. Adyeri decides to rise and go back home. We are told of the story of Adyeri's concubine (Birungi) who was his secretary and how he squandered the school funds to build her a house at Burungu. He then moved to live with Birungi after being fired from his job. He sold his land and financed a shop she had opened at Mugusu Trading Centre. He began to deteriorate and was admitted for having HIV/ AIDS and wondered who might have infected him with the disease since he had many concubines (He was a maniac). After the TB treatment he goes to shelter himself at Birungi's house but she chases him away.

Chapter 6
Atwoki becomes famous and successful.

Atwoki becomes famous and successful. He scores two goals that send his team to the African Cup of Nations. He becomes famous all over Uganda. He is Nicknamed "Fort Portal Bullet". He receives gifts and money from his fans and the President offers him a brand new car plus fully paid holiday trip to the Queen Elizabeth National Park in Kasese. Adyeri lives miserably but has categorically stated that he will not kneel and ask any financial assistance from Atwoki. Amoti is happy because of the tragedy that has befallen her husband and says let him learn. An old woman comes to beg her to forgive him but she refuses. Then the football fans of Atwoki bring Adyeri in a stretcher. One man speaks for the group and begs Atwoki to forgive his father.

Chapter 7
Atwoki's life in Kampala

Atwoki has been invited by his friend David in Kampala. Before going home they go to a restaurant where David influences Atwoki to have a girlfriend. Atwoki refuses since he has never slept with a girl in all his 22 years of age. David even tells a girl named Edda to kiss him. Reaching home, Atwoki receives a warm welcome. After lunch they gather to watch a film that is full of sexual scenes. Then Atwoki is given a room in the visitors' quarters full of pornographic magazines and pictures of half naked women. David tells Atwoki 'if you cannot change the world allow the world to change you'. pg 33. He is given another offer at the Sheraton but before going they watch a TV program on AIDS. The victim narrates his state how AIDS has affected him. He also says how he suffers from stigma from his friends and relatives. As the announcer educates on the ways HIV spread from infected person to another, David's father ignores him calling him old-fashioned. They go at the Sheraton and David's father picks girls at their presence. We are told that David is a Makerere University reject, he influences Atwoki to take beer and he fees nice. From that point he begins reflecting on Edda. At the end Edda gets hold of Atwoki.

Chapter 8
Vicky and Aliganyira Visits the witchdoctor

Aliganyira and Vicky are eating supper when her husband suggests that they should go to visit the witch doctor in Kihina to find out why they don't get a child 10 years since they got married. At first she refuses, but due to the pressure from her husband she agrees. The pressure was coming from his folks especially his mother that if Vicky is unproductive he should throw her out and bring in a replacement. They leave in the midnight. Finally they reach the witchdoctors house. They find six sick people laid down on the floor. Two were very thin and had lashes. When their turn comes Aliganyira and Vicky are asked whether they want a boy or a girl. They prefer a boy. He tells them that to make one boy costs 1 million or else they go home. The witchdoctor uses a small sharp knife to prick Vicky's stomach and tattoo it with his wizardly doze. Vicky remembers the TV programme she had watched on AIDS which warned on the danger of sharing sharp instruments. Vicky was desperate and in need of a baby but now she was receiving something else.

Chapter 9
The death of Adyeri and Sickness of Amoti

Adyeri has passed away. His drinking mates say a lot about him. They even have a discussion on whether the bazungu (whitemen) are also dying of HIV/AIDS. They talk about the origin of AIDS. Some say it originated from Zaire through green monkeys, some say it was brought by bakombozi soldiers from Tanzania during the Idd Amin war. One said that the virus was manufactured in the genetic laboratory in California. They concluded that the problem with AIDS is not where it came from but rather where it is going. That is to say "it is going to finish Uganda" Back in Katumba Abooki is alone nursing her sick mother. He has sent several messages to Atwoki but he is tied up to Edda and is rarely seen. She decides to go to Kasese to seek financial assistance from Vicky only to find her as sick as her dying mother. Nevertheless, Vicky advices her not to go for money because it will kill her. Then Vicky gives her enough money to help her. Then a man named John becomes her best friend in need who helps her in taking care of the sick mother. One day he invites her to his house. He offers her a coke and when she goes out for a short call he drops a valium tablet in her glass of coke. She becomes drunk and wakes up in the morning and finds herself naked on John's bed.

Chapter 10
Abooki's frustration sends her for test

Abooki is frustrated and confused. She thinks of having got HIV or unwanted pregnancy. She gets thinner and thinner until her mother is shocked. One night she gets the idea of going to Virika hospital for blood test. She meets Dr. Jonathan who counsels her on the precautions to take when contacting the victims. She narrates the story of why she suspects to have acquired the virus. Then he takes her blood sample and asks her to come for results after two weeks. The results are good and she takes a pregnancy test which also proves nil. She is happy for that then Jonathan gives her a post-test counselling. In the process the two fall in love for each other. Atwoki comes back suddenly and finds that his mother has already died. He is sick. His friend David, David's mother and their house girl are also sick. David's father has perished already. Vicky and Atwoki go to visit uncle Araali at Kitangwenda, Ilunga village. Uncle welcomes them warmly and tells Atwoki, "My son... my dear son... welcome home, East or West, home is best..."

INTRODUCTION
Title of the Book

"Passed like a shadow" is a symbolic title. It represents most of the events that take place in the novel. It can be viewed in the following light.

1. It is a representation of human life capitalizing the need to do good things that will be left behind as a beautiful memory of you when you are gone. Living a worthless life on earth that leaves no any memorable mark is to Bernard Mapalala the same as having passed on this earth like a shadow. It is like you never existed because no one will remember you. You become like a shadow that vanishes away when the sun disappears in the clouds. Look at the following song sung by pupils of Kinyamasika Primary school on parents' day; pg 22

> What have I done in this world?
> What memories shall I live when I'm gone?
> If memories I shall leave are only those…
> Of having eaten and drunk;
> I shall be ashamed; there is no honor in that;
> And remembering you for the debts you leave behind;
> It is curses which precede you on your journey;
> Many people who die in anonymity;

They die in anonymity because the glorious thing they did were eating, drinking and sleeping. Then they crown their glory with death, a deed which is not hard even for the young on a breast. That is having passed on this earth like a shadow….

2. It also presents Adyeri's family that suffered a tragedy of AIDS pandemic and passed from the scene of life like a shadow leaving behind only one family member (Abooki) who is HIV free.

3. It also represents the fact that AIDS pandemic has invaded the whole of Uganda and washes people away in large numbers and within a very short time. This is compared to

the shadow that disappears quickly when the sun disappears in the clouds. Refer to how the following people pass away in a short time; Adyeri's family, David's family, Aliganyira's family, Birungi etc.

4. Apart from these families the whole society in Uganda and Tanzania AIDS is killing people so quickly. Most people have acquired the disease unawares and ignorantly spread it unknowingly. The whole community is passing away like a shadow.

CHARACTERISATION

1. **Adyeri;**
   - He is the father of Abooki and Atwoki and a husband to Amoti and caregiver to Vicky.
   - He is an ex-headmaster of St. Leos High school; he loses his job as a result of a financial scandal for the money he steals to build a house for Birungi at Burungu.
   - He is a heavy drunkard and greedy. He becomes a hopeless heavy drunkard after losing the job. He also sets high bride price that makes Vicky's marriage to Akena impossible
   - He is hot tempered. He is extremely hot-tempered and treats his family in as a dictator. He beats his wife and children often over just slight mistakes.
   - He is an irresponsible father. He fails to provide for the family. Due to his drinking habit he fails to foot the food bills in the house. That's why uncle Araali comes and finds children with no food and foots the food bills.
   - He is a reputed womanizer and a distinguished sex-maniac. He engages in extramarital affairs with his concubines who eventually make him acquire the dreadful AIDS pandemic. He is deserted by his family and goes to get shelter to Birungi's home but she throws him away.
   - He is a victim of HIV/AIDS. He remains hopeless and dies miserably of the disease passing like a shadow.
   - He is not worthy being emulated.

2. **Amoti;**
   - The wife of Adyeri and a mother of Abooki and Atwoki.
   - She is a responsible and caring mother. Despite Adyeri being a heavy drunkard and a womanizer, she remains stable and takes care of the children. Despite all her weaknesses, Amoti has a positive side. She manages to take a good care of her children even after family separation. We are told that until they reach High school, Atwoki and Abooki have never engaged in sexual affairs.
   - She is jealous. We are told that Amoti does not want Vicky to marry Akena because of jealousy. As a result she puts an obstacle that Akena is a Munyamahanga (a man from another tribe). Also she is jealous of the wife of the rich shopkeeper.
   - She is a tribalist. She denies Vicky to marry a man from another tribe calling him a Munyamahanga.
   - She is revengeful and unforgiving. She turns away from her husband at a time of disaster. Even when she is pleaded to forgive him she is so reluctant and believes that it should be a lesson to him.
   - She's suspected to be unfaithful in her marriage. We are told that she loves going to Kinyamasika in the mornings possibly she has an extramarital affair. Pg 18

- She is superstitious. Amoti believes that the sickness of her husband is due to witchcraft. She says that her husband has been bewitched by Birungi.
- She is a gossiper. Amoti and Abwoli are seen gossiping against the wife of a rich shopkeeper. In page 3 the author says, "Of course, she had spent more than one hour just gossiping against the wife of the rich shopkeeper whom she intensively hated and was jealous of. They had laughed and laughed with Abwoli, who was her best friend."
- She is a victim of HIV/AIDS. She is also wiped away from the scene by the pandemic which she contracted from her husband and passes away like a shadow.
- In some cases she is not worthy being emulated but in others, yes.

3. Atwoki;

- The son of Adyeri who suffers poor upbringing from his heavily drinking father.
- He is a handsome and famous football star. He is nicknamed "Fort Portal Bullet" when he is in high school. He plays for the national team and scores a goal which makes the president reward him.
- He builds his mother a house. He makes a lot of money and manages to build a house for his mother at Katumba near Kachwamba. Pg 25
- He is easily forgiving unlike his mother. He forgives his father when he is brought home by his fans at a time when Adyeri was seriously sick.
- He is a victim of peer pressure. He is influenced by his friend David in Kampala and begins chasing girls. Following his behaviour he gets HIV from his girlfriend {Edda} and is soon to die of AIDS.
- He has a changing behavior. At first we are told he is so disciplined and faithful. But later he changes and becomes a reputed womanizer like his daddy.
- He is a betrayer/traitor. He betrays his sister and his mother. When his mother is sick he does not provide any financial help to the extent that Abooki has to go to Vicky for financial support and relies on the support given by John which later turn out to be a trap

4. Abooki;

- She is a daughter of Adyeri and Amoti
- She is a good adviser. She advises Atwoki to be careful when in Kampala lest he dies.
- She is a faithful and disciplined girl. She managed to remain virgin until she reached high school.
- She unexpectedly falls into a trap of a hypocrite known as John who tricks her and sleeps with her out of her consent.
- She is caring and loving. She takes care of her sick mother and brother. Although Atwoki deserted her when he was in the hall of fame, she never revenged when he needed her help.
- She falls in love with Dr. Jonathan. After confirming that she is HIV and pregnancy free, the two fall in love and start honourable relationship.
- She is forgiving. She easily forgives her brother Atwoki when he comes back from Kampala despite neglecting her in his better days.

5. Vicky;

- She is an Orphan and Adyeri's niece who lives with him after her mother's death. She is not given good parental care.

- She exiles herself from home and meets Akena who wants to marry her. But the issue is complicated by her uncle who demands high bride price.
- She is exploited by Adyeri's family. We are told she went to Bundibugyo to pick tea in the plantation but the money was prepaid to Amoti who used it to pay the school fees for her children and Vicky got nothing from her seat.
- She becomes a prostitute temporarily. She decides to go for commercial sex as a result of the influence from her friends Tusiime and Kunihira.
- She marries Aliganyira but they are not blessed with a child. Her husband pressurizes her to go to the witchdoctor where she gets HIV/AIDS. She becomes a victim and dies of the same.
- She has no stand. She leaves Akena because of the complications made by her caretakers, she engages in prostitution following the advice from her friends and she agrees to go to the witchdoctor despite her knowledge of the potential dangers involved.
- She is a good advisor. She advises Abooki not to go for money. Its better she gets married to a beggar provided they love each other.

6. David;

- He's a son of a rich and important man both in government and Kabaka's Council in Kampala.
- He is Atwoki's friend and a university dropout (reject). He is the one who invites Atwoki to Kampala and influences him negatively.
- He is a womanizer like his father. The author says he was his father's perfect replica. He influences Atwoki to start hunting for girls.
- He gets HIV/AIDS and spreads it intentionally.
- He is a bad advisor. He advises Atwoki by misleading him. He says for instance "Look Atwoki, if you can't change the world, allow the world to change you" pg 33.
- He dresses expensively and his greatest hobby is to chat with girls.
- He is not worthy being emulated.

7. Birungi;

- She's Adyeri's concubine who lives in Burungu.
- She is very beautiful with attractive hair. She manages to get hold of Adyeri despite all the defences he put.
- She is a prostitute and exploiter of men. She exploits Adyeri who steals the school funds to build her a house and sells his plot of land to finance her shop.
- She is a former secretary of Adyeri when he was the headmaster of St. Leos High school.
- She is ignorant of the disease called slim/AIDS and spreads it unawareness.
- She is a betrayer. She betrays Adyeri by throwing him out when he needed her help while they spent good time together. She takes another boyfriend just the second day who takes over Adyeri's place.

SETTING

The setting of the book is specifically Uganda though in a broader and general sense it represents the whole of Africa. Furthermore down the line the setting can be subdivided into Urban and rural settings.

1. **Rural Setting;** The rural setting occupies the most part of the book and is evident in the following ways/scenarios:
    - Witchdoctors in Kahina- this is common in rural areas.
    - Spouse beating- this is also common in rural than in urban areas. E.g. Adyeri beating Amoti.
    - Uncle Araali is living in the village (Ihunga) where they are using bicycles as means of transport.
    - Names of Villages like Karambi, Bundibugyo, Kalimba, Burungu etc also sum up the rural setting.
2. **Urban setting;**
    - People like Akena own a garage. This is common in town.
    - The mentioning of urban centres like Kampala city, towns like Kamwenge, Pallisa, Kachwamba, Kasese etc.
    - Presence of restaurants, bars are common in town.
    - Prostitution (commercial sex) is also a feature of urban setting.
    - There are also school setting which is not clear whether in town or village. E.g. St. Leos High School, St. Maria Goretti, Kyebambe Girls Sec School, Kinyamasika Primary school etc
    - Hospital setting where Abooki goes for test.

STYLE
The novel is very rich in its style.

1.   **Point of view.** The writer has used all the three persons. However 3rd person is the dominant one. This is to say the author narrates the story.
2. **There is also frequent use of dialogue among characters.** E.g. the conversation between Adyeri and Amoti when Vicky comes with Akena.
    > "I have told you that Vicky has come with a visitor"
    > "A visitor"
    > "Yes a visitor"
    > "Is the visitor tall or short?" Asked Adyeri....
3. **Also there is the use of monologue / soliloquy.** A speech in a play or movie in which a character who is alone speaks his thoughts aloud. Look at Adyeri in pg 15 "this visitor has really caught us when we are dead broke" he lamented to himself. "What a pity"... I wish I was a rich man or millionaire..."
4. **There is the use of songs** as in pg 15. Adyeri sings when drunk; "God bless Uganda Ohoo Forward Uganda forward Bravery, honesty, peace ..." Another song is sung by Kinyamasika Primary Pupils on parents' day. Pg 22
5. **The novel has also used a flashback style.** Pg 22 Adyeri's background. "The story was that he had this lady called Birungi ....." the narrator tells the story of why Adyeri was sacked in from his job as a Headmaster and eventually became a heavy drunkard. Then in pg 24 Adyeri reflects his past "A film rewinded Adyeri's mind about the other partners he had had at the local drinking club. He had become some sort of a maniac and was picking women at random whenever he was drunk..."

LANGUAGE USE

The language used is simple, straightforward and easy to understand. Moreover the novelist has employed many idioms, sayings and literary devices as we are going to look very closely.

FIGURES OF SPEECH;

1. **Simile;**
   - The man will die like a dog. Pg 27
   - But don't worry, Vicky men are like buses you miss one today another comes tomorrow. Pg 16
   - She walked to him as fearless as a lioness. Pg 3.
   - The new disease was spreading like bush fire in the whole of Uganda. Pg 24
2. **Onomatopoeia;**
   - Uwi-uwi- the sound of crying. Pg 4
   - Ha ha ah! – Sound of laughing. Pg 7
3. **Reiteration**. To repeat something that you have already said usually to emphasize.
   - I really regret... I really regret I have married a pig. A pig. A pig I have married a pig mawe! Pg 3
   - Uncle Araali, Uncle Araali has come pg 14
   - Knock, knock, knock, knock. Pg 27
   - Hurry, hurry, pg 14.
4. **Metaphor;**
   - I have married a pig. Pg 3
   - For them marriage is just business. Pg 17
5. **Personification;**
   - Money will kill you. pg 42
6. **Understatement**- a statement that makes something seems less important.
   - "You must be the most poorly dressed girl in Fort Portal'. Pg 18
7. **Barbarism** – using more than one language.
   - The novelist has used a lot of words from other languages other than English. E.g., bazungu/muzungu, bakombozi, munyamahanga, matoke, waragi, oburo
8. **Symbolism;**
   - Pig = a useless man
   - Slim= AIDS
9. **Sayings and Idioms;**
   - "Like father like son" pg 39.
   - "East or West home is Best" 49
   - "In fact marriage is an institution for blind" pg 17.
   - "Building castles in the air" pg 19
   - "To hook a big fish" pg 19
   - "To add salt to the wound..." pg 23
   - "Exchanging hot potatoes with Adyeri" pg 23

THEMES IN THE NOVEL

The main theme in this book seems to be AIDS pandemic nicknamed 'slim'. Most of all other themes seem to be revolving around building up the main theme.

1. **AIDS PANDEMIC;** AIDS pandemic is a disease that has invaded the society and spreads like a bush fire, sweeping people in large numbers. However, the author shows that it spreads rapidly because of people's ignorance and superstitious beliefs that the traditional society is caught up with. Even the title of the book itself seems to suggest that a lot of people; young and old, children and parents, women and men, poor and rich perish miserably and within a very short span of time.
   - A lot of people/characters have fallen victims of the pandemic. These include; Adyeri, Amoti, Atwoki, Vicky, Aliganyira, Birungi, David, His father, mother and their house girl. The author reveals some of the incidents that expose them to the pandemic.
   - Moreover, the author gives education on HIV/AIDS: on transmission he uses the TV announcer to educate the society that; AIDS is transmitted from one infected person to another through exchange of certain body fluids (semen, blood, vaginal secretions). This exchange stems from immoral activities such as fornication, sodomy, intravenous drug abuse etc. On prevention he uses Dr. Jonathan to educate the society that the 100% guaranteed protection against AIDS is abstinence for unmarried people, mutual love and loyalty among the married couples, premarital and extramarital sex should be discouraged at all costs.

2. **PROMISCUITY/INFIDELITY;** Promiscuity is a situation of someone having many sexual partners who are not legally married to him/her. Infidelity is a situation of having other partners than your wife. This is a situation that Adyeri found himself included in. He has a concubine called Birungi beside his own wife. He also sleeps with a lot of women that he picks in the streets. He couldn't even identify whoever might have infected him with the disease. "A film rewinded Adyeri's mind about the other partners he had had at the local drinking club. He had become some sort of a maniac and was picking women at random whenever he was drunk..." Then he infects his wife and they both die of the disease. Apart from Adyeri other characters who are infidel or promiscuous include the following;
   - David is promiscuous; he picks girls at random and gets the disease as a result of this behavior.
   - David's father is both infidel and promiscuous; he's married but he picks girls at the bar and in the streets and even his own house-girl.
   - Birungi is promiscuous as we are told that she had other men apart from Adyeri.
   - Muzungu (Tusiime's boyfriend) is infidel and we are told that he is married but visits Tusiime secretly. Pg 19
   - Aliganyira is also sex maniac because we are told he had married and divorced 2 wives and now has got married to Vicky. Pg 35
   - All big people who could help Abooki demanded body pleasure before they could do anything. This is a sign of promosquity.
   - John also is promiscuous because he drugged Abooki and slept with her without her consent.

3. **PROSTITUTION;** this is a situation of doing sex for sale or in other words it is a commercial sex. We are told that one of the chief reasons for this behaviour seems to be poverty. The young girls who involve in this dangerous behaviour are motivated by the fact that they want to meet their basic needs and cope up with their peers.

- Tusiime and Kunihira are a case in point. As they get involved in this and are capable of handling their lives they don't care about the dangers associated with it. This makes them capable of influencing Vicky who comes from a disadvantaged background/ family. Vicky also becomes a prostitute and foots the bills in Adyeri's family. This activity is also dangerous as it may expose the person to AIDS pandemic.
- Birungi is also a prostitute as she exploits Adyeri the throws him out and takes another boyfriend just the next day.
- Edda is also a prostitute as she exploits Atwoki and makes his loose his control in life.

4. **PEER PRESSURE AND INFLUENCE;** Peer pressure implies the influence one gets from his/her friends, age mates, colleagues, or family folks on different decisions. In the novel the following people have fallenvictims of the peer pressure.
   - Adyeri falls into a prey to Birungi seductive approaches. He squandered the school funds to build a house for her in Burungu. This results to his dismissal from his job.
   - Vicky also becomes a victim of the peer pressure from her friends Tusiime and Kunihira and begins to engage in prostitution. They say to her "you must be the most poorly dressed girl in Fort Portal" pg 18
   - Atwoki is influenced by David, when in Kampala. He introduces Atwoki to beer drinking and girls and even finances their affairs. This makes Atwoki to become bold with girls and leads him to get HIV/AIDS.
   - The pressure from Aliganyira's relatives exposes both Vicky and Aliganyira to the disease. They go to the witch doctor in search for a baby but as the witch doctor makes small cuts on Vicky's skin he infects her with HIV. The author says; in pg 36 "So much pressure had been mounting from his folks, especially from his mother. They said that if she is unproductive, then he should throw her out and bring in a replacement"

5. **IGNORANCE AND SUPERSTITION;**
   - Most people in this novel seem to be ignorant. They are not only ignorant about the disease but also don't know the ways the disease spreads. In pg 27 the author says something about Amoti; "All in all, she was ignorant about the real disease her husband was suffering from, neither was she aware that herself was already infected with the same virus, healthy though she was." In the same page he shows the Amoti associated her husband's illness with witchcraft. "Whatever it is, your father has been bewitched"
   - Vicky's husband takes her to the witch doctor in order to get a baby, instead she gets HIV.
   - The victims of slim are taken to witchdoctors with a belief that they have been bewitched.

6. **POVERTY;** Because most people are unable to afford basic needs, they use any other possible meansto meet their needs. Some of these methods are not good because they are likely toexpose someone to the possibility of getting HIV. Poverty is portrayed in the followingscenarios;
   - Vicky, Tusiime and Kunihira are forced to engage in prostitution in order to meet their basic needs including food and clothing.

- Abooki falls prey to John's trap because of her poor condition at home and John offers financial support. She responds to his invitation knowing that if she refuses she might as well lose the financial support. This makes her lose her virginity.
- Due to poor condition at home, Atwoki is forced to move from home to Kampala. He goes to live with his friend David who comes from a rich family where he is influenced to city life and eventually gets HIV.
- Adyeri's family is so poor to the extent that sometimes the visitor (uncle Araali) foots the food bills in the house.
- Poverty is also evident among the government officers. Aliganyira laments in pg 36. "These hungry government officers...they are simply professional beggars. I wonder why they think I can finance them all the time..."
- Poverty also makes people trust that witch doctors can make them rich; as thus they go to witchdoctors in search for richness as Aliganyira tells Vicky. Pg 37 "This man is very powerful...he has very powerful juju. His charms have made people rich"

7. CONFLICTS;

a) FAMILY CONFLICT; Family conflicts also play a major and significant role in exposing both parents andchildren to the chances of getting infected with disease. Let's look at the following family conflicts.

- **The conflict between Adyeri and Amoti** makes them separated. This forces Adyeri to remain with his concubines where he acquires the infection.
- **Atwoki is forced to move from home due to constant conflicts with Daddy** and poor upbringing. He acquires the disease in exile.
- **A conflict between Vicky and her husband's relatives** forces her to visit the witchdoctor in search for a baby, instead she gets HIV. Talking about Vicky the author says: "She felt very much threatened by his relatives who were always eyeing his great wealth."

b) INTRAPERSONAL CONFLICT;

- **Abooki** suffers intrapersonal conflict after being raped by John. She wonders whether she has contacted HIV or Pregnancy. As a solution she goes for blood test which confirms that she is HIV and Pregnancy free.
- Vicky also suffers intrapersonal conflict first when living with her uncle who mistreats her. She runs away from home to get comfort somewhere else. Also she suffers intrapersonal conflict when she marries Aliganyira and fails to get a child. She is worried if her husband will throw her out and bring in a replacement. As a result she goes to the witchdoctor in search for a baby but she gets HIV.

8. PARENTS' INFLUENCE ON THEIR CHILDREN;

It is generally said "Like father like son". Parents play a big role in the future behavior of their children. Parents ought to be good role models to their children or else they will become bad models. If it happens that they shape their children in a negative way, it may increase their chance of getting HIV as in the following cases from the novel.

- **David's father** influenced David negatively by giving him too much freedom. He also goes to the bars with his father, drinks beer and picks girls without any reprimand from the parent.

- **Atwoki** also experiences poor upbringing from his heavily drinking and sex maniac father. He eventually picks up his father's behavior and exposes himself to HIV.
- **The jealousy of Amoti** influences Vicky to engage in prostitution and later finds a husband as a way of getting her basic needs. This makes Vicky acquire the disease.
- However, Amoti's influence on Abooki is a positive one. She takes good care of her and we are told that Abooki was a much disciplined girl.

9. **POSITION OF WOMEN;** Women occupy different positions in different societies. Some authors portray women in a positive way while others portray their negative aspects or both. In this novel, womenoccupy the following positions;

   a) **Women as portrayed as tools for pleasure by men.** Most men use women just to satisfy their sexual desires. The following examples illustrate the point. Abooki by John, Edda by Atwoki, Birungi by Adyeri, David with his father were using a lot of women and girls for the same reason. This increases their chance of getting HIV.

   b) **Women are portrayed as prostitutes.** In the novel we see some women/girls engaging in commercial sex as a solution to poverty. These include; Vicky, Kunihira and Tusiime.

   c) **Women are portrayed as weak and have no say.** A woman is shown as a weak vessel that men can manipulate the way they wish.Amoti receives constant beating from her husband. Also Vicky is denied the chanceof marrying Akena by her uncle because of bride price which she has no say about.

   d) **Women are portrayed as superstitious.** Women also believe in witchcraft. Amoti believes that the sickness of her husbandis due to witchcraft. She says that her husband has been bewitched by Birungi.

   e) **A woman is portrayed as a jealous person.** We are told that Amoti does not want Vicky to marry Akena because of jealousy.As a result she puts an obstacle that Akena is a Munyamahanga (a man fromanother tribe). Also she is jealous of the wife of the rich shopkeeper.

   f) **Women are portrayed as gossipers.** Amoti and Abwoli are seen gossiping against the wife of a rich shopkeeper. In page3 the author says, "Of course, she had spent more than one hour just gossiping against the wifeof the rich shopkeeper whom she intensively hated and was jealous of. Theyhad laughed and laughed with Abwoli, who was her best friend."

   g) **Women are portrayed as parents and caretakers.** Despite all her weaknesses, Amoti has a positive side. She manages to take a good care of her children even after family separation. We are told that until they reach High school, Atwoki and Abooki have never engaged in sexual affairs.

   h) **A woman is portrayed as a betrayer.** We are told that Adyeri loses his job because of the financial scandal that he squandered the school funds to build Birungi a house and sells his plot of land to open a shop for her. Yet when he is sick she throws him away.

   i) **As a good advisor.** Vicky advised Abooki not to go after money it will kill her, Abooki advised Atwoki to be careful when he was going to Kampala.

j) As a responsible person. Amoti takes all the family responsibilities while Adyeri is enjoying life with his concubines. Abooki also takes care of her sick mother while Atwoki is enjoying the city life with girls.

10. INFLUENCE OF POWER / MONEY; Sometimes the position one has in the society or his financial status may influence orexpose him to the risk of getting HIV/AIDS. The following examples from the novel arecases in point.

- Adyeri (The headmaster) is trapped by Birungi (his secretary) because of her seductive approaches.
- Atwoki falls under Edda's control because he is a famous football star and many girls are hunting him.
- David's father uses his money and position to trap girls.
- David also uses his Daddy's money and wealth to win girls' love and exposes himself to HIV infection.
- John uses his money to finance Abooki and uses that loophole to rape her.
- Aliganyira marries and divorces two wives and forces Vicky to visit the witch doctor since he is rich and Vicky agrees simply because refusing could mean divorce and go back to hand-to-mouth kind of life she had before she hooked him.

Other themes;

11. Irresponsibility; Adyeri is an irresponsible father and leader. As a leader he failed to do anything forwhich to be remembered for. As a father he fails to provide for the family basicneeds. Due to his drinking habit he fails to foot the food bills in the house. That'swhy uncle Araali comes and finds children with no food and foots the food bills. Healso fails to take good care of his niece and leaves her to get engaged inprostitutions and he doesn't care.

12. Tribalism; Amoti has a spirit of tribalism. She denies Vicky to marry Akena saying he's a man from another tribe calling him a Munyamahanga.

13. Bride price; Bride price is a stumbling block for African youths to get married to their lovedones. Parents and caregivers usually complicate the matter by setting high bride price beyond the youths' financial ability. For Adyeri, as long as the bride price is settled it doesn't matter who/what marries Vicky whether it is a person, cow or a donkey. The greed of parents has led to loss of humanity.

> 15 heads of cattle.
> 8 goats
> 50,000/= shillings for buying back cloth.
> 15,000/= shillings for buyingDaddy's walking stick and
> 2 jerry cans of beer.

At the end, the meeting ends without a consensus between the two parties. (Adyeri's side and Akena's side)

14. Wife battering/spouse beating; Adyeri is a hot tempered husband who beats his wife just for a slight mistake. Thisis not good as it may lead to family conflict and hatred among the married couples.As a result it leads to family separations as in Adyeri's family. This is a bad custom but it is common among African societies.

15. Stigmatization; This is the act of treating somebody in a way that makes them feel that they are very bad or unimportant because of some circumstances like disability, diseases etc.

- An AIDS victim narrates on the TV how his friends have run away from him, even his relatives detest him.
- But also Adyeri is stigmatized when he attends a parents' day at Kinyamasika Primary. Nobody chats with him. Amoti also treats her husband with stigma not knowing that she is also suffering from the same tragedy.
- It is not good to stigmatize people with HIV but we can interact with them while taking the necessary precautions.

16. The influence of the mass media; Like fire, the mass media can be a good servant or a bad master depending on howthey is used. The mass media have a great influence on people's behavior.David's family seems to be affected by improper use of the media. They watchtelevision film which is a romantic tale full of sexual scenes and enjoy. Atwoki isgiven a room in the visitors' quarters which is full of pictures of half-naked womenand pornographic magazines. This in part contributed to moral pollution thatAtwoki became in the future.

17. Betrayal; Birungi betrays Adyeri but throwing him out at the time when he needed her help. We are told that Adyeri loses his job because of the financial scandal that he squandered the school finds to build Birungi a house and sold his plot of land to open a shop for her at Mugusu Trading Centre. Yet when he is sick she throws him away. Atwoki betrays his sister Abooki and his uncle Araali for neglecting them when he was in the hall of fame.

MESSAGE;

1. It is important to spread HIV/AIDS education to people about its infection, transmission, prevention and treatment. Many people seem to get the disease unawares and spread it unknowingly.
2. Multiple sexual partners increase the chance of getting HIV/AIDS.
3. People should be careful in choosing friends and selecting the advice from friends. Peer pressure seems to have a strong influence in personal transformation.
4. Family conflicts and poor upbringing create a detrimental future for the children.
5. Spouse beating is an outdated culture as it may lead to family separation.
6. People should do good things when still alive so that they can be remembered for good when they are gone lest they pass like a shadow.
7. We should use the mass media fruitfully for getting valuable information and education.
8. It is not good to treat HIV victims with social stigma.

RELEVANCE

The book is relevant in any African society as it clearly depicts some common issues that are prevalent in African context. Issues like; AIDS pandemic, Superstition, Ignorance, Infidelity, Family conflicts.

1. The influence of peer pressure especially among the youngsters is also common.
2. Bride price and the related complications are common in African societies.
3. Stigmatization of HIV/AIDS victims, Irresponsibility and Betrayal among members of the society are common phenomena in Africa.

TITLE; WEEP NOT A CHILD
AUTHOR; NGUGI WA THIONG'O
SETTING; GIKUYU VILLAGE-KENYA

INTRODUCTION
Part I - "The Waning Light"

Weep Not, Child is set in a Gikuyu village in Kenya during the 1952-1960 Emergency, a tumultuous and violent period which would eventually lead to Kenya's independence from Britain. One day, the beautiful Nyokabi offers her youngest son, Njoroge, an opportunity to go to school. He enthusiastically accepts, even though he knows it will be a financial stretch for the family. His prospects are contrasted with those of his half-brother Kamau. Although Kamau is only slightly older than Njoroge, he has already been apprenticed to a carpenter, and will pursue that instead of going to school. Both boys hope that their training will lead them to a happy and successful future.

The village is located near Kipanga, a larger town where many of the villagers work. Kipanga is home to many colorful characters, including a funny barber who tells colorful stories about his experiences fighting in World War II. On this day, Njoroge and Kamau's father, Ngotho, is spending time in Kipanga. He soon returns home, proud that his son will be the first in the family to attend school. Ngotho works as a farmer for a British land-owner, Mr. Howlands, on land that Ngotho's family once owned.

Njoroge initially has a hard time adjusting to life at school, but his old friend Mwihaki helps him. Mwihaki is the daughter of Jacobo, a rich Gikuyu pyrethrum farmer who owns the land that Ngotho and his family live on. One evening, Ngotho tells his wives and children – Kori, Boro, Kamau, and Njoroge –stories about how the British stole the Gikuyu land. These events particularly upset Boro, who believes his father complicit in the injustice by working for Mr. Howlands. Boro has been troubled ever since he lost his brother when they were fighting together in World War II.

Njoroge enjoys learning how to read - and eventually, how to speak English. He continues to bond with Mwihaki, and also dedicates himself to studying the Bible. He sees parallels between the Gikuyu struggle and the oppression of the Israelites. Meanwhile, Kamau is frustrated by the slow pace at which his boss, Nganga, teaches him.

Word spreads through the community about a strike to advocate for more rights for Africans. Ngotho wants to participate, but is worried that Mr. Howlands will fire him. He decides to walk out anyway, and attends a rally where Boro and his friend Kiarie are scheduled to speak. The police bring in Jacobo, who urges the strikers to return to work. Ngotho is so enraged by Jacobo that he rushes the stage and attacks him, which starts a riot. The riot is put down immediately, and has dire consequences for Ngotho's family – he is fired from his job and evicted from Jacobo's land. Fortunately, Nganga allows the family to move onto his land.

Two and a half years pass. Njoroge's hero, the revolutionary Jomo Kenyatta, is arrested. Meanwhile, there are many incidents of violence by the Mau Mau, one of the revolutionary groups. The whole culture is in a state of flux and worry.

Part II - "Darkness Falls"

Njoroge's older brothers Kori and Boro both have run-ins with the police. An atmosphere of fear Permeates the village; people are afraid not just of the police, but also of the Mau Mau, which slits the throats of suspected traitors. Mr. Howlands and Jacobo plot ways to arrest Ngotho, whom they both resent for his insubordination and his attack on Jacobo. They arrange for Kori and Njeri (Ngotho's first wife) to be arrested, although Mr. Howlands is reluctant to harm Ngotho because he remembers how much his old employee loved the land. Meanwhile, Njoroge's school is threatened by the Mau Mau, but he continues to attend at Kamau's advice.

One day, Mwihaki returns to the villages after several years away at boarding school. She and Njoroge are happy to see each other, and she invites him into her home, where he is surprised that Jacobo is so kind to him. They promise to be together after she graduates. Not much later, Njoroge and some friends go on a church retreat. However, the retreat is stopped by the police, who murder their group leader for his attitude of independence. Meanwhile, Boro plots ways to murder Jacobo. Njoroge is promoted to high school, and Mwihaki, whose grades are not as strong, attends a teaching college. The differences between them become more apparent – Mwihaki is frustrated and hopeless about the state of the country, whereas Njoroge believes that educated young people have the power to change the future. At high school, Njoroge flourishes. One day, he meets Stephen Howlands, the son of Mr. Howlands. The two boys realize that they have much in common, and discuss the reasons that they were afraid to talk to each other as children.

At nineteen, Njoroge is pulled out of school to be interrogated by the police. Jacobo has been Murdered, and they believe that Ngotho is involved. Njoroge is tortured mercilessly, but he refuses to give up any information. The police reveal that Ngotho has already confessed to the murder and that they have castrated him. During the torture, Njoroge passes out, and Mr. Howlands, who has been present at the interrogation, arranges for Njoroge to be released. As it turns out, Ngotho did not commit the murder; he only confessed to help Kamau, who was being detained as a suspect. In fact, Boro killed Jacobo; he believed that it was the only way to avenge his brother's death in the war. Mr. Howlands eventually realized that Ngotho's confession was false, but allowed him to be tortured anyway. However, he could not bring himself to execute Ngotho. Several days later, Ngotho dies. Njoroge and Boro visit him before he dies, and after Boro sees his father's condition, he murders Mr. Howlands in the white man's home.

After Ngotho's death, Njoroge is obliged to give up his education and to work in a dress shop. These events emotionally destroy Njoroge, and he goes to the one source of comfort he has left: Mwihaki. They admit that they love each other, but that they cannot be together because they are obliged to support their families, both of which are now missing a father. Njoroge tries to kill himself, but Nyokabi stops him and brings him home.

Chapter 1
The story begins in the Gikuyu village of Mahua, in Kenya.

Nyokabi is a beautiful woman, though she has been aged prematurely by a life of poverty and hardship. She offers her son, Njoroge, a chance to go to school – something the family has never been able to afford for his older siblings. He is delighted, even after she warns him that he will not be able to afford lunch there, and that he must attend every day. He rushes to tell his half-brother Kamau the good news.

Kamau, who is working as an apprentice carpenter, is happy to learn Njoroge's news. Although they are nearly the same age, Kamau cannot attend school because of his apprenticeship. The boys discuss their bright futures. Both hope that their training will make them as rich as either Jacobo, a wealthy and educated local villager, or Mr. Howlands, an English man who had lived among the community for a long time. Though both figures are the subject of local controversy - Mr. Howlands for his race and significant land ownership, and Jacobo for the compromises he makes to please Mr. Howlands – they are both admired because of their wealth. As we learn later, Njoroge and his family also live on land rented from Jacobo.

The narrator then speaks about the local community and landscape. He describes the black, paved road that passes through Mahua, heading far into the distance. It was built by Italian prisoners during World War II, and offers an alternative to the less-defined paths through the forest that natives would otherwise take when traversing the area.

The narrator then muses on the insularity of village life, and how difficult it is to understand white people. He tells of what the locals do for entertainment. When the men of Mahua get bored, they travel to the nearby town of Kipanga, where they shop and loiter. Kipanga is bigger and more diverse than Mahua – it has a large population of Indian traders, who maintain a fraught relationship with the native Gikuyu. One of the most popular figures in town is the barber, who tells stories about his time fighting in the war; in particular, he likes to tell about sleeping with white prostitutes in Jerusalem.

The narrator shifts back to the current day, on which the barber is speaking about the prostitutes. When he finishes his story, Ngotho- husband to Nyokabi, and father to Njoroge and Kamau - sets off for home. We learn that Nyokabi is Ngotho's second wife; his first is named Njeri. A man's first wife is favored in Gikuyu custom, but despite some occasional problems over jealousy, Ngotho's wives and children get along well. As he walks home, he reflects on his own experiences serving in World War I, and those of his sons, Boro and Mwangi, who fought in World War II. When he arrives home, Ngotho learns that Njoroge will soon start school, and he feels proud that his son will be educated like the daughter of Jacobo.

Chapter 2

On Monday, Njoroge's friend (and Jacobo's daughter) Mwihaki walks with him to his first day of school. Njoroge has admired her ever since he saw her being bullied by herd-boys many years before. She has been attending school for a while. When they arrive, the other boys shock Njoroge with their shouting and lewd jokes. They make fun of him, calling him a *Njuka*, or newcomer. They try to force him carry their bags, but Mwihaki saves him by claiming that Njoroge is her Njuka, and so only she can order him around.

146

Time passes. At first, Njoroge has a hard time adjusting to school life. He likes his teacher, but becomes afraid of her after she beats another student. Because he always returns straight home after school for fear of angering his mother, he does not make many friends. One day, Mwihaki walks home with him and they dawdle, chatting and throwing stones. When her son does not return immediately, Nyokabi sets out in search of him, and is upset to find him playing with a girl from a higher social class. One day after school, Njoroge begs his mother to tell him stories. Earlier that day, his teacher had asked him to tell the class a story, but he, in his nervousness, forgot all the stories he knows. Nyokabi agrees to honor his request after she finishes her chores.

Njoroge heads out to play, after taking off his school clothes. He passes Jacobo's large house, and recalls an instance in which Jacobo's wife, Juliana, hosted a party for all the children of parents who worked for the family. At the party, Njoroge giggled during Grace, and Juliana lectured the children about manners. Njoroge sees Mwihaki walking in his direction, and he hides, ashamed that she might see him wearing only his old calico loincloth. He instead meets up with Kamau, who complains that his employer, the carpenter Nganga, does not let him do enough hands-on work at his apprenticeship. Instead, Nganga only assigns Kamau menial tasks. Njoroge sympathizes with his brother's complaints, and invites him over for storytelling at Nyokabi's hut that evening.

That night, something unusual happens: Ngotho tells stories, instead of Nyokabi. He is known as an excellent storyteller. First, Ngotho recounts the traditional Gikuyu creation story, in which the Creator, Murungu, placed a man and a woman under his sacred tree. Next, he tells about how white men came to Kenya, forced him and others to fight in World War I, and then stole their land. (Ngotho's land now belongs to the wealthy Englishman Mr. Howlands.) According to Ngotho, a seer named Mugo wa Kibiro had prophesied all of this tragedy before the British even set foot in Kenya. She had also promised that the white men would eventually leave, a promise that gives many like Ngotho hope for the future.

The story enrages Boro, Ngotho's eldest son and a veteran of World War II. He has been troubled ever since losing his brother in the war, believing that his and his people are suffering seems to have no purpose. He demands to know why his father continues working for the man who took his land (Mr. Howlands), and then storms out before Ngotho can answer.

Chapter 3

Ngotho walks to work the next day, brooding over Boro's accusations, and reflecting on how the boy has changed since the war. As he walks through town, he remembers the various odd jobs he had held in his youth. When he arrives at the *shamba*, or tea plantation, the narrative shifts to Mr. Howlands's point of view. After fighting in World War I, Mr. Howlands grew disillusioned and decided to become a farmer in Africa, hoping to find inner peace there. He is completely dedicated to his work, and he admires Ngotho and his special connection with the land. Mr. Howlands brought his wife Suzanne – or Memsahib, as most of the characters call her – to Kenya, but he is oblivious to the fact that she hates it there. The Howlands have three children. Their eldest son, Peter, was killed in World War II, and their daughter became a missionary. Their youngest, Stephen, still lives with them.

As Mr. Howlands and Ngotho walk through the plantation together, Mr. Howlands confides in his employee about Peter's death, and about his doubts that Stephen can manage the plantation after he dies. Ngotho wonders to himself when the Howlands family will leave Kenya, and thinks that "Mr. Howlands should not complain [about Peter's death]. It had been his war" (33).

Chapter 4

At school, Njoroge enjoys learning to read from his funny and energetic teacher, Isaka. At home, he tries to teach Kamau what he is learning, but Kamau seems to resent the offer. One day, Mwihaki catches up with Njoroge after school, and asks why he never walks home with her anymore. He deflects the question, and they talk about their parents. Both of them fear their parents, even though they are good children. They both share a sense that their parents are sometimes wrong.

Njoroge recalls a time that an Indian boy tried to be friend him by giving him a piece of candy, and his mother made him throw it on the ground. When they pass Mr. Howlands' house, Njoroge mentions that his father works there, and they both speak around the fact that whites own land that once belonged to the blacks. Mwihaki mentions her father's belief that the natives were robbed because they were uneducated. Because she is a year ahead of Njoroge in school, she promises to teach him English once she learns it, but he is uncomfortable with learning from her. The following year, Njoroge skips a grade and is promoted to Standard I – the same grade Mwihaki is in.

Njoroge continues to urge Kamau to quit his apprenticeship and attend school, but Kamau insists that learning a trade is the only option for someone who owns no land. However, Njoroge and his father Ngotho continue to believe that education is the most important pursuit, although Ngotho thinks that "education [is] good only because it would lead to the recovery of lost lands" (40). Njoroge begins to sense that he is destined for something big.

Chapter 5

Njoroge and Kamau stand on a 'hill' of rubbish outside Ngotho's house. From the 'hill,' they can see the lights of the big city Nairobi. They discuss Boro, who has left to find work there. Njoroge hopes that Boro will return, but Kamau explains that "Boro is not of this place" – he is too resentful of the village elders, who failed to fight off the white people (44).

Kamau confesses he would like to quit his apprenticeship and leave for Nairobi like Boro did. This means he could not participate in a strike that some of the local men are planning, but he believes strikes are for old men anyway. Njoroge begins to talk to his brother about Mwihaki, but changes his mind and asks about a mysterious character named Jomo instead. Kamau says that Boro used to call Jomo "the black Moses," but does not offer much concrete information about him (46). That night, Njoroge prays that he will learn enough to both help his family and become smarter than Mwihaki.

Three years later, Njoroge and Mwihaki are in Standard IV, and beginning to learn English. They initially have trouble with grammar, which makes the teacher, Lucia (who is also Mwihaki's sister), very angry. However, they slowly progress, and begin to grasp the language. One day, a European woman visits the class, and Lucia is enraged when the students greet her with "good morning, Sir" instead of with the more appropriate "good afternoon, Madam" (49). Later, Njoroge realizes that the woman was Mr. Howlands' daughter, the missionary.

Time passes, and Kamau prepares for his circumcision ceremony, a rite of manhood amongst the Gikyu. Njoroge fears that once Kamau is a man, he will leave for the city and the family will disintegrate. As time goes by, Njoroge immerses himself in books, especially the Bible. He develops his own kind of religious faith, which combines Christian teachings with traditional Gikuyu values. He comes to believe that Africans are God's chosen people, and compares their struggles to those of the Israelites in the Old Testament. He wonders whether Jomo, "the black Moses," might in fact lead the Africans to freedom.

Chapter 6

The men of Mahua (the village) sometimes gather to discuss political affairs. Occasionally, Boro and Kori travel home from the city for these meetings, bringing friends from there. Njoroge loves to eavesdrop on these conversations. He listens in on one meeting, in which the men plan a strike to involve all black people - or at least all those who work under white people or the British colonial government. That night, Njoroge prays that the strike will result in a pay raise for his father. When he hears about the impending strike, Mr. Howlands threatens to fire any worker who participates.

Ngotho is torn with indecision – he wants to fight for better wages and fair treatment, but he also loves working the land and does not want to lose his job. He eventually decides to join the strike, which causes a bitter fight between him and Nyokabi. Although Ngotho and his wives usually restrain from fighting around their children, Njoroge hears the argument, and is deeply disturbed. That night, he asks God whether the strike will succeed, and falls asleep listening for an answer.

Chapter 7

At the beginning of the New Year, all the students gather at the school to learn whether they have passed and will continue to intermediate school. After a moment of suspense, Njoroge and Mwihaki learn that they have both passed, and they skip home merrily, holding hands. However, they separate as they approach their houses. When Mwihaki enters her house, her mood quickly dampens when she learns that something has happened to her father Jacobo.

The narrator tells what has happened. Earlier that day, Ngotho had left work to attend a rally in support of the strike. Boro, who has become a committed activist, and his friend Kiarie were scheduled to speak at the rally. Before they could begin, the police interrupted the rally and urged the audience to listen to Jacobo, who spoke to the natives about returning to work. Ngotho, who suddenly found himself furious at this "Traitor," rushed the stage to attack Jacobo (62). The other workers in the audience joined him, and a violent riot began. Jacobo was saved by the police's quick intervention, and Ngotho was hailed by the village as a hero.

The narrative jumps forward a few days. A group of men congregate near the barber's shop. They discuss how the strike has failed, and how Ngotho's family has been expelled from their home on Jacobo's land. Additionally, Ngotho has lost his job working for Mr. Howlands.
The events at the rally cause many changes for Njoroge and his family. Though the family is initially homeless, Nganga the carpenter allows them to set up new huts on his land. Without a

job, Ngotho cannot pay the rising fees at Njoroge's school, but Kamau and Kori use their salaries to ensure the boy can continue with his education. Meanwhile, Mwihaki has left for a boarding school far away.

Chapter 8

About two years have passed. Njoroge hears many stories about events occurring in the far-away towns of Nyeri and Murang'a. Often, these stories have a mythic element to them. For example, a boy named Karanja tells him one about Dedan Kimathi, the leader of the African Freedom Army, who tricked the police into expecting him to arrive, at which point they would arrest him. However, the leader instead turned himself into a white man, and borrowed a motorcycle from the police. The next day, he turns into an airplane, and drops them a letter explaining how he fooled them.

Jacobo has meanwhile become a chief. He is surrounded by bodyguards at all times, to protect him from guerilla resistance fighters. Mr. Howlands has become the district officer, and he and Jacobo often patrol the huts for suspicious activity. Njoroge has continued in his new school despite his family's precarious finances. One day, Njoroge comes home to find Boro and Kori in the house, both dirty and tired. There has been a police crackdown because Jomo will soon go to trial. Kori had been arrested, but he leaped from the moving police truck when he realized he and his fellow revolutionaries would be killed. Though he was shot in the knee during his escape, he has made it home. Everyone listens to his story.

There is an unmistakable tension in the house, both from fear for the future and from the problems between Ngotho and Boro. Boro has not forgiven his father for inciting the riot two years before; Boro and Kiarie are strong believers in nonviolent resistance, and Boro believes his father undermined the movement by attacking Jacobo. Another point of contention is the fact that Ngotho will not join the Mau Mau. Though Ngotho believes in the cause, joining would entail taking an oath, and Ngotho believes it shameful to have an oath administered to him by his son.

Chapter 9

At school, Njoroge and his friends discuss Jomo's trial and the various rebel splinter groups that have formed. Njoroge asks the difference between the KAU and the Mau Mau, two of the most powerful groups. Most of the other students explain that they "like KAU and fear Mau Mau" because the Mau Mau slit the throats of black people reputed to be traitors (79). The boys all daydream about fighting in the forest.

Everyone is disappointed and afraid when they learn that Jomo Kenyatta has been found guilty during his trial, and will hence not be released. Ngotho suffers a crisis of conscience – he worries that his actions at the rally will keep the prophecy (that the whites will leave Kenya) from being fulfilled. He also ponders his problematic relationship with Boro, and wonders whether he has made other mistakes as a father. Meanwhile, to her family, Njeri analyzes why Jomo lost his trial. She believes that it is impossible to win a trial when white men have made all the laws. Boro exclaims that black men must rise up and fight, and Njoroge is deeply moved by his brother's passion.

Chapter 10

In the district office, Mr. Howlands waits for Jacobo to arrive for a meeting. He reflects on his failure to live a simple life in Africa, realizing that he has become immersed in politics despite his intentions. He had reluctantly accepted the district officer post because he wants to defend his land, the only thing he truly believes in. He has never bothered to think about the Gikuyu perspective; to him, black people are like "donkeys or horses in his farm" (84). Like Ngotho, Mr. Howlands often feels that he does not understand his children – especially his missionary daughter.

Jacobo arrives. The rebellion has caused Mr. Howlands to hate Jacobo, whom he sees as a savage despite the black's man wealth and their long history of working together. Jacobo tells Mr. Howlands that he believes Ngotho and Boro are secretly participating in the rebellion; he even believes Ngotho might be the secret head of the Mau Mau. He asks permission to send them to a detention camp, and Mr. Howlands instructs him to arrest Ngotho and his sons for any minor infractions. As Jacobo leaves, Mr. Howlands reflects on how he has never forgotten Ngotho. That night, most of the family is gathered in Nyokabi's hut. When Njeri and Kori leave to sleep in Njeri's hut – only a few yards away – they are arrested for breaking the 6 p.m. curfew. Ngotho pays the fine for the crime, but only Njeri is released. Kori is sent to a detention camp without trial. Meanwhile, Jacobo continues to plot ways to arrest Ngotho.

One day, Njoroge arrives at school to find the students huddled around a letter that has been posted on the wall. The letter threatens that the headmaster and forty children will be killed if the school does not close down; it is signed by the resistance leader Dedan Kimathi. Njoroge does not understand the threat, because he "thought Mau Mau was on the side of the black people" (91). Kamau urges his brother to keep going to school, since he is no safer at home anyway. Njoroge agrees, and continues to attend.

Chapter 11

As conditions continue to deteriorate and daily life becomes more dangerous, Kamau becomes the family's main support. Njoroge, still in school, often thinks of Mwihaki, whom he has not seen since the riot several years before. One day, Kamau tells Njoroge that six villagers, including Nganga and the barber, have been taken into the woods and murdered.

One day, Mwihaki, home from boarding school on a vacation, surprises Njoroge as he is walking along the road. She has become a beautiful young woman, and Njoroge realizes that he must also appear more mature than he had before. They talk briefly, and Mwihaki asks Njoroge to spend more time with her. She gains his sympathy by confessing that everyone in the village avoids her because she is Jacobo's daughter. Njoroge reluctantly agrees to attend church with her.

Two days later, they walk to church together. When they arrive, their old teacher Isaka – who has become a Revivalist – reads a selection from the Book of Matthew about enduring hardship. After church, Mwihaki invites Njoroge into her home. Jacobo arrives unexpectedly, and wishes Njoroge good luck in school, explaining that Njoroge's generation will have to rebuild Kenya. Njoroge is briefly pleased at the attention, but grows uncomfortable when the sight of Jacobo's bodyguards reminds him of the dead barber.

Mwihaki and Njoroge discuss how Kenya has changed in the past few years. Mwihaki wonders why Jesus did not prevent the violence in their country. Njoroge, unshaken by her doubts, replies that God works in mysterious ways. They speculate about whether the Gikuyu are being punished for someone's sins. Mwihaki proposes they run away together, adding that she "could be such a nice sister" to Njoroge (104). Njoroge immediately argues the foolishness of the plan, but Mwihaki quickly assures him that she was joking. However, she promises to rejoin him once she finishes school.

Chapter 12

Over the years, Mr. Howlands has grown to enjoy crushing the resistance. As they often have, he and Jacobo discuss how to deal with Ngotho and Boro, although Mr. Howlands remains reluctant to directly attack Ngotho. To counter this reluctance, Jacobo shows him one of several threatening, anonymous notes he has lately received; he believes they have been sent by Ngotho.

Meanwhile, Isaka brings Njoroge and several other youths to a church retreat nearby. On the way there, the police detain the group and ask to see their papers. The girls are allowed to go free, and Njoroge is released because he has his papers. Isaka does not have papers, but is unfazed by the officers. He insists that he would never join the Mau Mau because he has devoted his life to Jesus. Nevertheless, the officers bring him into the forest and shoot him. Njoroge feels sick As it turns out, the officers were actually looking for Boro and his guerillas, who are staked out in the forest. The narrator focuses on them. Boro constantly broods about his brother Mwangi, who died in World War II. In fact, his entire life is devoted to avenging Mwangi's death. He believes that killing Jacobo will serve this goal, though he has yet to develop a plan for the assassination. He discusses the issue with his lieutenant, who is eager to help. However, Boro insists that he must perform this task alone.

Chapter 13

Njoroge is the only boy in the area to pass intermediate school and progress to high school. The villagers, proud of his accomplishments, chip in to pay his tuition. Mwihaki also passes her exit exams, but does not do well enough to continue to high school. Instead, she will attend a teacher's training college.

The day before Njoroge leaves, he and Mwihaki meet one last time. Mwihaki warns him not to forget the people he knew at home, and not to put on airs. Njoroge suspects she is jealous, and chatters about his hopes to go abroad after high school but to eventually return, since he believes Kenya needs him. Mwihaki angrily replies that the country has grown so dark that no one can fix it. Njoroge argues that that things will get better. After they say goodbye, Mwihaki walks home alone, trying to cover her tears.

Chapter 14

At first, Njoroge is puzzled by the diversity of his high school. For the first time, he interacts with white teachers who treat him with kindness and respect. He is also surprised to find that his classmates, who are from other tribes, are not so different from the boys he knows at home. One day, a school for European boys competes against Njoroge's school in football. Njoroge sits out the match, chatting with a white student who turns out to be Stephen Howlands.

Stephen admits that he often wanted to introduce himself to the black boys in Kipanga, but was afraid they would not want to talk to him. Njoroge sometimes saw Stephen around, and felt the same way. The boys ponder the strangeness of this coincidence. They comment on the tension that prevents people of different races from interacting with each other, but Njoroge reassures Stephen that the tension will one day pass and Kenya will be peaceful again. Stephen fears he will not be around to see it – he is being sent to England for boarding school.

Meanwhile, Mwihaki writes Njoroge frequently. In her letters, she confesses that she misses him, and confides that life at home has changed – "fear," she writes, "is in the air" (123). Jacobo has grown paranoid and unpleasant, and the villagers are terrified. Njoroge admits to himself that he is glad not to be at home.

Chapter 15

The chapter begins during Njoroge's third term at high school. Stephen and his sister have left for England. Njoroge remains very happy at the high school, which is an oasis of peace in a troubled country. The headmaster keeps order through both severity and a fervent belief in "the white man's rule and civilising mission" (126). One day, the headmaster pulls Njoroge out of class to tell him that his family has been involved in a "sad business," and that he must remain open to Christ. He then hands Njoroge over to the custody of two police officers (126).

The officers take Njoroge to a station known as the "House of Pain," where he is surprised to find Mr. Howlands waiting. The policemen interrogate Njoroge about Boro's whereabouts, and eventually reveal that Jacobo has been murdered. They beat Njoroge mercilessly when he cannot give them any information. Eventually, they inform him that his father Ngotho has admitted to the crime, and that they will castrate Njoroge if he does not confirm his father's guilt. Njoroge refuses to say anything, and passes out when they put the pincers to his penis. Mr. Howlands then leaves, without saying anything. A few days later, Njoroge and his mothers are released from confinement.

Meanwhile, Ngotho writhes in pain in his hut, remembering recent events. The narrator is ambiguous about who actually killed Jacobo, but implies that Ngotho was not guilty. Nevertheless, Ngotho was pleased when he learned of his rival's death, and he walked tall for the first time in years. However, Kamau was soon arrested for the murder, and Ngotho confessed to save his son. Mr. Howlands, who had come to consider Ngotho as a nemesis, interrogated him with such violence that even the other police officers were frightened. Njoroge's latest experiences finally break his optimism. He is overcome by guilt because he believes he has brought this "ill luck" on his family by associating with Mwihaki (131).

One night, he runs away from home. As he passes Jacobo's house, he realizes he wants nothing more than to hold Mwihaki and run away with her. He sadly returns home because he now knows he cannot leave either Mwihaki or his family. That night, he does not pray.

Chapter 16

Ngotho becomes desperately ill as he tries to recover from the wounds he sustained in torture. When Njoroge visits him, Ngotho rambles incoherently that the British have detained Kamau because they want "young blood" (134) When Ngotho hears a knock at the door, he fears it is

Mr. Howlands, but it turns out to be Boro, who is thin and unkempt after months of fighting and hiding in the woods. Boro apologizes for not coming sooner, and Ngotho begs him not leave the family again. However, Boro explains that he must continue to fight. He leaves not long afterwards, and Ngotho wishes him well, and then urges Njoroge to look after his mothers. As Boro walks out the door, Ngotho dies.

Chapter 17

Five months later, Njoroge works as a sales assistant in an Indian dress shop. He hates his job, and is ashamed that his big dreams have amounted to nothing. Mr. Howlands died on the same day as Ngotho did, and Boro and Kamau have been charged with his murder. The narrator recounts how Mr. Howlands died. After letting Ngotho go, he returned home to brood. Although he gave Ngotho wounds that would ultimately kill him, Mr. Howlands felt he had not yet received ultimate restitution. He was forced to let Ngotho go free because he found a notebook with Boro's name on it at the crime scene.

Over time, Mr. Howlands gradually realized that Ngotho truly had nothing to do with the murders. In fact, he even thought Boro was merely covering for Kamau. Seeing Njoroge tortured shamed him, and he grew guilty with the remembrance of how he had once been an idealistic youth who was subsequently disillusioned by violence. Boro entered Mr. Howlands's house on the day Ngotho died, and admitted that it was he who killed Jacobo. Boro then accused Mr. Howlands of stealing the Gikuyu land and raping their women. Mr. Howlands responded that it was *his* land. Boro laughed at this claim and then shot Mr. Howlands, after which he surrendered himself to the homeguards gathered outside. In the present day, Njoroge sulks at his job, and his miserable mood frightens the children who come into the shop. His boss fires him, and he leaves to seek comfort from Mwihaki.

Chapter 18

Mwihaki receives a note from Njoroge asking to see her, but she is reluctant because of Njoroge's association with her father's murder. She was devastated when she learned that Jacobo was dead. Eventually, she agrees to meet Njoroge. When he arrives, Njoroge apologizes for what happened to her father. Mwihaki believes that he could have warned her before the murder if he chose, but Njoroge insists that he knew nothing about it. Finally, he tells her that he loves her. Mwihaki confesses that she loves him too, and Njoroge proposes they run away to Uganda together, as she once proposed. However, Mwihaki insists they must stay because they have a duty to help make a brighter future for their people. She adds that she cannot leave her mother to be with him. Njoroge feels forsaken by everything he once cared for – education, God, country, Mwihaki. He walks to the outside of the village, prepared to hang himself. At the last moment, Nyokabi appears, and urges him to come home. He feels guilty for shirking his father's last command, which was to take care of his mothers. As he walks home, a voice in his head calls him a coward for attempting suicide.

Characterization;
1. **Nyokabi;** She is the second wife of Ngotho, a plantation hand and the patriarch of the novel's main family. Nyokabi cares deeply for her children, and strives to maintain peace in the family.

2. **Njoroge;** Njoroge is the novel's primary protagonist, and Ngotho's youngest son. He is the first in his family to attend school, and he aspires to use his education to make Kenya a better place. Ngugi describes him as —a dreamer, a visionary who consoled himself faced by the difficulties of the moment by a look at a better day to come‖ (130). The challenges to his optimism in large part constitute the novel's primary arc.

3. **Kamau;** Njoroge's slightly older half -brother and the son of Njeri. He is apprenticed as a carpenter, and thus cannot join Njoroge at school. Because he goes directly into a career, he is forced to mature more quickly than Njoroge does. As his father ages and his brothers join the Mau Mau, Kamau becomes his family's main support.

4. **Jacobo;** A wealthy chief and pyrethrum farmer – indeed, he is the first African to be allowed to grow the crop. He owns the land that Ngotho and his family live on, and he works against the Mau Mau uprising as it starts to intensify. He is also Mwihaki's father.

5. **Mr. Howlands;** He is a British tea farmer who moved to Kenya to escape a troubled past. He owns the land that once belonged to Ngotho's father, a source of tension between the men despite the fact that Mr. Howlands is Ngotho's employer. As time passes, he is appointed district officer, and viciously fights the rebellion.

6. **John;** Jacobo's son, who at the beginning of the novel is planning to study abroad in England,.

7. **The barber;** He is a humorous African who works in Kipanga. He likes to tell raunchy stories about his exploits fighting in World War II.

8. **Ngotho;** He is the patriarch of Njoroge's family, and a World War I veteran. He is married to Njeri and Nyokabi, and is the father of Boro, Kori, Kamau, and Njoroge, as well as another son, Mwangi, who died in World War II. He works on Mr. Howlands's plantation, and longs for the white people to leave Kenya so he can have his family's land back.

9. **Njeri;** She is Ngotho's brave and intelligent first wife and the mother of Kamau.

10. **Boro;** He is One of Ngotho's elder sons, who fought in World War II. He drinks frequently and seems to suffer from post-traumatic stress disorder. He is particularly troubled by the death of his brother Mwangi in the war. He eventually finds a sense of purpose through fighting in the Mau Mau rebellion, where he becomes the leader of a guerrilla group.

11. **Mwihaki;** She is Jacobo's daughter and one of the wealthiest girls in the village. She is close friends with Njoroge, and eventually becomes his love interest. Their shifting attitudes on the country's prospects in large part constitute the novel's primary arc.

12. **Lucia;** She is Jacobo's temperamental adult daughter, who teaches at the elementary school.

13. **Juliana;** Jacobo's wife, described as fat and stern.

14. **Nganga;** He is the village carpenter, who apprentices Kamau. Although he is initially characterized as stingy and mean, Nganga later shows his generosity by giving Ngotho's family a place to live after they are evicted from Jacobo's land.

15. **Mwangi;** He is One of Ngotho's elder son, who died while serving in World War II alongside his brother Boro. His death is a primary motivation in the resentment that fuels Boro.

16. **Kori;** He is Ngotho and Njeri's adult son. He works at the Green Hotel tea shop in Kipanga.

17. **Mugo wa Kibiro;** A seer who predicted that white men would come and take people's land, long before the British came to Kenya. However, he also predicted that they would one day leave, a prediction which gives Ngotho hope.

18. **Murungu;** The Gikuyu name for the Creator.

19. **Memsahib;** She is Mr Howlands's moody wife, who —mattered [to her husband] only in so far as she made it possible for him to work ... more efficiently without a worry about home (30).

20. **Isaka;** First introduced as a jovial teacher at Njoroge's school, with a reputation for drinking and womanizing, Isaka later appears as a Christian revivalist after the rebellion begins.

21. **Jomo;** Though he never appears directly in the novel, Jomo Kenyatta's reputation as the Gikuyu leader of the KAU makes him a hero to the village and Njoroge in particular. Kenyatta is a real historical figure who would become the first Prime Minister of Kenya after it achieved independence.

22. **Kiarie;** He is One of Boro's politically active friends from the city, who joins him in many events amongst the Gikuyu.

23. **Karanja;** He is a boy in the village who brings the village news about the rebellion.

24. **Dedan Kimathi;** He is the leader of the African Freedom Army, and an important figure in the uprising. Though never directly featured in the novel, his reputation strikes fear in the hearts of the villagers and Njoroge. He is another real historical figure, and remains very controversial for his use of violence. Eventually, there developed a schism between Kimathi's Mau Mau and Jomo Kenyatta's more moderate followers in the KAU.

25. **Mucatha;** This is One of Njoroge's friends at school.

26. **Stephen Howlands;** He is Mr. Howlands's youngest son (and the only one alive during the period of the novel). He is shy and thoughtful, and Mr. Howlands has doubts about whether he is suitable to inherit the plantation. He and Njoroge have an important conversation late in the novel.

Themes

1. **Grief;** In some ways, grief is the primary driving force behind the action of *Weep Not, Child*. Boro is driven to join the Mau Mau to assuage his grief over his brother Mwangi's death in World War II. Ngotho's resentments are fueled by grief over losing his family's land to the British. Similarly, grief drives Njoroge's spiritual evolution. Nothing can undermine his faith in God until Ngotho dies, at which point Njoroge stops praying. Similarly, Jacobo's death prevents Njoroge from being with Mwihaki, because she must care for her mother. As the characters cope with the deaths of their loved ones, their overwhelming grief slowly dissolves into a sense of duty that allows them to transcend

their misery. Although Njoroge is nearly driven to suicide by Mwihaki's rejection and his father's death, it is the necessity of caring for his mothers (which he would not have to do if Ngotho were alive) that ultimately saves him.

2. **Social class;** As Ngugi notes on several occasions, race is not the only obstacle that prevents the characters from pursuing their goals in life. They are arguably even more hampered by their social class. This applies to poor characters like Kamau, who must persist with the carpentry apprenticeship he dislikes in order to support his family. However, even upper-class characters find that their upbringing prevents them from being truly free. For example, Mwihaki's affection for Njoroge is hampered by her famiy's wealth, and the expectations that come from that. Similarly, Stephen Howland must attend boarding school in England even though he feels more at home in Kenya, and does not want to leave. Njoroge has a great hope that education will help bridge the gap of social class, but circumstances cede his education before he can test that theory.

3. **The land;** Ngotho and Mr. Howlands share a fierce dedication to the land. At the center of their relationship is the central problem of the colonial presence in Kenya, and hence to the novel's main conflicts. Each has his own deep connection to the land. Land is an important part of Gikuyu culture, an indicator of a family. Mr. Howlands seems to have embodied some of this sentiment, despite his racism. However, 'land' does not refer only to the physical space used for living and farming. By the end of the novel, it has acquired a multi-dimensional meaning. In addition to Mr. Howlands's *shamba*, the concept of land has come to include the people who live on it. (Indeed, Ngugi suggests that dispossessing a people of their land is not enough to separate them from it; the connection is too strong.) —When the time for Njoroge to leave [for secondary school] came near," Ngugi writes, "many people contributed money so that he could go since he was no longer the son of Ngotho but the son of the land‖ (115). Land, with all its profundity, is what the Africans lost to the British, and what they are fighting to regain.

4. **Love;** One of the major questions that *Weep Not, Child* raises is whether love is a strong enough force to transcend suffering. The pure love between Njoroge and Mwihaki certainly proves resilient over the course of novel: —Her world and Njoroge's world stood somewhere outside petty prejudices, hatreds and class differences," Ngugi writes (97). However, the novel's ending suggests that love may endure, but that it cannot change a person's circumstances. Although the two young people want to run away and live together in Uganda, they are ultimately bound by a stronger sense of duty to their parents and their country. Part of the story's tragedy is that individuality is helpless before greater forces beyond anyone's control.

5. **Infighting;** *Weep Not A Child* is full of evidence that infighting between Africans was a major problem during the Mau Mau uprising. Ngugi suggests that some of it may have been justified; for instance, Jacobo is a truly villainous character, and we are meant to sympathize with Ngotho when he attacks him. However, Ngugi is very explicit about the fact that such infighting ultimately platg xyed into the hands of the British, driving wedges between Africans and making the conflict more violent than was necessary. The difference between the reputations of Jomo and Dedan Kimathi reveal how significant the ideological differences amongst Africans had become. When Njoroge and Stephen Howlands discuss the causes of prejudice, their insights offer a way for Africans to move beyond their differences and fight for the common good. The tragedy is that individual desires are often useless before larger social forces that in many ways hurt everyone.

6. **Women's role in society;** certain aspects of Gikuyu society, like polygamy, female circumcision and wife-beating, may be foreign and even uncomfortable for modern Western readers. But despite its uncritical portrayal of these realities, *weep not; Child* is thoughtful about the role of women in a traditional society. Mwihaki's failure to continue to high school is not a reflection on women's abilities to succeed in general, but it does highlight the difficulties that bright, motivated young women face if they try to pursue an education. The narrator suggests that Mwihaki's sense of obligation to her family, and the restrictive convent atmosphere of her school, prevented her from doing as well as she might in other circumstances. Njoroge's mothers, Nyokabi and Njeri, are other examples of strong women, although they occupy more traditional roles in society than Mwihaki or Lucia do. Njeri in particular shows a strong intellect and courage when she is arrested, and Nyokabi takes great initiative in arranging for Njoroge to attend school. Together, the mothers show that women play just as important a role in improving society as men do - provided they live under a relatively tolerant patriarch like Ngotho.

7. **Family loyalty;** Njoroge turns to many different sources of comfort as conditions deteriorate in his village: school, religion, and his love for Mwihaki are some examples. Yet the only force that stands between him and suicide at the end of the book is his sense of duty to his mothers, who will be alone and destitute if he dies. Mwihaki rejects him because she, too, must care for her mother. For Ngugi, family loyalty is the ultimate bond. One of the primary challenges his characters face is deciding how to best stay loyal to their family in a time of conflict and contradictions. Boro is a particularly complex example of this question. Ngotho orders him to stop fighting with the Mau Mau, but Boro feels he must continue in order to avenge his father's death, and to fight for a better future for his younger siblings. Whether to defend one's family by immediately providing or by fighting for their progeny (in terms of rebellion or, in Njoroge's case, education) is a question posed, but not answered, by the novel.

TECHNIQUE;

1. **Point of View;** Weep Not, Child uses a third person omniscient narrator to weave seamlessly through the perspectives of different characters, as well as providing objective descriptions of events and settings. As the book is written as an exploration of a society at a given point in time, this style of narration provides the reader with access to the histories and points of view of people on different sides of the political spectrum. For example, we are told about Mr Howlands' struggle to reconnect with his homeland upon his return from World War I from his perspective, and can then see a similar battle playing out within Boro. Similarly, Jacobo's statement to Njoroge that he will be needed to help rebuild the country echoes Njoroge's unexpressed belief in his own destiny as a savior.

2. **The use of dialogue;**
   - Teacher; Say Ah.

     Class; Aaaaa.
     'Teacher; Again.
     Class; Aaaaa.

3. **Use of story-telling;** e.g. Ngotho tell stories to his children.

4. **Use of religious language;** e.g.God's chosen people
5. **Language use;**
    a) **Symbolism;**
        - **Light and dark;** the references to light and dark throughout the novel speaks to optimism and despair, to write and wrong, to hopelessness and salvation. Njoroge's focus on the light helps to buoy him through Kenya's dark times, but when the light goes out for him, he waits for literal darkness in order to attempt to take his own life. Right from the epigraph onward, there is a discussion of light and darkness. When Isaka is preaching about the Second Coming in church, darkness falls over the building, but Njoroge talks also about the sunshine following the night. Even the two parts of the book - The Waning Light and Darkness Falls - evoke this symbolism.
        - **Land;** In this novel, the land symbolizes different things to different people: for Mr. Howlands, it is a representation of his ability to restrain, control and subdue, whereas to Ngotho...
    b) **Metaphor;** *e.g. 0, mother, you are an angel of God,*
    c) **Repetition;** e.g. *you are, you are.*
    d) **Simile;** e.g.It was not as big as the second
    e) **Hyperbole;** e.g.the barber himself was a short brown man with hair very carefully brushed.
    f) **Onomatopoeia;**
        - (The barber lets his clippers go flick -lick -lick -lick.
        - What with bombs and machine guns that went boom-crunch! boom-crunch! troo! troo!
    g) **Barbarism;**
        - She had brought them up to value *Ustaarabu,*
        - That was the time he went to work for Mr Howlands - as a Shamba-boy.
        - 'Good morning, Bwana.'
        - 'Ndio Bwana.'
        - *'Kwa nini Bwana.* Are you going back to-?'
    h) **Personification;** e.g.the voice of Boro had cut deep into him, cut into all the lonely years of waiting.

MESSAGE;
1. Betrayal is the source of misunderstanding.
2. Exploitation is an obstacle towards development.
3. Race is not the only obstacle that prevents the characters from pursuing their goals in life.
4. Love may endure, but that it cannot change a person's circumstances.
5. Injustice is the source of misunderstanding.

TITLE; WREATH FOR FATHER MAYER
AUTHOR; S.N NDUNGURU
PUBLISHER; MKUKI NA NYOTA
SETTING; TANZANIA
YEAR; 1997

BOOK SUMMARY

The book opens with a special Sunday prayer, after which we are introduced to a cholera epidemic at a Catholic Mission station, Songea. Many people die of cholera just within a short period of time. The death cases include children. In grief, some of those who have died were very good and active parishioners (Christians) (page 1).

The cholera epidemic had left behind the number of widows and orphans. Moreover, the calamity has brought tense and great conflict in the society and leads to the fight between the societies e.g. the conflict between Father Moyo sand the young man, Adolfo Theodor. This young man was complaining about his son's illness, he was accusing his grandmother as a witch. So, he followed her to the church when she was praying at St. Theresa's statue.

The child was not being witched but suffering from diarrhea and vomiting. But the people always believe in superstitious. It is also due cholera which led to the theft and murder e.g. on 9th September, Papandreou's gang invaded brother Nyoka and took a carton of medicine.

Another notable event in this course is the murder of Father Moyo's house servant, called Kalistus. The man was murdered on a way when he was trying to save the stolen medicine. He is killed by one of the Papandreou's gang (Mohamed Said). We get this evidence of killing from the confession of Miteo.

On the murder of Kalistus, the innocent person had cleared the way to the truth because we are told in the book that once police were asked or given information which probably needed a quick measure but they could not come on time, as Father Moyo claims.

In the process of exploring the information about murderers, Musa who is said to have detected the death of Kalistus was taken by police at a hidden place. Musa was tortured and highly humiliated by the police who forced him to mention the names of the murderers. Musa saw them from far what they were doing but he could not notice them. The investigation was therefore, in vain because no arrest was made. In the mean-time the cholera appears to be waning.

Fr. Moyo continued to help his villagers with the use of kerosene and tried to find a permanent solution to the villagers' problem of water supply. In pursuance to his objectives at Songea, Father Moyo left Mkongo to present his two-fold plan before the Bishop.

Father Moyo's journey to Europe starts with a problem in Dar es Salaam where a young British who introduces himself as James O' Brien (Michael Dinglefoot), a hashish dealer who becomes a Father's friend.

The friendship between Father Moyo and O'Brien did not end in Dar es Salaam at the airport, but they were together in the flight, all the way to Britain. O'Brien decided to do so because it was the only way that he could succeed to export his hashish. He, therefore, hide his hashish packets into Father Moyo's bag. Father Moyo did not have knowledge about that drug until his bag was caught by the police at Charles de Gaulle Airport.

While in the DC 10 flight O'Brien wrote a note for Father Moyo which directed him to his friend at Crichton Hotel 95' Kensington place where O'Brien's friend, a Hotel manager would provide Father Moyo with full board and lodging. And it was that note which facilitated the handing over of Calabrini's gang at the Hotel Crichton.

Fr. Moyo's Mission to Europe is all about looking for assistance from his fellow Christians in Europe so as to help the Mkongo people who had been suffering from cholera for a long time, and to find the solution of water problem at Mkongo village.

Hiss mission was successful, first in Birmingham, then in Munich, Switzerland. While in Birmingham, Father Moyo he was captured by the two Calabrini's men who took him to unknown place.

Father found himself in the gang's house. In the gang's house Father Moyo met Dr. Benet, a scientist and a medical doctor in Calabrini's organization. Dr. Benet had joined the Calabrini's organization ten years ago but he helped Father Moyo to escape.

Before Father Moyo had left for Mkongo he met Dr. Benet and the he convinced him to go to Tanzania. At the end Dr. Benet agreed and promised him to work in one of the mission's hospitals or dispensaries at Mkongo.

Father Moyo arrived at Songea in a third week of December. Many people, particularly parishioners are happy to see him back. But the only thing that seemed to Father Moyo's home coming back is the impeding hearing of the theft case. He called brother Nyoka and asked him if he knew the person called Miteo. Miteo is the name proclaimed by Father Moyo to have dreamt that he is the one who hacked Kalistus to death. Miteo's name is Christopher who is then called so by the name of his late father (page 131).

The claim presented by the Inspector includes Mkongo priest to be responsible for the murder of Kalistus but all the presented claims are neglected. In the course of exploring information about theft Cyprian meets Pau, aged twelve, the last born, a son of late Julius Ndiwu Miteo, the youngest and most loved wife of Bwanapima. Paul tells the whole situation at home and that's why sometimes his mother does not cook for him when he returns from school (page 154).

After listening for the explanations given by Father Moyo, Mr. Milinga promised to take measure on this case without any delay. It took only few hours in that night when all the suspects are arrested. We see this on page 160-161 when Mr. Milinga phoned Father Kafupi to tell him about the matter concerned. After conversion with Mr. Milinga, the RPC, Fr. Kafupi, returned to his fellows and told them what is going on.

All suspects are interrogated, but the most interesting and most important of all statements is that made by Christopher Miteo who declared being involved in the stealing at priest's house. He mentioned names of all who participated; these were Papandreou Kaguru, the Boss, Athmani Abdallah, Alias Msumari, Barnabas Kipingu, Alias Madondo and Mohamed Said who killed Kalistus and Miteo himself. Miteo began to confess on page 162.

At last of the confession, we find that the culprits were jailed, we see this judgment on page 167. Having sentenced, the accused are allowed to appeal within fourteen days. Only Constantine Kaguru and Omari Bwanapima appealed. Unfortunately, they were enhanced the sentence of twenty years each.

Going around of the end pages, we are introduced to the sugar crisis in Songea. This is revealed by Bwanali. Bwanali is big trader at Songea who used any means to obtain goods from the big companies during crisis e.g. he once acted as a good Muslim so as to get access to Mecca to pilgrimage intentionally to bring back goods and commodities from Arabian countries which are seen to be marketable in Tanzania. Other time, he used the behind door to get sugar bags from Regional Trading Company during the sugar crisis.

At the end, we are exposed to the arrival of Dr. Benet at Songea Airport at 11:00 hrs. He was welcomed with joy at the Bishop's house. A simple discussion was made about where Dr. Benet shall be posted. It was suggested that Dr. Benet should visit first the two working places Peramiho and Mkongo then, he will decide himself where he could work. After one month had elapsed Dr. Benet told Bishop Makita that he preferred working at Mkongo to Peramiho.

CHARACTERS AND CHARACTERIZATION
1. **FR.DENIS MOYO:** A parishioner at Mkongo parish and a main character in the novel. He is caring, committed and good hearted. He cares about the health of other people. For example, he deals effectively with the problem of cholera outbreak at Mkongo. He is well informed about the causes of cholera and measures which can be taken to alleviate the problem. He helps people to get rid of cholera. He does it by educating people the importance of boiling drinking water. He is an outstanding character due to his critical thinking and humanity.
2. **BWANAPIMA:** A witchdoctor at Mkongo village. He is a swindler and cheats people at Mkongo that he can cure cholera using traditional medicine. He is superstitious since he believes in magic power. He uses his magic power to earn income from illiterate villagers. He gets hens, cows and money from people to cure them. He is a very exploiting as he uses peoples' problems and ignorance to get money from them. He tells people that he knows much traditional medicine. He likes money more than anything. He

uses any possible way to get money. For example, he assists Miteo to accomplish the mission of stealing cartons of medicine from Mkongo parish.

3. **CHRISTOPHER MITEO:** Bwanapima's brother-in-law. Works at Mkongo parish on behalf of the late Kalistus. He is portrayed as a thief. He is charged of Kalistus murder and theft. He admits that he is daring in crimes, plundering and robbing. He apologizes for committing murder and stealing. He is a dishonest character. He is a person not to be trusted. He caused the death of Kalistus due to his mission of stealing medicine at the parish.

4. **PATRICK MILLINGA:** A Ruvuma regional Police Commander (RPC). Portrayed as a cooperative, keen and diligent man. He cooperates with the Mkongo parishioners under Fr.Kafupi on the pending case of the murder of Kalistus when Inspector Mpangala fails to handle the matter. He is very attentive when listening to peoples' problems.

5. **YOMBAYOMBA:** A chairman of Mkongo village. He is superstitious as he believes that magic power can assist him in his leadership. He consults the witchdoctor in whatever he wants to do. He is hypocritical since he pretends to be good and helpful when he sees that there is something to gain from the matter. He is an envious person. He wishes that some privileges that other people have should be his. For example, he is envy of Kalistus' work at the mission.

THEMES IN THE NOVEL

1. **THE ROLE AND POSITION OF RELIGIOUS INSTITUTIONS IN THE SOCIETY:** The role of religious institutions is to promote spiritual growth of people. The churches and Mosques established have that primary role. Apart from spiritual growth of people, religious institutions also provide social services to people. The church provides health, safe and clean water services. This can be seen at Mkongo parish where the church has built a dispensary which treats all residents of Mkongo. The church also fights against evils prevailing in the society that hinder spiritual harmonization of people. The church also educates the society on the causes of diseases like cholera. People are advised to go to hospital whenever they fall sick rather than going to witchdoctors.

2. **CHOLERA (WATERBORNE DISEASE):** The writer focuses on the eruption of cholera at Mkongo village. The church and the government took initiatives to help people. Cholera is caused by poor hygiene, ignorance, poverty and superstition. The dirty environment with lack of latrines contributes a lot to the spread of the disease. Poverty can be another major cause of the disease since people cannot afford to buy utensils for boiling drinking water and buying soaps to wash their hands as part of cleanliness. The persistence of cholera is accelerated by the level of ignorance of the people. Lack of good social services especially clean and safe water for drinking forced people to drink contaminated water from river Mbuchi. Cholera causes death. The disease kills many people especially those who go to the witchdoctor instead of going to the hospital. People at Mkongo village are ignorant and think that they are bewitched.

3. **SUPERSTITION:** A deep rooted belief in the community. The belief is based on magic power, witchcraft and invisible evil spirits. Witchdoctors use that loop hole to collect money from ignorant people. For example, Adolfo believed that his grandmother bewitched his child. Superstition is seen as a source of all conflicts in the society. Adolfo severely beats his grandmother suspecting her of bewitching his child while the child suffers from cholera. Superstition is typically based on deceit and trickery. Superstition is

a source of mistreatment of people in the society. People with beliefs on superstition suspect others for bewitching them. For example, Adolfo suspected his grandmother for bewitching his child.

4. **SOCIAL CRIMES AND IMMORALITY:** The author reveals various social crimes and immorality facing his society. Some of these crimes include murder, drug trafficking and theft. Drug trafficking face many countries in the World. Drugs are transported and distributed in various parts of the country through secret and illegal means. For example, Fr. Moyo is implicated in transporting hashish. He carries these illegal drugs without knowing since they were planted in his bag by Michael. Drug traffickers are detected using dogs and technology at Airports and other transport centers. People involved in drug trafficking use skilled people and technology. Kidnapping is another social crime shown by the author. Drug traffickers tend to kidnap whoever gets to know their network. Fr. Moyo was kidnapped in Birmingham since he revealed the secrets of the network. Theft and murder are social crimes that threaten harmony of the society.

5. **IRRESPONSIBILITY:** Bad leadership is revealed by the author. The police force is accused of failing to apprehend the culprits. Inspector Mpangala and sub Inspector Kapela failed to capture the killers of Kalistus. Instead of apprehending the culprits, the police oppressed Mzee Mussa and forced him to name the culprits he did not see. Yombayomba also proved to be an irresponsible leader. It took him hours to gather the villagers when Kalistus was killed. Superstition beliefs can also encourage irresponsibility among leaders as they believe that whatever they want to do, they have to see the witchdoctors first. This reduces confidence of the leader and spoils their decisions.

6. **POVERTY**: Most of the Mkongo villagers are poor, makes so they don't have sufficient utensils for boiling water in order to avoid cholera. Also their poverty is shown when Fr Moyo shows a picture of a villager's house which covered by grass in order to raise funds to buy water pipes and kerosene tins for them.Fr. Moyo helps them by providing the empty tins to each house in order to boil water. At the end the disease disappears, although Fr. Moyo has a plan to build water pipes. Also, their poverty shows that instead of sending their patients to the dispensary, they send them to Bwanapima who lies to them; by saying somebody bewitched them which made them to become sick. E.g. Adolfo sent his child to Bwanapima and believed that his grandmother bewitched his child (p. 3), But Fr. Moyo insisted him to send his child to the dispensary and he was cured.

7. **CONFLICT;**

a) **Family conflict:** Conflict rises between Adolfo and his grandmother. He went in the church where his grandmother was in playing and accused her of bewitching his son, who was sick at that moment. "She killed my sister last month and now my little son is sick. She wants to kill him, too" (p. 4) it was Fr. Moyo who saved the old woman from being hurt by that young man.

b) **Individual Conflict:** Fr. Moyo has individual conflict, he asks himself."How could these poor people boil the drinking water when they did not even have proper utensils for boiling water? How could they be expected to keep clean when they did not even have soap? (p. 2) .Therefore, due to this individual conflict, Fr. Moyo decided to collect empty kerosene tins and distribute one to each house. This individual conflict helped the people of Mkongo to remove cholera.

8. **BETRAYAL:** Bwanapima and Papandreou's gang betray Fr. Moyo and the society of Mkongo after stealing the medicine for curing cholera. That situation caused Fr. Moyo to have trouble and to search for the thief and another solution.

9. **WOMEN'S EMANCIPATION:** In this society of Mkongo, women are portrayed negatively and positively. Negatively, women are seen as liars and blackmailers, for example, the wife of Bwanapima, Rosina, cooperates with a thief and his young brother, called Miteo, to keep the stolen tetracycline. Also, women accept polygamy because Rosina agreed to be the fifth and youngest wife of Bwanapima. Positively, women are kind and care for the sick, for example sister Gaudiosa who cares for the sick in the Mkongo parish dispensary as a nurse.

10. **TORTURE AND VIOLATION OF HUMAN RIGHTS:** During the investigation, policemen do not show regard for humanity. We see in the book Constable Hilary Mhagama pulling Mzee Musa's hair and Mr. Chowo twisting Musa's hand at the back despite the truth and cooperation he is giving. Also, the policemen mistreat Musa by pointing a gun at him, threatening to kill him (p. 38). Acts done by policemen are against the principles and rule of law and human rights; consequently the people lack confidence in their own police force, something which is dangerous.

Use of literary devices in A Wreath of Fr Moyo

1. **Symbolism:** Symbolism as a literary device is shown in the title of the novel which is "A Wreath for Fr. Mayer. The word "wreath" means an arrangement of flowers leaves or stems fastened in a ring and used for decoration or for lying on a grave, (Burges, 1993). Hence, in this novel it is a symbol for love and honor for the soul of the departed priest (Fr. Vitus Mayer)….. (P. 109). Therefore, Fr. Denis Moyo put the wreath on the grave of Fr. Vitus Mayer on behalf of Mkongo Parish, where the late Fr. Vitus Mayer used to work.Ndunguru uses symbolism in the title of his book to foreshadow the story so that readers' interest is amplified in order to find the meaning or the title. Hence on (p. 109) the symbol Wreath brings its meaning which is love and honor for the soul of the departed priest Fr. Vitus Mayer. In this way Ndunguru uses symbolism to spice up his writing.

2. **Imagery:** Imagery is also used in the novel, for example on (p. 112) where Fr.Vitus Mayer and Kalistus appear to him in a dream and tell him about causes of Fr. Moyo's death. When he wakes up he realizes that he was actually at St. Otliien Monastry in Germany and that Fr.Vitus Mayer and Kalistus had died. The author uses imagery to hide the ways or investigation he uses to get thieves who steal the carton of tetracycline. Also, the author creates mental images for the reader in discovering the murder of Kalistus and the ones who steal the medicine.

3. **Dialogue:** Dialogue is portrayed in each chapter. On (p. 4) there is the dialogue between Adolfo and Fr. Moyo: 'What's the child suffering from?' 'Diarrhea and vomiting'. When did it start?' 'Five O'clock this morning' 'where's the child now?''At home'. 'Go and take him to the dispensary at once.' Also on (p. 19) there is conversation between Sister

Abuntantia and Justus. 'What's it Justus? Asked Sister Abuntantia, a little irritated. 'Oh, there's a man outside who says he must see Fr. Moyo at once'. 'Can't you tell him to wait?' 'I told him so, but he wouldn't listen 'Alright, close the door, father will come out in a minute.'(p. 19) 'Hey, Father, didn't you have lunch?' asked Fr. Cyprian 'No, I didn't feel like having any' 'Why, malaria again?' 'Not quite, I simply didn't have the appetite for any food (p. 24)

4. **Allusion:** This is another literary device used in the story. On (Page 124) the author introduces Paul Bwanapima, before proceeding with the story. Now we must pause for a moment to introduce this personage, Paul Bwanapima, Paul aged twelve was the last born son of Bwanapima, the medicine man.

TITLE; UNANSWERED CRIES
AUTHOR; OSMAN CONTEH
SETTING; SIERRA LEONE

CHAPTERS SUMMARY

CHAPTER ONE

On the day gods wanted her circumcised, Olabisi is shown to sit restless, on a low stool washing dirty dishes in a large plastic bowl. As she begins to scrub the dish, the wind brings her news of an approaching group of singers. She sits up and tries to listen like a dog sensing an intruder. It is a sound of drums and singing. The sound keeps getting closer; this makes Olabisi to say, "I must see this". She drops the dishes back into plastic bowl and springs to her feet. Her mother appears and decides to stop her until she finishes her work as she says, "Finish your work Olabisi. My husband will be here soon and he hates waiting for his meal".

Olabisi insists on going and tells her mother about the camera given to her by her father from Freetown. Her mother (Makalay Kamara), gets angry with her and says, "I don't want to hear a word about your useless father in this house. Hear me?" Then Olabisi replies by saying, "Yes mama" The singers and drummers are seen to be closer than before, this makes Olabisi to remember her camera and mentions the name of her father again, she says "I have to take pictures. Daddy told me….. Before she finishes saying, her mother interferes her and says, "Are you deaf? You are here to spend the holidays not to sing your father's name in my ears."

She keeps complaining and says, "Useless man. Skirt chaser. Is he still chasing women? (pg 6) Olabisi is heard to reply by saying, "No mama. Except that lawyer, Oyah, and she has never called him useless". Her mother finishes by saying, "Hmmmff! You lie with a straight face, just like your hopeless father". Makalay is lastly shown to agree with Olabisi and then they go together to watch the dancers. Olabisi asks her mother about the group of young girls and elders, and she is finally told that they are women of Bondo society and she can become a member if she gets circumcised. Makalay releases a sweet smile and asks her daughter, "Would you like to become a member? " And Olabisi replies by saying, "I just want to take pictures" The smile is now shown to freeze on Makalay's face.

Olabisi sprints ahead of Makalay, dashing into the house through the backdoor. She is told by her father to get close to any object she wants to photograph, wild animals excluded. "Where is my camera?" her eyes are shown to search the room. Olabisi becomes frantic and begins to fling out of the bag anything that does not feel like a camera. Brassieres smelling of sweat, unwashed panties, she would kill for if anyone else tried to see them, dirty jeans slaughtered at the knees, slips, skirts, over-size T-shirts, stolen lipstick and finally her camera is found.

Two drummers and female masked dancer appear to lead the group, and then came the group of Half naked girls. The oldest is said to be about twelve, two years younger than Olabisi. The youngest looks six years old. Each is seen with lappa, a piece of cloth, tied under the armpit. They dance barefoot on the stony road, for the girls who come from town like Olabisi, could end Up with bleeding feet.

Olabisi appears to dance her way down the steps, singing along the Bondo girls. Suddenly Makalay's hand clamps down on her shoulder and yanks her back. She skids backwards, as if she had stepped on a banana peel, and landed down. "Where are you going, singing and dancing like that? Do you think this is Freetown? Makalay warns Olabisi not to dare to go nearby them and she calls her gborka.

Olabisi seems to get confused with the word gborka and asks her mother if that word refers to the half-naked dancers as she says, "You mean those girls? Her mother replies by saying, "They are not girls! They have become women, so talk respectfully when you talk about them. Olabisi does not understand as there is a six-year-old child among them and tries to ask more questions to her mother, this makes her mother (Makalay Kamara) to grab Olabisi's left ear and twist it hard like a driver twisting the ignition key of a stubborn car. "If you ever try to go near them again, I will beat you until your skin peels. Do you understand me?" Olabisi rubs her left ear. It feels so hot and says, "I just wanted to take pictures and ask few questions about the Bondo Secret society". This makes her mother tiresome and gasps, "Subanallah, go away from here before I lose my temper. In fact, go and finish your work. Gborka" (pg11)

Olabisi tries to hide her true color as she used to live in Freetown. She becomes very respectful to her mother. In Freetown, Olabisi used to be face to face with danger and survived without a scratch. She used to sneak out of the house and go with Edward Cole (Eddy), her boy friend to join the students' demonstration against the government. Olabisi is now shown to sit on the three legged stool and continue to wash the last dish again. Her mother gets closer to her and says, "If you get circumcised, you will no longer be called a gborka. You will be respected as the real woman, fit to be the wife of paramount chief". The words of her mother do not work as the daughter replies by saying, "I do not need a paramount chief". I have Eddy. Her mother continues to advise her by saying, "If you do not get circumcised, no one in this village will ever respect you. No man will ever want to marry you. The riff-raff boys will be after you for sexual fun like dogs. But if you get circumcised, none of these ugly things will happen to you". She pauses to let her words sink into Olabisi's heart. "Would you like to be a Bondo woman? I can arrange everything"

Olabisi finds the words get lost as she says, "I…., Daddy will…" Makalay tries to encourage her that her father would never know until she told him. Makalay still insists that Olabisi would be taught how to be a real woman, how to cook a meal that would make her husband lick his fingers like a child, but Olabisi rejects and says, "Eddy eats with a spoon not with his hands" Makalay does not get tired, she tells her that she would be taught to be a good house wife, to be a wonderful mother and tells her to think of the passing out ceremony, graduation day as she would be dressed in the most beautiful clothes ever, with good earrings, good trinkets and all types of jewelers. Olabisi keeps on insisting that if Makalay loves her, she could still dress that way without being circumcised.

Olabisi is taken by a flash memory as she thinks of Eddy's mother who had given birth to a boy called Durosemi. When Duro was circumcised, his little penis was wrapped up with fine gauze and regularly socked with baby oil to take away the pain of urinating. She then calls her mother, "Mama" and Makalay replies while smiling, "Yes dear" then Olabisi continues, " How do you circumcise a girl while she is not a boy, boys have penises but girls don't,. How do you……? Before she finishes the question makes Makalay's smile to vanish and serves a slap like a small bomb. She finally says, "You have started sleeping with boys! Gborka"

CHAPTER TWO

Olabisi is seen to return home from a stream. There are two girls called Rugiatu and Salay. Salay is short and stocky like a well fed pig, while Rugiatu is tall, skinny and hungry looking like a shaved bird. They are expert bucket carriers as they balance buckets on their heads, Olabis tries to do the same but her bucket appears to slide down and her bucket becomes half empty. The girls walk bare foot confidently; Olabisi is seen with the T-shirt with words BEACH BUM. She then calls out, "Hey, Rugiatu, are you a gborka or have you been….." The words die in her throat as the girls become angry. They fight and push her down, Olabisi tries to apologize to them, but they do not care and finally Rugiatu spits in her face, a thick wad of mucus. Olabisi without stopping to think, she kicks Rugiatu in the stomach unexpectedly as she had been taught by Eddy. Rugiatu falls down like a cut wood. Salay rushes forward with fingers ready to scratch Olabisi's face but Olabisi manages to step aside and grip Salay's lappa; she rips it off her body.

Salay's eyes fly open with shock; she is seen to stand naked except for a pair of cotton pants. Around her waist, there are several layers of color beads. Rugiatu immediately attacks Olabisi like a mad dog, Olabisi lashes with her fist, the first blow misses, the second one catches Rugiatu on the side of her head and she falls like a sack of rotten potatoes. Olabisi tears the lappa of Rugiatu to shreds, and then goes for the pants and beads around Rugiatu's waist. She gives them a sharp jerk and says, "Now I am going to see what you have between your legs that were circumcised". Suddenly the shadow rushes at her, then something blunt and heavy hits on her head like falling coconut. She sees stars, plenty of them before the dark of clouds comes. Olabisi finds herself in her bed staring up at Makalay's worried face.

Makalay blames on Olabisi for what she does to Rugiatu and Salay. She asks why she brings trouble instead of peace in that village. She also wonders if that is the way Olabisi used to live in Freetown. Olabisi is seen to examine her body with her fingers and say, "At least my head is not broken" Makalay informs Olabisi that Rugiatu and Salay are the daughters of Yah Posseh, the Digba Sowey, and the head of circumcisers. Olabisi responds by saying that she does not afraid of her, since her daughters are the ones who started fighting. Makalay tells Olabisi that Yah Posseh is very powerful. She controls the spirits, the Bondo gods whose laws Olabisi has broken. She accuses Olabisi of stripping two Bondo girls naked and looking at their private parts. Olabisi complains by saying that the girls did not look away when she was bathing. They kept staring at her.

Makalay's hands shake Olabisi's throat, she calls Olabisi stupid and gborka. Makalay tells Olabisi that the girls can look at the Olabisi's nakedness but she cannot do the same to them. This makes Olabisi to say, "But they are not boys' mama. What do they have that I don't have" Then Makalay says, "They are virgins" and Olabisi talks back to her mother by saying, "Me too". Makalay becomes angry and says, "Liar" and continues to say that she examined Olabisi while she was unconscious, Olabisi flushes with shame. She feels invaded, assaulted, raped by her on mother. Her mother is seen not to care anything, and says, "I will reduce your appetite for boys, you will be circumcised" Olabisi keeps insisting that she does not want to be circumcised.

Suddenly uproar is heard outside like that of outraged mob of women, yelling for blood. It is Yah Posseh with Bondo women, waving knives, machetes, sticks and other ugly weapons. Makalay is then seen to get out and talking to them. Yah Posseh is as black as midnight with flat eyes like a snake. She is very powerful, Olabisi's voice is full of fear and she begins to feel like a mouse watching a cat. Yah Posseh's mouth is full of missing teeth. She looks at Makalay and says, "Your daughter from the city has offended the spirit of our ancestors, the gods of our tradition. The spirit demands that she must be circumcised. This makes Makalay to respond by saying, "Whatever the spirits say, I will do" Olabisi hears it and says, "Is mama crazy?"

Yah Posseh commands Makalay to take Olabisi to the camp in that evening and if she disobeys, the spirits would make things difficult for her during child birth. "Don't say that, I am pregnant" Makalay is heard to respond. Olabisi is seen to close the door. She steps out of her skirt and wriggles into the jeans. She is then seen to run as if her feet are on fire. Makalay and her husband try to give a chase. There is nothing to fear from Makalay as she cannot outrun a snail. Dauda is as stubborn as brainless goat. Olabisi keeps running, Dauda tries to shorten the distance. Olabisi then sees her bucket beside the foot path, an idea comes into her mind, and she stoops, scoops up the empty bucket and flings it behind her in one smooth move. The bucket flies towards Dauda's legs and crashes into them. Dauda falls on his face as if he wants to eat the earth. It must take sometimes before he feels like running again. Olabisi disappears into the thick bush.

CHAPTER THREE

Olabisi runs into the dark forest and gradually the foot path begins to resemble a tunnel as if the forest wants to swallow her. "Don't scare" Olabisi tells herself. "Just keep running". Her mind begins to think of wild animals, tiger, leopard, elephants and lions. She remembers that her teacher told her that there are no lions in Sierra Leone. What if the teacher was wrong? She is in the middle of the jungle not class. She feels the foot steps behind her. She feels like the creature chases her. Branches smack her face, rip her T-shirt, bruise her hands but she feels nothing. Her eyes go wide at the sight before her, her kneels feel weak.

A mud hut with thatched roof is seen standing in the middle of a clearing, few yards off the main path. It is the fenced hut. She begins to run, the creature does the same. She decides to stop, the creature does the same. It is invisible creature, some kind of magic "juju". Olabisi begins to think of Yah Posseh. Her ears catch the sound of echoes. She then hears the footsteps and voice, this makes Olabisi to ask herself, "Who are they, what are they doing here? Are they the owners of the mud hut? Olabisi glances up the tree; she catches hold of the low branch and begins to lift herself up the tree. The branch bows under her weight and then breaks. She falls like a stone. With one great leap, she catches hold of another branch, a stronger one. Quickly she lifts herself upon to the branch and makes her way up to the tree again. It is the Bondo camp.

Olabisi body breaks into goose flesh. The two women and the ten- year-old girl enter the camp. The girl looks like a fly being led to a spider web. The girl breaks away from the women and runs as faster as her legs could carry her. She gets caught with another woman; she falls, rolls and screams. Her cry goes unanswered. She fights like a wild cat, kicking and punching without any success. The fat woman goes over and sits on her small chest. Two women grip her hands. Two other grab her feet and spread them wide. An elderly woman comes out of the hut, holding a sharp object. The elderly woman reaches her hand down to the genitals of the girl and starts to cut her flesh. The camp breaks into a song. Olabisi screams, "I must get out of this place" She tastes the salty tears at the corner of her mouth; she realizes that she was crying and suddenly she lets herself drop to the ground. She then finds herself get caught. "Welcome to Bondo camp" Yah Posseh and her two daughters surround her.

CHAPTER FOUR

Makalay dreams of Yah Posseh with a cock ready to punish her. She lifts the cock by the neck, cut off its head and throws the body in the air. It takes a blind dive and falls at Makalay's feet. The immediate effect appears on Makalay's face. Her face begins to distort like a rubber mask brought close to a flame. She touches her throat as she struggles to breath. She screams and wakes up. She then says, "Thank God, it was just a dream" Dauda enters the room; he shows Makalay the bruises on his hands and knees. Makalay lights the lamp as it is getting dark. Makalay is then seen to run into the forest to find Olabisi. "You fool woman" snaps a man's voice, "I could have shot you" It is Pa Amadu, he keeps asking, "What are you doing in this part of wood? You frighten my animals" Makalay explains about her daughter and asks him to help looking for her but Pa Amadu rejects by saying, " I hunt wild animals not human beings". Makalay says, "This is the matter of life and death" and promises him a gallon of palm oil. Pa Amadu complains that his family is tired of eating fish; he wants animals which have been frightened by Makalay. This makes Makalay to promise him a goat; Pa Amadu agrees with her and disappears among the trees.

CHAPTER FIVE

"I said welcome to Bondo camp" Yah Poss repeats to Olabisi. She tells Olabisi that the spirits want her circumcised but Olabisi rejects that she is not ready for circumcision. Yah Posseh cracks with laughter. Her mouth is like the cave where bats go to sleep. (Page 36) Yah Posseh lifts the cock in her hand and pulls out a knife. The drumming and singing in the forest fill the forest with Bondo music. The tension increases to Olabisi, without wasting time, Olabisi attacks the two girls just as Eddy taught her. They both twist on the ground like salted earth worms. Olabisi manages to run away. She keeps running until she sees the river and says, "Oh God I can't swim". It becomes difficult for her to swim across the river, she then says, "No I can't go back. Yah Posseh and the Bondo women will be looking for me". She tests the depth of river with her right foot and gets into it. A few yards away, something splashes into the river. She firstly tries to think of monkey that falls while straining for a drink from a branch of a tree. She then sees the outline of a long body like a log moving towards her. It is crocodile. She explodes out of river quickly and screams as if her hair was on fire. She runs until she collides with Pa Amadu, the hunter.

CHAPTER SIX

In Freetown, Ade Jones is seen to be in conflict with Oyah because of Yamide. Ade Jones tries to explain to Oyah that Yamide is just an ordinary friend. He says, "I have told you that a dozen of time". Oyah becomes angry with him and tells him not to touch her. She also demands to know why she found herself in Ade Jone's bed room while she slept on the sitting roam coach. Ade Jones explains to her about the party with few friends that took place in the sitting room is the reason behind her movement. Oyah becomes offended and blames on Ade Jones for allowing his friends in the sitting room. She hits Ade's chest with a small fist and says, "You know I snore, Ade. Oh my God I was half – naked last night" She beats him with her fist again and finally asks, "Which friends came to the house?" Ade Jones responds by saying, "The one that gave you Malaria last time. The mosquitoes". He explains to her that it is that reason that made him to get her into his bed. At 34, Ade Jones was five years older than Oyah. Oyah is seen to have no trust in Ade Jones because of his bad behavior of being a womanizer. She pushes him out of her way and leaves. "Wait" Ade goes after her, his face is as sad as a tortoise. He says, "I need you Oyah" and asks her to marry him. Oyah decides to forgive him.

Suddenly the sound of the running feet is heard. It is Olabisi. She runs as if the angel of death is close by. As Oyah turns to look, Olabisi throws herself at her, hugging, crying and clinging. Ade Jones listens to his daughter who is seen with tears welled up in her eyes. She says, 'I'm backing home with my daddy. Thank you God" She tells her daddy that she would never go back to her mama's village because of Female Genital Mutilation (FGM), planned by her mother and other Bondo women. His father becomes upset but Oyah interrupts as she is seen to come from the dinning and wants the story of Bondo women to wait. She takes the child to the bathroom to clean her and change her into some flesh clothes.

In the bathroom Olabisi pulls her T-shirt over her head and wriggles out of her jeans with Oyah's help. She rolls her pants down her feet and begins to step out of them. Oyah is seen to smile and asks Olabisi, "Are you not ashamed to stand naked, big as you are?" Olabisi pulls her pants up her legs again and asks, "Tell me aunt, am I a woman or just a girl?" Oyah tells Olabisi that she has entered a period in her life when she is neither a girl nor woman. It is called adolescence. Oyah teaches Olabisi about relationship and asks Olabisi, "You don't have a boy friend, do you? Olabisi says, I have Eddy, no I don't have a boy friend aunt" Oyah advises Olabisi to wait until she gets married.

She is then seen to help Olabisi to scrub her back, gently and says, "When did you lastly have a birth? The water is filthy around your feet. If it gets to the sea, the fish will die of the worst kind of pollution". Olabisi asks her aunt to make a promise if she would never get offended with the question she wanted to ask, and then Oyah promises her not to get offended. Olabisi asks, "Were you circumcised?" Oyah answers by saying, "Yes". Olabisi continues to ask Oyah more questions as she wants to know whether Oyah felt pain or not, then Oyah responds by saying that it was a long time ago when she was about eight or nine years old. She can therefore not remember. Olabisi asks Oyah if she can circumcise her daughter but Oyah rejects by saying, "No

I am wiser today than yesterday" Olabisi breaks into a huge smile and asks Oyah to be her mother.

A bang noise comes from the living room as if someone wants to break the front door. Olabisi becomes worried and says, "Mama is here". Oyah tells Olabisi to remain there and leaves the girl, she is stopped by Ade Jones who says, "Go back I will take care of her" He continues saying that he does not need a body guard. Makalay shouts and bangs at the door like some wild man. She shouts, "I want my daughter". She becomes very stubborn and says that she cannot go without her daughter. Ade Jones tries to fear Olabisi by saying, "If you go near her I will kill you". He tells Makalay that Olabisi is his daughter she cannot leave that house. This makes Makalay to say, "Who told you Olabisi is your child, I was pregnant in trouble and needed a father for my child. You were handy. Does that make you father? Ade Jones becomes upset to hear the words from Makalay. He gets confused as he does not believe his ears from what Makalay says. Makalay continues and says, "I came to Freetown to complete my secondary school education and go to college. I fell in love with Abdurrahman…... before she finishes Ade Jones panics and says, "I don't want to hear his name in my house" Makalay informs Ade Jones that Abdurrahman is the father of Olabis and he's dead. Ade goes crazy, he grips Makalay's throat, and Makalay begins to struggle with him, fighting for her life. He forces her to confess that what was said is wrong as he says, "Confess your lies woman. Tell me you were lying" Makalay runs out of breath, she decides to follow what she is told but Ade and says, "I lied, you are the father" Ade releases her through. Ade commands Olabisi to get out of his house and promises to see his solicitor. Makalay cries out, "I know you would run for a help to a lawyer" She turns away.

CHAPTER SEVEN

It is in the morning, Olabisi is told to take her breakfast by Ade, before going to the court. Olabisi fears for her mother to win but Oyah encourages her. Oyah tells Olabisi that judges are like referees to lawyers. She teaches Olabisi common words used in the court like "Objection" that is said when the lawyer does not want his/her client to be asked questions and "overruled" which means disagrees. Bondo women are all over the streets of Freetown. In groups of hundreds, they are shown with their banners splashed with these words, **FEMALE CIRCUMCISION! A MOTHER'S DECISION!**

Two hours later Olabisi makes her first appearance in the court. She is called by Oyah in the witness box. She asks Olabisi many questions and then she wants Olabisi to explain what happened on the fifteen of August. Olabis narrates everything about Bondo and her struggle to go back to Freetown. She explains how he gave enough money to Pa Amadu (The hunter) to buy two goats in order for him to take her to the main road and put her into the vehicle that goes to Freetown. Oyah asks Makalay if she wants to be circumcised, then Olabis says, "No" Oyah finishes, then Makalay's lawyer, Salaam Sesay takes his turn to ask Olabis questions.

Olabisi becomes in difficult situation as she is asked whether she has a boy friend or not? She becomes worried and says, "No sir" Then Makalay's lawyer says, "You mean you are virgin" Olabisi gets confused as her mama's voice rings in her ears. She says, "Yes…eh…No" This makes Makalay's lawyer (Salaam Sesay) to say, "You are confused, let me unconfused you. Do you know Edward Cole" Olabisi rejects by saying "I do not him" Laughter rolls out from the

172

spectators. It makes Olabisi to feel stupid. Salaam Sesay continues to insist on Edward Cole and he reminds Olabisi of another name which is Eddy. Olabisi seems to agree and she is asked another question, "Had you ever sex with him?" Olabisi closes her eyes and says, "Yes, once" This makes Edward Cole to shout, "Several times" Olabis feels ashamed and shouts, "That's lie" Tears run down Olabisi's face.

Salaam Sesay continues by asking, "Did your father know about it?" Olabisi says, "No" Olabisi is asked about her age and she says that she is fourteen. Salaam Sesay wonders how could Olabisi manage to fool her father at that age. Salaam Sesay asks Olabisi if she knows the main reason for circumcision, Olabisi says that her mother told her that circumcision would make her a real woman. Salaam Sesay adds one question to Olabisi, "You want to be able to reduce your sexual appetite, don't you? After a long silence, Olabisi answers the question by saying, "Does cutting off a person tongue reduces appetite for food or his enjoyment for it?" Ade gives a faint smile and Makalay stares at Olabis with a disgusted look. Salaam Sesay finishes by saying, "No further questions". Oyah calls Ade Jones as her next witness. Ade is asked several questions by her. He answers all the questions and insists on his disagreement to Female Genital Mutilation (FGM) by saying, "There is no medical or religious reasons either in the Bible or Qur'an for hurting my daughter" He is then told that he is not a medical doctor, pastor or imam. He is not qualified to say that.

Makalay's lawyer (Salaam Sesay) rises to Ade and asks him some questions. He reminds him of his weakness of being fooled by her daughter. Ade Jones' face becomes tight with anger. He then asks him, "Do you have a wife" Ade is seen to adjust his tie and says, "No I don't have a wife" This makes Salaam Sesay to say, "You answered trustfully. For you have had five girl friends and you are now living with a woman who is not your wife. Judge Kanu interferes and says, "That is out of order" Finally the judge hit the bench with his gavel, BAM! The court is adjourned until ten o'clock on Monday morning. Songs of protests fill the air sung by Bondo women. Eddy smiles and follows Olabisi, he says, "I'm sorry about what happened" Olabisi spits in his face and says, "Judah! How much did they pay you?" Ade keeps calling, "Bisi" but Olabis kicks him away. Makalay's lawyer rushes out and say, "You can charge her for that" but Eddy says, "She is my girl friend" Olabisi becomes furious and promises to show him her other side. Ade continues by saying, "I love you" Olabisi answers, "Me too, I love me" Ade tells Olabisi that she does not know what is she going to miss but Olabis says, "You mean sexual transmitted diseases and unwanted pregnancies". Eddy's mouth falls open; this makes Olabisi to say, "Close your mouth before you swallow a fly". Olabisi runs off.

CHAPTER EIGHT

Olabisi confesses to her father. "Please forgive me, daddy. It will never happen again" She breaks down and cries. Olabisi asks her father not to hate her. This makes her father to say, "I hate what you did but I love you" Olabisi is taken to the gynecologist (Dr. Asiatu Koroma) who proves that Olabisi is not pregnant. On Monday, in the court Oyah is seen to call Dr. Asiatu Koroma in the witness box. She is asked to say how long she has been the gynecologist; she then says that she has been working as the gynecologist for ten years. She is then told to explain how Female Genital Mutilation (FGM) takes place, she says, "There is the sensitive part in the sexual organs of a woman called the clitoris. Many Bondo women believe that this part of a woman is filthy, ugly and makes a woman immoral" She also says, "Here in Sierra Leone, it is amputated, cut off completely. In other parts of Africa, after cutting it off, the lips of the vagina are scrapped with either a blade or knife". Oyah asks Dr. Asiatu Koroma about the instruments used in performing this operation, she then mentions about lazor blades, pieces of glass, scissors and knives. It depends on the sowey. She also says that it is possible to be infected with diseases if the operation is carried out without sterilization. Oyah continues to ask Dr. Asiatu Koroma if they give girls any pain killers and Dr. Asiatu Koroma says, "Never. A girl is supposed to bear the pain like a real woman" She says that the death is attributed to witchcraft. If the girl dies, she is said to have seen the Bondo spirit, the god of female circumcision.

She also talks of Olabis, "I have examined Olabis over the weekend and I find her healthy and normal. There is no medical reason for amputating any part of her body or genitals" Oyah finishes her questions. Dr. Asiatu Koroma is asked by Makalay's lawyer. She is asked whether she underwent circumcision or not, she agrees that she was circumcised. She is asked if she was infected with hepatitis, tetanus or HIV/AIDS and she says, "No" Makalay's lawyer continues to ask her if she suffered from excessive bleeding and difficulties in child birth, Dr. Asiatu Koroma said, "No, except the normal" Makalay's lawyer says despite the fact that Dr. Asiatu Koroma was circumcised at the age of twelve, she suffered no risk to her health, no excessive bleeding, no diseases, no death, no complication during birth instead God gave her a gift, a healthy bouncing baby girl who would be thirteen that Thursday.

Before Salaam Sesay finishes, Dr. Asiatu Koroma interferes him and says, "And she is dying of AIDS" Everybody in the court sits up and gets shocked. Dr. Koroma says, "My daughter was infected with HIV/AIDS six years ago at the Bondo camp. This information makes Makalay's Lawyer to say, "I'm sorry to hear that, Doctor" Olabisi stands up and shouts, "You don't feel sorry at all. You want the same thing happen to me". Makalay's lawyer tells Dr. Koroma that, "Teenagers now days are not like virgin Marry, you know". This makes Dr. Koroma's eyes to flush with anger and says that her daughter (Umu) has never done drugs, has never taken blood transfusion and still virgin Salam Sesay finishes and says, "I have no further questions".

CHAPTER NINE

Yah Posseh walks into the witness box. She is the old woman and has an orange gown with enough shoulder folds to hide an elephants. She says that Female Genital Mutilation (FGM) was inherited from her great-great grandmother. The Bondo tradition is as old as Africa. She mentions the advantages of Female Genital Mutilation (FGM) by saying that women are taught to be committed in marriage, to manage house hold, to prepare tasty meals. Oyah asks Yah Posseh if she doesn't think that there are millions of women who become wonderful wives, skilful cooks, great parents and are committed in their marriage without being circumcised" Yah Posseh takes a minute to gather her thoughts like a hen gathering her chicks under her wings. Oyah keeps insisting for her question to be answered, Yah Posseh panics and says, "Don't rise your voice at me young woman. I may be older than your grandmother"

Later on Makalay is also called to walk into the witness box. She is asked by Oyah to tell her age when she was circumcised and she says, "Ten" Oyah asks if Makalay was yet circumcised when she became the girl friend of Ade Jones but Makalay defends herself that she was a teenager and inexperienced. She is then asked how old was she by the time she was pregnant, she says, "It's none of your business" She then says, "Sixteen" This makes Oyah to say, "You were circumcised at the age of ten, you started having sex at the age of fourteen and becomes pregnant at the age of sixteen out of wedlock. Circumcision did not help you, did it? Oyah continues to ask Makalay about Dauda Kamara, and still insists that circumcision does not work.

INTRODUCTION
THE TITLE

The title of the book can be discussed looking at both literal and non-literal meanings. On a broader sense the latter implies to refuse to grant/fulfil someone's desires, claims or wishes as expected. In this novel we see a lot of claims that are not, answered/fulfilled. So we have the following cries that are unanswered;

1. First, there is a literal cry that is made by a young lady but her cry is literally unanswered. Look at the following paragraph from page 29. "Suddenly the bondo women started pounding their drums and the whole camp broke into a song. The shrieks of the girl were drowned. Her cries went unanswered. Her clothes and pants were torn off her body. She fought like a wild cat, kicking and punching and shrieking and scratching. Without any success."

2. Second, in a more general sense it refers to the cry of many girls who are forced by their parents to undergo FGM against their wishes. Their cries are not answered because nobody cares. Their parents never listen to them. For example Olabisi is not listened to by her mother.

3. Third, the cries of the whole traditional society led by Ya Posseh in wanting all their girls to be circumcised including Olabisi are not answered. They claim it up to the court demanding that their cause is right and defend their position but eventually the court judge gives a decision against them. This is to say their cries were not answered.

4. Fourth, Makalay's desire and wish to have her daughter Olabisi circumcised are not answered. Makalay and other traditional women led by the Bondo secret society, believe that through circumcision a girl would be able to prepare adequately for parenthood, be submissive, faithful and loyal to her husband and possess self-control over her sexual appetite. This cry is also unanswered as the court judges against her.

5. Fifth, the cry of Eddy to have Olabisi back is not answered. Edward Cole apologizes for what he did to Olabisi by revealing their relationship to Salaam Sessay who later humiliates her in the court in front of her daddy. Eddy's cry is not answered as Olabisi kicks him and runs away signifying the end of their relationship.

CHARACTERISATION

1. OLABISI

- She's Ade Jones and Makalay's daughter. She almost becomes a victim of traditional practices by being forced by her own mother to undergo female genital mutilation.
- **She is inquisitive and curious** -she asks a lot of questions for knowledge. Her curiosity lands her in trouble when she ignorantly asks Rugiatu and Sallay whether they are Gborka (a disparaging term for an uncircumcised girl). They get furious and fight vigorously. Her experience of living in town makes her believe that only boys undergo circumcision so she wanders what in the woman is being circumcised in the process.

- **She is very intelligent and streetwise.** Being streetwise means having the knowledge and experience that is needed to deal with the difficulties and dangers of life in a big city – this is evident to Olabisi if we consider;
  a) First, the way she flung the bucket behind her towards Dauda who fell on his face like a log of wood and hence stopped chasing her.
  b) Second, the way she fought off attacks from Rugiatu, Sallay and Yah Posseh hence avoiding grievous and actual bodily harm and forced FGM.
  c) Lastly the way she maneuvered her way out of dangerous situations in Freetown whenever students went on rampage.
- **She is Religious**- she repeatedly calls upon God for help whenever she finds herself in a dilemma or difficult circumstances. For instance when she finds herself in the unfamiliar and unfriendly territory around Bondo women's circumcision camp with Ya Posseh and her girls closing in on her, she said 'what am I to do? God if you are there help me''
- **She is so brave**, courageous and risk taker- Olabisi is a daring girl in many ways. By standing up against her mother and saying no to female circumcision, she showed great courage and fearlessness and also by manoeuvring herself out of danger after danger the way she did when escaping from the village back to the city, she showed great courage and heroism.
- **She is an agent for change /revolutionist.** – She is a revolutionist who wants to see FGM stopped since it is mostly done against the girls' will. Although in Sierra Leone female circumcision is considered to be sacrosanct, and the only best rite of passage that every girl must undergo, Olabisi finds no value in it. She advocates for change in the society by tabling a dialogue whether or not FGM is important for girls today because she is aware of the dangers of FGM and thus protests being circumcised according to bondo tradition
- **She is a fornicator.** Fornication means to have sex with somebody that you are not married to. She is engaged in premarital love affairs with Edward Cole. Their relationship is exposed by Sessay in court and she feels humiliated.
- **She is remorseful and apologetic** – when her secret relationship with Edward Cole is finally disclosed, she regrets for having done so against the wishes of the parents and apologizes by promising to take care of herself not to offend her daddy again. She even breaks her relationship with Eddy in public. On pg. 65 we are told that she apologized for the hundredth times the moment they stepped into the house. In some cases she is worthy being emulated in the society.

2. **MAKALAY**
   - This is Olabisi's mother, an educated woman and a school teacher.
   - **She is uncivilized and very abusive.**- she uses lots of abusive and foul language against Ade and Bisi; for instance she calls Ade a skirt chaser, useless man and a hopeless father. She also calls Bisi a stupid girl and a Gborka which is a derogatory term for uncircumcised girl; pg 19 ('you did worse than that you stupid girl, you stripped two bondo girls naked and looked at their private parts. You! A Gborka!'')
   - **She's quite strict and a hot-tempered mother.** She treats Olabisi rudely to make her behave well. This is exhibited by the way she easily gets angry at the slightest provocation. For instance she slaps Bisi for being too inquisitive and she's also angry at Bisi for dancing pg 14 (Makalay's slap hit Olabisi on the face like a small bomb, toppling her off the stool), she also twists Bisi's ears pg11(''Makalay grabbed

Olabisi's left ear and twisted it hard like a driver twisting the ignition key of a stubborn car'')

- **She is an upholder and custodian of African culture.** She implores Bisi to be circumcised and also advocates for her to learn her native tongue. We see her telling Bisi 'one day you will come and stay with me permanently and learn your native tongue'' she further goes on to claim that the only way people will ever respect and stop calling her (Bisi) Gborka is if she gets circumcised.
- **She is Superstitious** – She believes in the power of spirits. She trusts the spirits would make her childbirth difficult if she doesn't obey them. That's why on page 22 we see her meekly submitting herself to the fate of the spirits by saying 'whatever the spirits say I will do'' and 'don't say that. Please! I'm pregnant.'' Pg 22.
- **She is Desperate-** She is so desperate to get her daughter circumcised (all in the name of obeying the fictitious spirits) that she is ready to move heaven and earth just to ensure her beloved daughter is circumcised. Some of her desperate acts include; bribing Pa Amadu the hunter with a goat of his choice from her husband's herd if he brings Bisi back to her. She represents those people whose education has only helped them to solve their financial problems and never the change in attitude. She forces Olabisi to be circumcised because she fears the bondo spirits.
- **She is a Hypocrite** – This is a person who pretends to have moral standards or opinions that they do not actually have. She believes that FGM helps to reduce sexual appetite to girls and makes them committed to their husbands, but fails to explain why FGM failed to make her committed to Ade as she conceived Olabisi at the tender age of 16 years of age and out of wedlock but she later moved again to Dauda. Pg 83
- **She is a traditionalist and Conservative** – Despite her education, she supports FGM which she was supposed to condemn with all her mighty. She is resistant to change despite the fact that she is educated and knows the potential dangers of FGM and the belief in fictitious spirits, she still holds on to these outdated traditional practices. Because she doesn't want changes in the society she is not worthy being emulated.

3. YAH POSSEH

- She is Salay and Rugiatu's mother.
- She is Superstitious and traditionalist. She is believed to have powers even to speak with the spirits. Like Makalay she also believes that FGM has a way of making girls real women and creating a sense of commitment to their husbands.
- She's the Digba Sowey i.e. the chief circumciser. She is among the women who perpetuate FGM in the name of ancestral tradition..
- She is a strong custodian and champion of African traditions and practices. She undertakes this responsibility with great zeal and pride as it can be evidenced through her words in the court. "I am the Digba Sowey, the head of the female circumcisers." Pg 74
- She does not want changes in the society and thus not worthy being emulated.

4. DR. ASIATU KOROMA

- She is a medical doctor by profession.
- She uses her education and position in a positive way educating the people on the effects of FGM. She helps the court in reaching the decision of setting Olabisi free from the traditional practices.

- She is aware of the possible complications that can arise as a result of going through FGM both immediate and long term.
- She advocates for change in the society. She is worthy being emulated.

5. OYAH

- She is professionally a lawyer and uses her education positively by defending the rights of women. She stands as an advocate in Olabisi's case and helps her to come out a winner and Makalay with her Lawyers become losers.
- She is forgiving – She She is aware of Ade Jones unfaithfulness in relationship and asks for more commitment unless otherwise they should stop the relationship. Notwithstanding Ade Jones infidel and promiscuous behavior, and fake promises to marry her, she still finds it in her heart to forgive him like a mother forgiving a spoilt child. pg 43
- She is Supportive and caring – she supports her husband-to-be when he has a brief conflict with Makalay over Bisi's circumcision. She categorically states that ''if I'm going to be your wife, I must stand by you'' pg. 47.
- She is Responsible and has true love– she has true love for Olabisi and wants her to be happy by protecting her from traditional influence. She exhibits qualities of a responsible parent by giving Olabisi motherly advice to stay away from boys until she gets married. She also helps clean Olabisi like a loving mother would do to her own daughter, as Olabisi's soon to be Surrogate/ substitute mother; she thrives in this role which only serves to forge a strong bond of friendship between the two. Pg.45
- She is Liberal and agent for social change – she is an open minded person, someone who changes with the changing times. Despite being circumcised herself, she's against this barbaric tradition.
- She later becomes Ade Jones wife officially. She represents women who are revolutionists and in need for change in the society so she is worthy being emulated.

6. ADE JONES

- This is Olabisi's father married to Oyah.. He has true love for Olabisi and wants her to be happy by protecting her from traditional influence.
- He is Promiscuous/womanizer – He is a womanizer as we are told he has five girlfriends apart from Oyah. He also had Makalay with whom they bore Olabisi. Makalay referred to him as a 'skirt chaser', Oyah also said something to that effect i.e. ''I've been doing that for the past three years while you chase after girls''. Pg. 41
- He is Funny and comic – He tells Oyah some cock and bull story about being attacked by several friends (mosquitoes) they hosted the previous night. This joke shows how funny, inventive and humorous Ade is. Pg.40
- He is against FGM – He also wants changes and doesn't want her daughter to be circumcised against her will. He firmly supports his daughter who refused to be circumcised. This can be evidenced from his words in the court where he firmly declared, 'No Bondo woman is going to circumcise my daughter for the sake of superstition or tradition'' pg. 62
- He is Irresponsible parent – he has been a bad role model to his daughter since he keeps on changing women day by day and tells his daughter "do as I say not as I do". This makes Olabisi to start having a love affair with Eddy right under his nose. If he was responsible, maybe he would have detected this early on and stopped it. But then they were both embarrassed when the issue was revealed in the court.66

- He is hot Tempered – he easily gets angry, he threatens Makalay that he would kill her if she doesn't vacate his premises.
- He has a changing attitude. He finally comes to his senses and admits that he has been a bad father and promises to change. In page 66 he tells Olabisi "from now on, it will no longer be 'do as I say' but 'Learn from watching me'"

7. SALAAM SESAY

- He is professionally a lawyer. He also represents people who would do anything in the name of money. Although he is educated and certainly knows the harmful effects of FGM, he supports FGM to get money from his clients. He is among the people who are a stumbling block in the way leading to development because to him what is important is money not humanity or dignity even when he knows the effects. He is not worthy being emulated.

8. JUDGE KANU

- He is professionally a lawyer who uses his position to grant justice where it is due. He conducts Olabisi's case and makes a wise decision that Olabisi should not be forced to undergo FGM against her will or the will of the father. He is among the people who fight for the oppressed. He is also after changes thus worthy being emulated.

SETTING

The novel is set in Sierra Leone, although scanning through the themes one can realize that the setting in a more general sense represents African communities where FGM is common. Moreover, to drive the message home the author has employed (rural) village and urban (town) setting.

1. The village/rural setting includes the following sub-settings
    a) Home; Olabisi always quarrels with her mom at home based on their disagreement on the issue of FGM. FGM is rampart in rural areas than in urban.
    b) Bondo camps; we are also introduced to the practices at the bondo camp and what is going on there.
    c) Forest; we also see a large forest where hunting is taking place. Hunting is typical feature of rural setting. Additionally, drawing water from the stream sums up the village setting.
2. Urban setting in Freetown is also portrayed with the following sub settings.
    a) Home; the urban home is different from the rural one. For example we are told that Olabisi went to take a shower in the bathroom. 'Exactly, Olabisi turned on the shower' pg 45. This is common in town Courtroom. We are also introduced to courtroom setting and how the case proceedings take place. Most courts are in town.
    b) Streets in Freetown. Bondo women are seen all over in streets of Freetown.

STYLE/TECHNIQUE

1. The novel is rich in its style. The novelist has employed the **straightforward narration.** We are told of Olabisi in the village, and the experience there, then forced to undergo FGM runs back to town then to court. In the middle there are cases of flashbacks like when Olabisi narrates what happened to her and when Ya Posseh narrates the history of FGM

2. The story is told using a **narrative technique.** But also there are cases of dialogue especially in the courtroom.

3. **POINT OF VIEW**
   - The author has employed all types of points of view. Omniscient point of view. The narrator seems to know what characters are thinking, e.g. "nothing exciting happens in this place, she thought" pg 5
   - First person point of view. At times Olabisi and other characters speak in first person. E.g. "I must see this" pg 5
   - Third person point of view. In most cases the novelist has employed this kind of point of view. The narrator tells the story in 3rd person. E.g. "she dropped the dish back into the plastic bowl and …

4. **DICTION/ LANGUAGE USE;** the language used is not only simple and easy to understand for an ordinary reader but also rich in its use of registers. The author has employed legal language, religious language and common language.
   - **Legal language;** There is the use of legal vocabulary like "sustained, overruled, objection … etc to suit the courtroom setting"
   - **Religious language.** There is also the use of the language common in religious context. 'Dear God I will start going to church this Sunday. Just make Mama lose this case.' "You answered truthfully. For you have had five girlfriends and you are now living with a woman who is not your wife"

FIGURES OF SPEECH

The novel is rich in its employment of various figures of speech as follows;

1. **Barbarism;** The use of more than one language in a literary work.
   - "gborka, bondo, subanallah" etc
2. **Onomatopoeia** -imitation of natural sounds by words
   - BAM! Pg 63,
   - He hit the bench with his gavel BAM! Pg.86
3. **Simile;** specific comparison by means of the words "like" or "as" between two kinds of ideas or objects.
   - "Sleeping like Lazarus" pg41
   - "She sat up listening like a dog sensing an intruder" pg 5
   - "She fought like a wild cat" 29.
   - "You are as hopeless as your father" pg 8
   - "Makalay sucked her teeth like a cobra"
4. **Apostrophe;** This is a device by which an actor turns from the audience, or a writer from readers, toaddress a person who usually is either absent or deceased, an inanimate object, or an abstract idea.
   - "Dear God I will start going to church this Sunday. Just make Mama lose this case."
   - "God if you are there please save me!" Pg 26, 61
5. **Rhetorical question** (Olabisi asking herself)
   - "Who are they? What are they doing here? Are they the owners of the mud hut?" Pg 27
6. **Satire**

- "Welcome to the bondo camp, white woman" (This is Ya Posseh mocking Olabisi because she doesn't want to be circumcised)

7. Imagery

- "She fell down rolling and screaming" pg 29
- "The whole village broke into a song" pg 29
- Olabisi running through the bush
- "Camera bulbs were flashing all over the place" pg 88

8. Metaphor;

- (The bondo tradition) "It is mama Africa" pg 74
- "A child is a bundle of joy" – pg 76
- "Death is the enemy..."

9. Personification; this is a representation of inanimate objects or abstract ideas as living beings.

- "Death is the enemy who has no respect for people and their privacy. He will come knocking at your door while you are sleeping …"
- Bondo tradition is also referred to as mama Africa.

10. Allusion;

- "You answered truthfully. For you have had five girlfriends and you are now living with a woman who is not your wife". pg 62 (referring to the Samaritan woman in the bible).

11. Hyperbole

- Daddy says you are the best lawyer in the whole world." Pg 47

12. Symbolism

- The gavel – symbol of authority.

13. Saying

- "Never laugh with your enemy, otherwise you might end up as friend"s pg 75
- "Do as I say, not as I do" pg 45

THEMATIC ANALYSIS

1. FEMALE GENITAL MUTILATION (FGM);

- The whole novel seems to be centred on the debate whether or not female genital mutilation is worthy passing on. The novelist uses the main character Olabisi Jones who despite having half knowledge about FGM still determines that she will never undergo FGM. On the other extreme he uses Makalay, educated school teacher as a mockery to people whose education has helped them only to solve their financial problems and not to change their mindsets. Despite the fact that Makalay is educated, she supports FGM in fear of the spirits and bondo gods.
- Successfully, the author has set up a debate for the matter. He shows that education is needed to help those who support the bondo ritual to view it with another perspective. Through judge Kanu he says; "I can see that there is an obvious need for dialogue between both groups for a better understanding of each other's position"
- Arguably, female genital mutilation is an outdated tradition that undermines the dignity of women and robs them of their privilege to enjoy marital life. It also carries along with it a lot of complications at childbirth, excessive bleeding,

psychological torture; infections of diseases and even the catastrophe of death are just few cases in point. This is to say FGM should be uprooted with both hands.

2. SUPERSTITION AND IGNORANCE

- FGM seems to be carried along in this society simply because the society is wrapped in the vicious cycle of superstition and ignorance. Even educated people like Makalay are afraid of speaking against the practice in fear of the bondo spirits. E.g. in page 85 Makalay says "when a circumcised woman reveals to a gborka the secret of the gods, something terrible will happen to her "
- Additionally, complications at child birth are attributed to the disobedience of bondo gods than to FGM.
- She continues to say "that is one reason why many women suffer complications during childbirth. They talk too much"
- Ya Possey is believed to be very powerful because she can communicate with the spirits.
- Moreover, many people especially women seem to cheer up the practice because they are ignorant of the problems it carries along.

3. AWARENESS; awareness has been revealed in different scenarios.

- First, Olabisi is aware of the harmful effects of undergoing FGM and her rights of decision making thus she protests to go through the process.
- Second, Dr. Asiatu and Oyah are also aware of the medical complications and potential dangers that come along with FGM thus they help to prevent Olabisi to undergo FGM.
- Third, Ade Jones is aware of her child's right to decide whether or not she should undergo FGM.

4. CONFLICTS

a) FAMILY CONFLICT

- There is a family conflict between Makalay and Olabisi. This results when Olabisi refuses to be circumcised according to bondo tradition. It increases when Ya Posseh threatens that if Makalay doesn't take Olabisi to the bondo camp something bad will happen to her at childbirth since she is pregnant. She decides to look for Olabisi no matter the cost.
- Between Makalay and Ade Jones. This results when Makalay wants to take Olabisi by force to undergo FGM. They decide to take the matter to court where it is resolved.
- Between Oyah and Ade. These results from infidel behavior of Ade Jones who sleeps with many women and has not officially married Oyah. It ends when Ade promises to marry her and they eventually get married

b) SOCIAL CONFLICT; **There** is a conflict between Ya Posseh's family and Makalay's family which results when Rugiatu and Sayah fight against Olabisi for asking whether Rugiatu is a gborka. Also from the fact that women want Olabisi to be circumcised but she doesn't.

c) CULTURAL CONFLICT; Ever since the coming of whites the issue of cultural conflict has become a common phenomenon. There is a conflict between old culture (traditionalism) and modern culture (modernism). While on one hand people like Makalay, Ya Posseh and other bondo women uphold outdated culture like FGM, belief in spirits and bondo gods, on the other hand there are people like Olabisi, Oyah, Ade

Jones and Dr. Asiatu who embrace modern culture and see no need to carry on with such superstition.

d) **INTRAPERSONAL CONFLICT;** There is intrapersonal conflict within Olabisi on different matters.

- One, because she is forced to undergo female genital mutilation. Two, because her relationship with Eddy is revealed and wonders what her father will do to her. She plans to kill herself. Three, she fears if Makalay wins the case what will happen to her.
- Makalay also suffers intrapersonal conflict for the fear of what Ya Posseh will do to her if she fails to take Olabisi to the bondo camps. She even dreams about Ya Posseh.

5. **POSITION OF WOMEN IN THE SOCIETY;** Women have occupied different positions both good and bad.

a) **Women are used as tools for pleasure by men.** Ade is using Makalay for pleasure after impregnating her he goes to Oyah. We are told he has some more five girlfriends. "You answered truthfully. For you have had five girlfriends, and you are now living with a woman who is not your wife" pg 62. Olabisi is also used by Eddy for the same reason since they are not yet married.

b) **Women also show a picture of ignorant and foolish people.** They should have been the ones to oppose FGM but surprisingly enough they are the ones supporting it. They are also ignorant of the dangers brought by FGM but they think only of the benefits ignoring the harmful outcomes.

c) **Women are portrayed as cruel people who perpetuate a cruel custom.** If we consider how FGM takes place, we wouldn't imagine a woman standing in court to defend it. Oyah asks Makalay "Mrs Kamara, do you not find it surprising to see a college educated woman supporting and defending cruelty to a child…"

d) **Women are portrayed as superstitious.** The whole process is carried out on the basis of superstitious grounds. The belief in bondo gods and spirits. For example Makalay says "when a circumcised woman reveals to a gborka the secrets of the gods, something terrible will happen to her." Pg 85

e) **Women have been portrayed as revolutionists.** In this case we see Olabisi, Oyah and Dr. Asiatu standing firm to fight for the freedom of women and rights of the child of decision making.

f) **Women have also been portrayed as child bearers and caretakers.** Makalay is the mother of Olabisi who is very strict in ensuring that Olabisi observes good family standards like avoiding boys until she gets married. Also Oyah takes good care of Olabisi as her child although she is not her real biological mother.

g) As agents for social change. We see Oyah, Olabisi and Asiatu standing firm as agents to bring about changes in this society particularly as far as FGM is concerned.

6. **CORRUPTION AND BETRAYAL**

- Although it takes only a small part but that isn't a reason to ignore discussing it. There have been cases of corruption in the novel. Pa-Amadu -The hunter is given a task by Makalay to look for Olabisi in which case he would be given a goat if he succeeded to find her. Unfortunately, she finds her and receives some money from her and helps her to escape. This shows how our society fails to reach some intended goals because of individualistic tendencies of few members of the society who use every opportunity coming their way for private gain. Olabisi says:

- "I ran back and… and bumped into this man, a hunter. He said if I gave him enough money to buy two goats instead of one, he would show me the way out of the forest instead of taking me back to my mother"
- Makalay is betrayed by Pa Amadu the hunter in this case. Olabisi is also betrayed by her boyfriend Edward Cole by revealing their secret relationship which is later used in the court to humiliate her in front of her daddy.

7. **INFLUENCE OF EDUCATION;** Meaningful education is that which helps to build a person by helping him/her to change the society by changing the way he/she thinks. When education fails to change a person's mindset and the way he/she looks at things, that education was but a waste of time.

- In the book both scenarios have been manifested. Makalay and Salaam Sessay represent a group of educated Africans who for them education is just a means to earn salaries and manage the family budget. She still upholds the harmful traditions despite the fact that she learnt in school how harmful FGM is.
- On the other hand there are people like Asiatu and Oyah who have used their professionalism to bring about changes in the society by condemning what is bad. Without fail, they join hands and fight for Olabisi until they successfully snatch her from the bondo ritual. This is the positive effect of education.

8. **HUMILIATION and OPPRESSION**

- There are many cases that show humiliation to women in this novel. But generally the act of forcing young girls to be circumcised against their will is by itself humiliation. Most girls are taken to bondo camps at the age when they are unable to defend themselves. Olabisi narrates how she saw a girl trying to escape for her safety but was overpowered by older women who held her screaming but her cries went unanswered.
- Also Olabisi is humiliated by her mother for examining her secret parts when she is unconscious and discovers that she has lost her virginity. The author says;
- "Olabisi flushed with shame. She felt invaded, assaulted, raped! By her own mother. How could you do this to me, Mama?"
- Also Olabisi feels humiliated in the court when her secret affair with Eddy is revealed. She thinks of throwing herself into a fast moving truck to cover up her shame.

MESSAGE
There is actually a lot to learn from the novel.

1. Female Genital Mutilation is very dangerous and risky as it may lead to death or HIV infection.
2. Parents should respect children's right and not simply press their wills on their children even when they affect the children.
3. Some of our traditions like FGM are outdated so they should be discarded.
4. Not every educated person is necessarily civilized. So education should be used as a means to bring about social change and not to prevent changes.
5. Parents should be good role models to their children lest they pick bad behaviors. They should also be responsible for taking care of their children.
6. Ignorance and superstation are obstacles to development.

7. Corruption and betrayal are obstacles to development and the building of an ideal society. We should fight against corrupt people like Pa- Amadu.

RELEVANCE
The novel is relevant in a number of ways;
1. FGM is still a common practice among most African societies. It is practiced in rural communities by ignorant masses ignoring all the consequences that come along with FGM.
2. There are educated people who support outdated customs like FGM, Superstition etc as did Makalay.
3. Most girls are forced by their parents to undergo FGM and when they stand against such practices nobody listens to them. Their cries go unanswered. This is common among the Kuryans of Northern Tanzania.
4. We also have girls who are now aware of the effects of FGM as a result they are now protesting to undergo the process.
5. Corruption, ignorance and believing in superstition are also common phenomena in our country and Africa in general.

TITLE; THE INTERVIEW
AUTHOR; PATRICK M NGUGI
SETTING; NAIROBI CITY-KENYA

PLOT SUMMARY.
CHAPTER ONE; THE ACCIDENT

Joe wakes up and prepares himself to go for an interview. He completed form four at Nairobi Central Academy but was not given the certificates since he had not cleared the 40000/= he owed the school as school fees. As a result he could neither get any job nor go to college. We are told that their parents were killed in ethnic cleansing thus Joe and his sisters were sheltered by their maternal uncle – Jonathan. Joe leaves for the interview and he goes through the newspapers headlines. One of them reads "ELEPHANT GROUP TAKES OVER NAIROBI BOTTLERS".

As he reaches the bus stop he sees an old woman who seems to be mentally disturbed across the road. The matatu are nowhere to be seen to take him to the interview on time. Then the old woman starts crossing the road. Unfortunately, the fast moving matatu knocks her down but Joe dives to rescue her from the full impact. He then calls the police who arrive with an ambulance and collects the old cucu to the hospital with Joe for further police interview at the hospital police post. Joe wonders whether he would be able to make it on time to the interview.

CHAPTER TWO; AT THE HOSPITAL

At the hospital Joe is so depressed for having missed the interview. One medic named Freddie Mwasi tries to comfort him thinking that Joe is depressed because of the old cucu. A full flashback is given on how Joe's parents and other people were killed and children massacred. Joe and his sisters managed to escape and found themselves in Nairobi city. Together with their brother David, were sheltered by their uncle – Jonathan.

Joe is taken to the hospital's police post for further interview with Chief Inspector Margaret Kinyua. Joe narrates what happened up the time the police and the ambulance arrived. After the interview with Joe, she then orders Constable Kilonzo to take Joe to the interview by the ambulance. It was then 9:15 while his interview was scheduled at 8:30. He was 45 minutes late. Before they leave he rushes in to see cucu, who's been admitted. He meets Dr. Ochieng' who's examining the old cucu. He thanks Joe for calling them in time. He asks Joe if he is related to cucu and Joe refuses. After that Joe is rushed to the City Soap Industries Kampala Road in the Industrial Area for the interview.

CHAPTER THREE; JOE ARRIVES FOR THE INTERVIEW

Joe enters the building and asks for Mr Daniel Kung'us office at the reception. The receptionist confirms if he is one of the interviewees. She wonders why he is so late, as his interview was scheduled at 8:30. She allows him go upstairs. Another flashback is told of a girl named Gladwell who happened to be Joe's closest friend. The two met at the church when they were both choir members and Joe loved her.

Joe enters the office of Mr. Kung'u and finds a lot of young men and women who are also for the same job. The secretary informs Mr Kung'u of Joe's arrival and he gives him an appointment to meet him at noon. He is happy and hopeful that at least the boss has agreed to meet him. As he was leaving Gladwell stops him. He is so impressed to see her. After a brief chat they arrange to meet later and she goes back to the office. At exactly 11:30 he comes back and is allowed in without the usual formalities. He explains why he was late for the interview. Mr Kung'u says that they cannot hire him since he failed the interview in the first place by not showing up on time for the interview and their policy does not allow lateness for whatever reason. Then Joe is asked to leave his paper and he leaves the office.

CHAPTER FOUR; JOE AND GLADWELL GO OUT

David comforts Joe for the bad news. Then Joe tells him how he met Gladwell in the office. Joe and Gladwell meet at Ogden Cinema and they stride to Silver Moon Restaurant. They talk a bit about Gladwell sister Georgina who died of Tuberculosis. Joe then tells Gladwell how he rescued the old cucu. Joe feels a bit depressed that they decide to change the topic. They leave each other while Joe is wondering if cucu was to die, would she be buried anonymously. He hoped that cucu had a family somewhere, and that someone somewhere might be looking for her.

Joe decides to go to the hospital to see cucu's progress. He goes to the ward number three and meets Mildred Amiti – the nurse who is attending cucu. She gives him a brief summary of cucu's progress ever since he left. After staring at her and having some more conversation with the nurse he excuses himself and leaves promising to visit the following day.

CHAPTER FIVE; JOE SECURES A JOB AT THE NATIONAL LIBRARY

Joe suffers a sleepless night because of cucu's vision that keeps visiting his mind. He leaves his bed and goes to watch the CNN. David also wakes up and goes to have a chat with him. David informs Joe of the job he has found for him as a librarian at the national library. Although it was the last occupation he expected, for that moment it was better than nothing. He becomes a bit happy and the two go to sleep. In the morning Joe reports at the National Library and is directed to the Chief Librarian's office, Mr. Julius Kimeu who was David's old schoolmate. That's how Joe gets a part-time job at the National Library.

As Joe is engaged in reading, suddenly the memory of cucu comes into his mind and fails to ignore it. He asks for permission and goes to see her. At the hospital he finds a crowd of people examining a dead body of a pastor who flung himself from the 8th floor because he was HIV positive. Joe meets Freddie – the medic and the two go to see cucu. Dr. Ochieng' gives them a summary of cucu's condition that she is now conscious only that she suffers from amnesia (loss of memory) as she couldn't remember anything.

CHAPTER SIX; AT THE HOSPITAL

Cucu is happy to see Joe and she blesses him for saving her life by spiting on his face. Cucu asks for the discharge and says Joe will direct her to her home. Dr. Ochieng', Freddie and Joe try to reason together what is to be done to cucu but later they agree to meet the following day. Joe wonders how in the world a pastor can get HIV but Dr. Ochieng' informs him that HIV gets anyone including Bishops, Doctors and other important dignitaries.

After leaving the hospital he thinks of Gladwell and decides to go to the choir practice at St. Bernadette Church where he meets her. After the practice the two walk home together. Joe tells Gladwell of cucu but she doesn't seem to be happy by the way Joe is getting concerned with cucu and calls him RED CROSS. Joe changes the topic and tells her that he has got a job as Assistant Librarian at the National Library. Later on they talk of a Pastor who jumped from the 8th floor and died. Then Glad says even her sister Georgina was there and she died of AIDS not TB as it was announced.

CHAPTER SEVEN; JOE GETS THE CONTACTS OF CUCU'S RELATIVES

Joe recounts the day's events to his brother but he ends up discouraging him to continue with cucu's case. The next day he went to work but did not go to visit cucu. The following day he goes and Dr. Ochieng' gives him a brief summary of cucu's accusation on him why he had not shown up the previous day. As they talk to cucu she mentions that her home is in Kariobangi. They are so impressed because at least they have got where to start the house hunting mission.

When Joe goes back at work Joe receives a call from Glad who informs him that she has got the job at the City Soap Industries. They plan to meet and have a drink together but he remembers the house hunting mission with Dr. Ochieng' and Mildred then they postpone instead they agree to join the hunting mission. He goes back to work and decides to peruse the past newspapers. He comes across an announcement of a missing person and discovers that it is cucu. He reads the caption below the photo. Page 45

"Leah 'Chiki' Nyaguthii (above) went missing from her Muthaiga home about one month ago. She is 70 years old. Light complexion and of slightly heavy build. She was dressed in a light green frock and sweater when she was last seen. She speaks Kikuyu, Kikamba, Kiswahili and a little English and is slightly mentally disturbed. Anyone who might see her can telephone her son Johnson K Njogu at 3345643; or call nearest police station. A reward of Sh 100,000 will be given to whoever helps in locating this woman.

CHAPTER EIGHT; JOE CONTACTS JOHNSON NJOGU

Joe notes down the telephone number of Johnson Njogu the old lady's son. He asks Mercy Muraya – the receptionist to ring it. Unfortunately he doesn't get Njogu directly because this is a home telephone. He asks for his office number and rings him directly. The man sounds so hostile that Joe wonders whether he has done a mistake. Njogu thinks that Joe is just one of those nitwits who called him just because they were after money. Joe calls him the second time, tells him where the lady is and bangs down the phone. Joe wonders how God orchestrated this plan in a mysterious way; that he could get the library job, find cucu's relatives and finally claim 100,000/= which would help him redeem his certificates.

Glad comes over and the two head to the hospital as he gives her a summary of the exciting news. Arriving at the hospital Joe tells Dr. Ochieng' the news. Dr. Ochieng' is impressed for the updates. They wait for Njogu to call but they are finally disappointed. Back home he tells the story to his brother David who confirms that it should be the well known Njogu since there is just one Njogu – the billionaire and the Chairman and Chief executive of Elephant Group of Companies.

CHAPTER NINE; JOE'S BACKGOUND IS GIVEN AND CUCU IS TAKEN

A flashback is given on how Joe escaped with his sisters since all men and boys were killed only girls and women were spared. Some unlucky ones (girls) were raped and abducted. They were collected at the Catholic Mission by his brother and their uncle. They lived with their uncle who provided them with both physical and psychological needs. He sent them to school and David finished and got a job as a bookkeeper. He helped his uncle to provide for financial needs to his young siblings. By the time Joe completed his Fourth Form he owed the school 40,000/=. Mary (aged 22) completed her training and got a job as a nurse at Nairobi Metropolis Hospice. She had to pay for Lucy who was a secretarial student at City Polytechnic.

Joe thinks of his paternal grandparents since he had seen them when he was so young. We are told that their grandfather was Kibe and grandmother was Wacheke. We are also told of Joe's paternal uncle John Kibe who got a scholarship and went to America to study Business Administration. Then a full flashback of Joe's family is given. Joe calls at the hospital and Mildred says that cucu is still there despite being discharged. Joe and Gladwell go to the hospital to see cucu. Surprisingly they find someone else on cucu's bed. They wonder whether cucu is dead or released to roam in the streets. Later Freddie tells him that Mr. Njogu came to collect her.

CHAPTER TEN; A CHAUFFEUR COMES TO PICK JOE

For two days Joe becomes a zombie but later he becomes normal again. He goes back to work and colleagues are happy. He is informed by Mercy that someone needs to see him. A man who introduces himself to be Tony Kibe tells him that he has come to pick him to go and meet Mr. Njogu. He seeks for permission and is allowed. The chauffeur opens the car door for Joe and he feels like a VIP. Tony and Joe talk a bit about cucu and her improvements. Joe thinks that he is daydreaming but he finally realizes that it is real. He feels embarrassed when the chauffeur opens the door for him. He wonders whether he is already a celebrity.

CHAPTER ELEVEN; JOE IN NJOGU'S MANSION

Joe enters Njogu's living room which is full of modern and expensive items. Joe scans all these in a few seconds as he stands mesmerised by the luxury of a modern high-class living room. Joe meets Njogu's family members who welcome him warmly and interview him how he found cucu. Joe tells them everything including how his actions had cost him a chance of an interview. Joe tells how he failed to get his certificates for lacking 40,000 as fees.

Uncle Dan comes in, in the middle of the conversation. He looks familiar to Joe but his memory fails him where in the world they had met before. After a while Joe remembers that he is Daniel Kung'u the Personnel Manager at the City Soap Industries who told him that the company does not tolerate lateness. They praise Joe for his good heart. Then Njogu promises to pay the 40,000 for him to be able to collect his certificates. He doubles the prize from 100,000 to 200,000 then offers Joe a job at the City Soap Ind.

They ask David to be fetched to come and celebrate with them. Meanwhile they ask Joe to tell them his family Background. In the process they discover that he is a grandson of Wacheke (cucu) and a nephew to Johnson Njogu and Daniel Kung'u and a cousin to Joyce and Tony (Njogu's children). What a coincidence!

CHAPTER TWELVE; THE REUNION PARTY

Joe is happy that he has more money than he expected. He will have enough to pay for his certificates and still have much left over. They inform their sisters Lucy and Mary to accompany them for the reunion party at Njogu's mansion. He also invites Gladwell to go with them. Gladwell is surprised to hear that Njogu is Joe's relative and on top of that Joe has been offered a job. Arriving at the mansion Joyce and Tony meet the newcomers; Mary, Lucy, Gladwell, Joe and David. The Njogus come out also to meet the newcomers. Cucu sends spittle of blessing on their heads to bless them. They all break into a song and dance while tears of joy welling in their eyes.

INTRODUCTION
THE TITLE OF THE BOOK

Perhaps the basic questions to ask ourselves before we move further into the book are;
1. What is the meaning of the word interview?
2. "What is (are) the interview(s) in 'the Interview?'"

The word interview can be understood as:
1. A formal meeting at which somebody is asked questions to see if they are suitable for a particular job, or for a course of study at a college, university, etc
2. It is to ask somebody questions about their life, opinions, etc, especially on the radio or television or for a newspaper or magazine
3. To ask somebody questions at a private meeting.

In The Interview there are several interviews that relate to the title of the book.
1. **Job interview at the City Soap Industry.** The major interview in the novel is the job interview which Joe has to attend but unfortunately he misses it because of volunteering

to save cucu. We are also told that a lot of candidates have attended the same job interview at the CITY SOAP INDUSTRY including Gladwell.

2. **Police interview with Joe.** The second interview is held by the police (Chief Inspector Margaret Kinyua) to interview Joe how the accident occurred and if he can recognize the plate number of the matatu.

3. **Hospital interview.** At the hospital also Joe is asked some questions including whether he knows the old woman he saved.

4. **Njogu's interview with Joe.** Njogu asks Joe several questions after inviting him to his home. In that interview they come to find out that they are related and Joe is Njogu's nephew.

5. **The life interview.** Joe's life is an interview by itself. From the way he sacrifices his job interview, to save cucu's life, then keeps on visiting her at the hospital, and helps to finds her relatives. All these are series of actions that later reward him the job he wanted plus other benefits.

CHARACTERS AND CHARACTERIZATION

1. JOSEPH KIMANI (JOE);

- He is the main character in the novel. He is a son of Bernard Kung'u and Nancy Mwihaki and a young brother to David Kibe, Mary Waithera, and Lucy Nduta and a grandson of Leah Wacheke.
- He is educated. He is a form four leaver from Nairobi city Academy but fails to collect his certificate due to debt of 40,000/= that he owed the school as fees arrears.
- He is an orphan. He lost both his parents in an ethnic cleansing that took place in Uasin Gishu district where he lived with his parents. We are told in page 62 that "Joe was orphaned at age ten".
- He becomes insomniac. Joe suffers from insomnia (the condition of being unable to sleep) due to different circumstances. One is his state of joblessness. Second is cucu's accident and the related nightmares.
- He is kind-hearted and sympathetic. He saves cucu from a fatal accident and takes care of her at the expense of his own job interview. Although he does not know the woman, he keeps on regularly visiting her at the hospital, even after being discouraged by his brother David and his girlfriend Gladwell, who mock him "Red Cross".
- He is quick in decision making. This is revealed from the way he saved cucu and immediately contacts the police. The author says; "he jumped into the road, got hold of the muttering woman and pulled her off road as he dived to avoid the speeding matatu." Pg 8
- He is lucky. His kindness to save and serve cucu opens doors for his future success. He gets a part-time job as an assistant librarian, which helps him to connect cucu with her family. He is awarded Ksh 240,000/=. He gets a job he dreamt of; furthermore, still he is reunited with his relatives. This shows that kindness pays.
- He is poor. He comes from a poor family that cannot afford to pay for his school fees. However this is due to the massacre of his parents and land grabbing. He is a good example in the society.

2. LEAH WACHEKE (CUCU);

- She is an old woman who at times is mentally disturbed. She goes mad after the death of her husband Kibe who is killed in ethnic cleansing at Molo. Pg 75 Her condition results to her involvement in a matatu accident and is rescued by Joe.
- She temporarily suffers from amnesia. {a medical condition in which somebody partly or completely loses their memory} Cucu loses her memory of who she is, where she came from, who her relatives are etc. later she gradually recovers.
- She is Joe's paternal grandmother. It is later discovered that she is a real biological grandmother to Joseph Kimani and a mother to Bernard Kung'u.
- She has a thanksgiving heart. After all that Joe did to her, the Njogus came to collect her at the hospital without acknowledging what Joe did but she insisted that Joe must be called to see her. The author says; {Tony telling Joe} "She even said we had to wait for you before taking her away...we thought she'd forget about it once she reached home but we were mistaken..." pg 76

3. GLADWELL;

- She is a sister to the late Georgina who died of AIDS.
- She is a singer. We are told that she was singing in a choir at St Benedette Church and that's where she met Joe who is also a singer.
- She is Joe's girlfriend. After meeting at the choir the two become friends and they spend some times together, going out etc.
- She is an avid reader of novels. We are told that she was an addict of romantic novels. Joe comments; "so Gladwell the romantic novel addict was after the same job." Pg 24
- She is pretty. We are told that she is so pretty that Joe hopes that one day when she is not in the middle of too much reading – he would get the courage to tell her how he felt about her.
- She is jealousy and selfish. She becomes uncomfortable and jealous when Joe keeps on paying regular visits to cucu at the hospital and his intention to look for cucu's relatives. She mocks Joe by asking him "Since when are you the Red Cross?"
- She gets a job at the city Soap Industry. Out of the great completion for just one post she becomes victorious and gets that job. She is even thankful that Joe was late for the interview because he might have qualified for the post instead.

4. DANIEL KUNG'U;

- He is a cousin to Johnson Njogu and Bernard Kung'u.
- He is the Personnel Manager at the City Soap Industries. He is the one who conducts the interview for the company to fill in the vacancy of a lab technician.
- He is very strict about time. Joe comes a bit late for the interview for having done a generous work but his excuse hits the wall. The receptionist tells Joe "Well, Mr Kung'u is very particular about time.".pg 21. In the office he tells Joe "I'm sorry but our policy does not allow lateness for whatever reason" pg 26
- He is inconsiderate. Although Joe is late for a genuine reason he does not consider him. He says that they can't hire him because he failed to show up and they will only consider those who are on time.

5. JOHNSON NJOGU;

- He is a rich billionaire and industrial tycoon. He is the one who owns Elephant Group of Companies.

- He is a son of Kibe and Wacheke and a brother of Bernard Kung'u.
- He is educated. We are told that he gets a scholarship and goes to study in America a five years' course in Business Administration.
- He is a very kind man. Although at first Joe thought he is a rude man, the way he talked to him on the phone he came to realise that he wasn't so at all. He treats Joe kindly after discovering what he did to his mother that Joe feels like a VIP.
- He has a thanksgiving heart. Although he had promised 100000/= to whoever will help them relocate their missing mom, he doubled the prize to 200000/= for Joe plus paying his fee arrears and offering him a job at the City Soap Industry. All these happen before even discovering that they are related.
- He is carried away by culture shock in America. He completes his studies but does not return back home on time. He even gets a job.
- He is remorseful and apologetic. This happens in different scenarios; first he apologizes for not taking Joe seriously when he called firstly, informing him of the found cucu pg 80. Secondly, he feels guilty and sorrowful for having abandoned home completely when in America. Pg 88

6. **DAVID;**
   - He is the older brother of Joe, Mary and Lucy.
   - He is educated. He grows up at Uncle Jonathan's place where he finishes school, and completes a six-month' account course.
   - He works as a bookkeeper. After getting the job, he takes over the responsibility of buying clothes for Joe, paying for his education and giving him a little pocket money.
   - He finds a part-time job for Joe. Due to the state of joblessness that is eating his young brother he decides to find a part-time job for him through his friend Julius Kimeu as an assistant librarian.
   - He is selfish: He discourages Joe from visiting cucu since he does not know her he even mocks Joe by telling him "I hope this time you will not witness another accident and play the Good Samaritan" pg 34.

7. **Uncle Jonathan;** a kind-hearted man who takes care of his sister's (Nancy) children after the death of their parents. He sends them to school and takes care of all the physical and psychological needs.

8. **Dr Ochieng':** He serves as a Doctor at the National hospital. He is also very kindhearted man since he gives maximum care to cucu and gives a hand of cooperation to house-hunt cucus relatives with Freddie the Medic and Mildred the nurse.

9. **Mercy.** The library receptionist who helps Joe to get his call through to Njogu.

SETTING

The setting of the book is in a modern city Nairobi in Kenya. It portrays the challenges in post independence African countries in urban areas. The setting is urban due to the following reasons:
1. Mode of Transport. Matatu transport is a common public transport used in Nairobi city. Also Ambulance services are common in town than in the countryside.
2. High unemployment rate. In towns most educated people have no jobs as evidenced by a number of young people who appear for interview just for one post.
3. Library services are provided in towns than in the countryside.

4. Life style. The kind of lifestyle described in Njogu's home symbolizes the kind of life the rich people live in big cities. Things like36-inch TV, video, and hi-fi equipment, computer, fax machine cum photocopier.
5. Industries. Many industries are located in urban areas like the City Soap Industry. There are also sub settings that sum up the urban setting.
6. Office setting. We see the office setting in the building that the City Soap Industry headquarters is located.
7. Hospital setting. We see hospital setting at the National hospital where cucu is admitted. But also incidents like suicide of HIV/AIDS victims take place there.
8. Restaurant setting. We see Joe and Gladwell going out at Silver moon Restaurant for a drink and some chats. This is common in towns than in countryside.

STYLE;

1. The book is rich in its style. The author has employed both the **narrative technique** to a large extent and **dialogue** to bring the characters to life. For example in page 73 Joe is taking to Tony.

> "Are you looking for me?" Joe asked.
> "Are you Joseph Kimani? He was asked in reply.
> "Yes, i am" Joe said politely but curiously.
> "Then you are the man I am looking for. Let's go....

2. **Point of view.** The writer has used all the three persons. However 3rd person singular is the dominant one. This is to say the author narrates the story. The author has employed the language of conversation with informal words like

> "Oh God Jeeysus! Pg 87
> "Aunteeeee! Ankoo is calling you! Pg 56

3. **Code mixing like;**

- What you guys call shamba?
- Very sad. Pole Sana.

4. Also the book has employed **the language of newspaper reporting.** E.g. In pg7 ELEPHANT GROUP TAKES OVER NAIROBI BOTTLERS. Also in pg 54 there is an advert for a missing person, common in newspapers.

LANGUAGE USE

The author has used a lot of figures of speech to enrich his style and get his messages across. Some of the figures of speech used are:

1. **Hyperbole;**

- He had polished his shoes...that he could almost use it as a mirror. Pg 7.
- The matatu were notorious for taking ages to appear pg 8
- The silence that followed the next few seconds was so heavy that you could hear particles of dust fly past your ears and settle on the ground. Pg 83

2. **Simile;**

- She is as fit as a fiddle. Pg 38
- She hugged me like hell. Pg 45
- Joe's heart skidded, stopped, then went wild beating like hell. 83

3. **Metaphor;**

- Even science can be an art in fact it is an art. Pg 34

- Since when are you Red Cross. Pg 45

4. **Euphemism;**
   - You see she seemed not to be of sound mind when I saw her before the accident. Pg 18 (meaning she was insane)

5. **Rhetorical question;**
   - Where did she come from? Where was she going? Who was she? What drove her insane? And who were her relatives? Pg 18

6. **Personification;**
   - His heart was racing vigorously. Pg 21
   - Sorry my mind was miles away. Pg 29
   - Thank your stars, Joe there is an opening for you. Pg 3
   - Then she smiled as his face registered in his mind. Pg 50
   - His heart raced madly. 53
   - The picture of his patient, the old cucu stared back at him. Pg 53

7. **Barbarism;**
   - Kwani, whom did you expect? Pg 33
   - Ngai fafa. Pg 85
   - It was their shauri. Pg 72
   - What you guys call shamba? Pg 85
   - Pole Sana. Pg 85

8. **Allusion;**
   - I hope this time you will not witness another accident and play the Good Samaritan. Pg 34 (referring to the Good Samaritan in the Bible)

9. **Oxymoron;**
   - And continued to daydream in the night pg
   - His new-old friend, cucu. pg 72

10. **Alliteration;**
    - They are very lively, lovely folks. Pg 94

11. **Reiteration;**
    - Oh young man thank you, thank you, thank you so much.pg 41

12. **Sayings idioms and proverbs;**
    - Survival for the fittest. Pg 8
    - Do you think that is just sour grapes or wishful thinking? Pg 27
    - The world will not end just because you missed the interview. Pg 27
    - Let's cross those bridges when we reach them. Pg42

13. **Religious language;**
    - May God bless you and bless your ways throughout your life. Pg 41

THEMATIC ANALYSIS

1. **NEPOTISM;** This is the act of giving unfair advantages to your own family if you are in a positionof power, especially by giving them jobs.
   - Joe gets a job through his brother who is a friend of Julius Kimeu – the chief librarian at the national library. David reports the matter to Joe by saying "there is a job for you somewhere. A friend of mine has fixed something for you" pg 33

- Also Daniel Kung'u is the Personnel Manager at the City Soap Industries which is owned by his cousin Johnson Njogu.

2. **CONFLICT;** This is a situation in which there are opposing ideas, opinions, feelings or wishes; asituation in which it is difficult to choose and sometimes the two opposing partiesend up fighting. In this novel there are two major types of conflicts; Intrapersonal (internal) conflict and social conflict.

   a) **INTRAPERSONAL CONFLICT**
   - This takes place within the mind of a character. The character struggles to make decision, take action, or overcome a feeling. In the novel we see Joe involved in this conflict due to some reasons.
   - One, is the fact that he misses the interview and consequently misses the job altogether.
   - Two, the accident he witnesses and the related nightmares that he tries to overcome but he fails. The author tries to explain this situation in page 32 by saying "Every time he closed his eyes he saw the pitiful figure of the old woman being knocked and dragged by the matatu. He tried reading a novel hoping to drift into sleep, but visions of the accident still crept into his mind"
   - Three, when he finds out that Njogu has taken cucu secretly from the hospital without informing him he becomes uncomfortable.

   b) **SOCIAL CONFLICT;** This conflict usually involves one community/society or any social group with another. In this society we see the Repercussion of social conflicts between communities as a result of ethnic cleansing that take place some years back in Uasin Gishu district. These repercussions include;
   - Massacre/massive killings. We are told that even at Kondoo area of Burnt forest in the rift valley one night some warriors raided the farms killing many people. Houses were burnt and people including children were massacred.
   - Raping. We are told in page 63 that during the massacre women and girls would be mostly spared but the unlucky ones were abducted and raped.
   - Family disintegration. Joe's family is completely disintegrated, and relocated. Joe and his siblings leave their area and go to live with their uncle Jotham, while the grandmother (Wacheke) and other relatives are separated.
   - Land annexation/appropriation. During the tribal crashes the land is taken from the owners by strangers/invaders. For example in page 6 the author says "When David visited what had once been their homestead years later, he found strangers living on the farm... They dared him to set foot on the compound if he valued his life" But also when Njogu comes back from America he tries to trace their home in Molo but he says "it was all in shambles with strangers living on the farm.

3. **POVERTY;** This is the state of living below the poverty line - the official level of income that is necessary to be able to buy the basic things you need such as food and clothes and to pay for somewhere to live. This society is characterised by poverty. More often than not poverty in this society is caused by the state of joblessness. This society is no exception. The author has portrayed the theme of poverty in the following scenarios.
   - Joe's family is so poor that Joe fails to pay the school fees. As a result he is unable to recover his secondary school certificates. He is out struggling and looking for the job that will enable him to help his financially burdened brother and pay for his school fees arrears and redeem his certificates.

- Many people are poor and can't afford the living. This is evidenced by the way they make prank calls to Njogu claiming to have located the missing cucu just to get money from him.
- Many educated people are jobless. This is evident in the office of the Personnel Manager of the City Soap Industry where a score of young women and men appear for interview just for one post. This shows how the state of joblessness is big and serious resulting to poverty in this society.

4. **UNEMPLOYMENT;** This is the state or the fact of a number of people not having jobs. Unemployment is acommon problem in developing countries especially among the youths. Manyeducated people are jobless. This is evident in the office of the Personnel Manager ofthe City Soap Industry –Daniel Kung'u- where Joe finds a score of young womenand men who appear for interview all clutching envelopes and other papers and satin nervous anticipation just for one post. This shows how the state of joblessness isabig and serious resulting to poverty in this society.

- Joe suffers the fate of joblessness and he tries to find any job that will help him to clear his school fees arrears. He gets a part time job at the National library and accepts it though it's not one that he anticipated. He accepts it nevertheless since something is better than nothing.

5. **AFRICAN TRADITIONS;** A tradition is a belief, custom or way of doing something that has existed for a long time among a particular group of people. In this society there are some few cases of African tradition though it seems to be a modernized society.

- Blessings. More often than not the elders bless the young by spitting on their forehead or on their palms. Cucu blesses Joe in a similar way. The author says; "After sending spittle of blessing upon his face, she released Joe from the tight embrace" page 4. Also in page 95 we are told that when the family is finally reunited "cucu spits over their head to bless them.
- Unity and cooperation in extended family. Africans have always been living in unity and cooperation among the members of extended family. In this book we see after the death of Joe's parents they are hosted by their maternal uncle who takes care of them including sending them to school and meeting their physical and psychological needs. David also cooperates with his siblings when his uncle is burdened.

6. **THE PLIGHT OF HIV/AIDS;** HIV/AIDS is a common theme in the contemporary African literature. Many authors write showing the ways it spreads and preventive measures. Most of them use characters as their mouthpieces to pass over the intended message. In this book AIDS is discussed in the following approach;

- There are suicide cases. People who suspect they have the disease jump off from the eighth floor where AIDS victims are taken care of and end their lives.
- HIV is indiscriminate as it gets anyone. Joe wonders how a pastor can be infected with HIV but Dr, Ochieng tells him that HIV does not care who you are as long as you indulge in risky behaviors you will be subjected to it. He says: "We know bishops, doctors and other important dignitaries who have succumbed to the disease. However what is important is that it can get anyone. No one is out of reach as long as they continue indulging in risky activities" pg 43
- AIDS has no cure yet but there are preventive ways. Using Dr. Ochieng' as his mouthpiece the author says that the only ways to stay out of AIDS are: To abstain from

sex if you are single, Be faithful to one partner, Practice safe sex- If you are not sure if your partner is faithful, Take HIV test if you eventually decide to get married.
- People are not telling the truth about AIDS. We are told the Gladwell's sister – Georgina died of AIDS. However to avoid stigma it was announced that she died of Tuberculosis (TB) pg 46

7. **LUCK AND FATE;** Luck refers to good things that happen to you by chance, not because of your ownefforts or abilities and fate implies the power that is believed to control everything that happens to somebody and that cannot be stopped or changed.
   - Everything that happens to Joe's life seems to be controlled by powers outside himself. Joe witnesses an accident that becomes a turning point in his life completely. The accident makes him miss the interview, thus he misses the job he desired. He gets another job that still works miraculously to help him locate cucu's relatives only to discover that he was helping his own cucu. The author expresses this luck and fate in the following way "Throughout the lunch hour Joe kept on thinking how, by a stroke of luck, he had come across the advert.
   - He continues to say "Was it by divine mercy that he had got the job at the Library in the first place? Was it through divine design that he had witnessed the accident, so that he could fail the interview and get this job at the library, so that he could be instrumental in helping the Njogu's find their loved one? God surely worked in mysterious ways." Pg 59
   - Eventually Joe gets 240,000/= and the job he desired just for helping their own grandmother unknowingly. Also this incident helps them to discover that the Njogu is their real relatives who got misplaced long ago. There was a power beyond Joe's control that was orchestrating all these things in Joe's life.

8. **CLASSES;** These are the groups of people in a society that are thought of as being at the same socialor economic level. In most post colonial African countries there are classes of poorpeople and rich people. In this society, this situation is evident.

   a) **The poor/low class**
   - The poor class as represented by Joe and his siblings are getting hard time to sustain their living. It is shown that due to poverty at home Joe is not able to pay for his school fees thus unable to get his certificates. This is contributed partly by tribal/ethnic clashes which result to the death of their parents and appropriation of their land where they could produce. It is also contributed by the state of joblessness that Joe faces. He gets a part time job at the National library and accepts it though it is not one that he anticipated. He accepts it nevertheless since something is better than nothing.
   - Many people are poor and can't afford the living. This is evidenced by the way they make prank calls to Njogu claiming to have located the missing cucu just to get money from him.
   - Many educated people are jobless. This is evident in the office of the Personnel Manager of the City Soap Industry where a score of young women and men appear for interview just for one post. This shows how the state of joblessness is big and serious resulting to poverty in this society.

   b) **The Rich/high Class**
   - The rich class is represented by the Njogus. These have everything they need; good houses, expensive cars, big income generating projects etc. The author

describes Njogu's home in a way that everything there symbolises wealth. In page 76 he says "the stately mansions behind the elegant gates and beautifully trimmed hedges mesmerized him".

- He continues to describe the mansion from inside that when Joe entered Njogu's living room he saw expensive items which displayed affluence to the point of obscenity and arrogance. The author says "Joe scanned all these in a few seconds, as he stood mesmerized by the luxury of a modern, high-class living room". Pg 78

9. **HUMANITY AND KINDNESS;** Humanity is the quality of being kind to people and animals by making sure that they donot suffer more than is necessary. The entire book seems to be centered on the theme ofhumanity and kindness. The author shows how some people play the role of goodSamaritans in helping other people in need of their help. The following cannot be leftunmentioned.

- Joe plays the role of a Good Samaritan by helping cucu at the expense of his own job interview. However the author shows that kindness pays. Joe eventually gets the job he aspired for and discovers that he was helping his own biological paternal grandmother.
- We are told that some good Samaritans were carrying refuges in Lorries to the Catholic Mission in Londiani.
- Uncle Jonathan takes care of his sister's children and becomes their guardian meeting their immediate physical and psychological needs, feeding, clothing and counseling them, until all four siblings become too much a burden for him and his young wife.

Other minor themes include

10. **Selfishness.** Both David and Gladwell show selfishness by discouraging Joe who keeps on visiting cucu and taking care of her since he is not related to her.
11. **Jealousy.** Gladwell becomes jealousy when Joe spends much time thinking about and visiting cucu than spending time with her (Gladwell) Sacrifice. Joe sacrifices his life to save cucu in a moving matatu. He could probably be injured as well but he never cared about that since he wanted to save cucu. He sacrifices his time to send cucu to the hospital and misses the interview but also to visit cucu at the hospital every now and then.

MESSAGE

1. **What goes around comes around.** Joe did his best to help cucu but he ended up benefiting more than he had expected.
2. **HIV/AIDS is indiscriminate as it gets anyone.** People should be careful by abstaining from sex if they are single, be faithful to one partner, practice safe sex – if one is not sure if their partner is faithful – This includes using a condom and taking HIV test if one eventually decides to get married.
3. **We should avoid social conflict in the society** as it may result to massacre of innocent people, raping of girls and women, family disintegration, and land alienation.
4. **Unemployment is a big problem among the educated youngsters.** Governments should create employment opportunities for the youths otherwise there will be much trouble in the future.

5. **Poverty is another crisis that is facing developing countries.** It makes people to be dishonest and selfish. It should be eradicated immediately.
6. People should not be given jobs depending on whom they know but what they know.
7. We should be thankful to people who have helped us as did cucu and Njogu.

RELEVANCE
The book is relevant in a number of ways.
1. AIDS is killing people day by day. Additionally there are many cases of people committing suicide when they suspect they have acquired the disease.
2. Unemployment and joblessness are common problems in Africa today especially Tanzania.
3. The gap between the rich and the poor is widening day by day.
4. There are few generous people in the society who can sacrifice their lives to save others as did Joe.
5. Nepotism is also rampant. People get jobs in the government offices not on the basis on technical know-what but know-whom.

POETRY ANALYSIS

GROWING UP WITH POETRY BY D RUBADIRI

A FREEDOM SONG BY Marjorie Oludhe Macgoye (Kenya)

Atieno washes dishes,
Atieno plucks the chicken,
Atieno gets up early,
Beds her sacks down in the kitchen,
Atieno is eight years old
Atieno yo.

Since she's my sister's child
Atieno needs no pay
While she works my wife can sit
Sewing every sunny day,
With her earning I support
Atieno yo.

Atieno's sly and jealous
Bad example to the kids
Since she minds them, like a school girl
Wants their dresses, shoes and beads
Atieno ten years old,
Atieno yo.

Now my wife has gone to study
Atieno's less free,
Don't I keep her, school my own ones,
Pay the party union fee
All for progress: Aren't you grateful,
Atieno yo?

Visitors need much attention,
All the more when I work at night.
That girl stays too long at the market
Who will teach her what is right?
Atieno rising fourteen,
Atieno yo.

Atieno had a baby
So we know that she is not barren
Fifty-fifty it may live
To repeat the life she had,

Ending in post partum bleeding
Atieno yo.

Atieno soon replaced
Meat and sugar more than all
She ate in such a narrow life
Were lavished in her funeral
Atieno's gone to glory
Atieno yo.

THEMATIC ANALYSIS

1. **CHILD LABOR;** The issue of child labor has become a burning issuethat attracts the attention of most social activists.Many children are employed informally, in the streets,homes and some workplaces. We see those sellingplastic bags, candies, washing cars, helping the militaryrebels etc. Atieno in the poem is just one case inpoint. She represents this class. She is working as ahouse girl at the age of 8 and strangely enoughwithout pay. At this age she should have been in STD2. Yet she is employed in her uncle's home (stanza 1)

2. **EXPLOITATION AND OPPRESSION;** Despite the growing awareness of the violation ofhuman rights, the world is still facing the problem of exploitation and oppression. The young girl in the poem is not only exploited but also oppressed by her own uncle. Although she works and does all the domestic chores she is not paid norgiven any good care. The poetess suggests that sheeven desires to have the dresses, shoes and beads ofher cousins since she is not given one. Here says thepoetess "Atieno's sly and jealousy/Bad example to thekids/ since she minds them like a school girl/Wants their dresses, shoes and dresses".Again in the second stanza she shows how Atieno'sefforts are wasted without gain. "Since she is my sister's child/Atieno needs no pay"(stanza 2)

3. **EARLY PREGNANCY;** This is another common problem among theteenagers today. Parents are now very busy than atany point in human history. As a result teens havebeen left without proper parental care. Many girlstoday have failed to reach their educational goalsbecause when they get pregnancy, they are kicked outof schools altogether. At the age of fourteen Atienobecomes pregnant. This is partly due to poor parentalcare. As the poetess says that her aunt has gone tostudy and uncle is busy with the work while poorAtieno has no one to teach her what is right.Since she is still young to handle the deliverycomplications she dies of excessive post partumbleeding (stanza 5)

4. **HYPOCRISY;** There is hypocrisy from family level to national levelwhen you come to think of it. Most step parentsmistreat their step children at home but in the outsidethey want everybody to believe that they are takinggood care of them. If you hear the tone of Atieno'suncle you will certainly discover some points ofsympathy. But the question is; who is mistreating theyoung Atieno? It's her uncle. This is hypocrisy. On thefuneral, we are told that meat and sugar more than allthat Atieno had eaten in such a narrow life werelavished in her funeral. That translates into somethinglike, "I loved the child" what a hypocrite! (stanza 7)

5. **POOR PARENTAL CARE;** While we are not told the reasons why Atieno is notliving with her own biological parents; it is evidentthat most parents have left the responsibility of takingcare of their children to the community like schools, churches or relatives. Because the parents are busy, they have no time to make regular follow-ups to check the

kind of upbringing their children go through. Parenting is the most important responsibility thatparents are now avoiding. Atieno goes to work in heruncle's home at the age of eight, and her parents' are not making follow-ups. Atieno's uncle is alsoportrayed as a bad parent since he mistreats his ownniece.

RELEVANCE;

As we have seen child labor, hypocrisy, exploitation, oppression, poor parental care and early pregnancies are all common phenomena in our country today. We see many children in the streets selling things like plastic bags, washing cars; helping the military rebels etc. many girls drop their studies due to early pregnancies. Every day we hear of violation and abuse of children rights and parents are very busy today to the point that they cannot spare time to be with their children and listen to their problems.

Figures of speech/ poetic devices;
1. **Refrain;** Every stanza ends with a refrain line "Atieno yo"
2. **Alliteration;** "Pay party union fee" "Atieno needs no pay"
3. **Rhetorical question;** who will teach her what is right? Aren't you grateful Atieno yo?
4. **Simile; e.g.**"She minds them like a school girl"
5. **Metaphor;** the poet tried to compare "sacks" and beds.
6. **Repetition;** e.g. Atieno.
7. **Imagery;** e.g. "Atieno has gone to glory" produce a picture that the girl has gone to a holly place.

BUILDING THE NATION by Christopher H. M. Barlow (Uganda)

Today I did my share
In building the nation
I drove the permanent secretary
To an important urgent function
In fact to a luncheon at the Vic.

The menu reflected its importance
Cold Bell beer with small talk,
Then fried chicken with niceties
Wine to fill the hollowness of the laughs
Ice-ream to cover the stereotype jokes
Coffee to keep the PS awake on return journey.

I drove the permanent secretary back.
He yawned many times in the back of the car
Then to keep awake, he suddenly asked,
Did you have any lunch friend?
I replied looking straight ahead
And secretly smiling at his belated concern
That I had not, but was sliming!

Upon which he said with seriousness
That amused more than annoyed me,
Mwananchi, I too had none!
I attended to matters of state.
Highly delicate diplomatic duties you know,
And friend, it goes against my grain,
Causes me stomach ulcers and wind
Ah, he continued, yawning again,
The pains we suffer in building the nation!

So the PS had ulcers too!
My ulcers I think are equally painful
Only they are caused by hunger,
No sumptuous lunches!

So two nation builders
Arrived home this evening
With terrible stomach pains
The result of building the nation –
- Different ways.

THEMATIC ANALYSIS

1. **DISILLUSIONMENT;** The kind of disillusionment portrayed in the poem is that which Africans have towards their leaders who have adopted the very tenets of the colonizers from whom they got power. Essentially, the idea of nation building turns out to be a very complicated phenomenon where those who are central to the process have their efforts wasted by leaders who can implement policies. The persona shows more disillusionment by stating that at the meeting *"the menu reflected its importance/ ColdBell beer with small talks/ then fried chicken with niceties/ wine.../ ice cream .../coffee…* (Lines 6-11). This reflects the triviality of a meeting where serious issues were supposed to be discussed.

2. **LIES AND HYPOCRISY;** This has been a vital tool for most politicians when they want to win more votes from their ignorant masses. They make heaps of lies on the optimistic crowds but eventually everything turns out only a nightmare. The PS lies to the driver that he did not have any meal just as did the driver yet you and I know that he had a very heavy and sumptuous lunch. He even shows his hypocrisy more clearly when he asks this question. *"Then to keep awake hesuddenly asked/Did you have any lunch friend?"* It is rather sad to note that he does not ask whether the driver haseaten anything because he is concerned about his welfare, but it is simply to keep him awake through thejourney.

3. **CLASSES;** In a broader way the poem thoroughly depicts two classes in one society. There is middle class and lower class. Both of them are supposed to mutually benefit from the national resources. Yet the middle class that is represented by the PS exploits the lower class that more often than not comprises those who are involved in the modes

of production. For example the driver drives the PS to the place where there is feasting (eating) while the driver does not take part in the feasting. The role of both classes is building the nation, but the middle class has just become the parasites who feed on the national resources at the expense of the masses. They are not building the nation at all but building their stomachs.

4. **MARGINALIZATION AND EXPLOITATION;** Furthermore in the poem, the two parties represent the two strands of nation builders that are in most African states. On one side there are those represented by the driver (the local masses) while on the other hand we have high class being represented by the PS. The later is very busy misuse the public funds which can be used to rebuild the nations. The masses are the hardworking people whose benevolence is easily taken for granted by those in power. There are those who eat extravagantly and those who work on empty stomachs. The persona himself comes from the marginalized class. His disillusionment is caused by lifestyles of African leaders and informs his fellow countrymen what is actually happening.

5. **AWARENESS;** The poem paints a picture of awareness that those who are oppressed are now aware that those in power are exploiting them. This is an important step as long as the liberation of the oppressed is concerned. It is also a significant step if the nation is to realize sustainable development where the national resources will be mutually utilized for the benefit of not only the ruling class but the masses as well. If we examine the end of the poem it seems to induce a kind of anger that should lead to vengeance (revenge). The persona is appealing to the oppressed to raise the occasion and deal with the ruling class. The fact that *"two nation builders/ arrived home this evening/with terrible stomach pain/the result of building the nation/different ways"* is more like an appeal to emotions where the persona seeks actions from the masses. In a way, the persona calls for a reaction towards the ruling class's hypocritical nation building where they pretend to have welfare of the masses at heart while in real sense they just want to capitalize on their efforts.

6. **VULNERABILITY OF HUMANITY;** Nevertheless, the persona seems to have hopes in some facts that both the African bourgeoisie and the proletariats have their points of vulnerability. They both suffer in one way or another because of their own actions and lifestyles. For instance the driver becomes sick because of lack of food while the PS becomes sick for eating too much.

> So Ps has ulcers too!
> My ulcers I think are equally painful
> Only they are caused by hunger,
> No sumptuous lunches!

RELEVANCE

The poem is relevant in our country in a number of ways. Today we have a lot of leaders who misuse the public funds while those who are involved in the means of production live in dire poverty. Hypocrisy has also become a way of life. Classes, exploitation and marginalization are also major issues in our society.

Figures of speech;

1. **Alliteration**
   "Highly delicate diplomatic duties...
   And secretly smiling…

Cold Bell beer"
2. **Barbarism;** e.g. *Mwananchi, I too had none!*
3. **Onomatopoeia;** e.g. *Ah,* he continued yawning again. This is the sound of yawning
4. **Satire;** Lunch is called an important urgent function, this is very satirical
   "To an important urgent function
   In fact to a luncheon at the Vic"
5. **Irony;** The title of the poem '***Building the Nation"*** is ironical because the guys in the poem were not building the nation.
6. **Repetition;** e.g. " Building the nation"
7. **Rhetorical question;** e.g. " Did you have any lunch friend"
8. **Sarcasm;** bitter words have been used e.g. " menu reflected its importance"

AFRICA BY David Diop (Senegal)

Africa my Africa
Africa of proud warriors in the ancestral savannahs
Africa of whom my grandmother sings
On the banks of the distant river
I have never known you
But your blood flows in my veins
Your beautiful black blood that irrigates the fields
The blood of your sweat
The sweat of your work
The work of your slavery
The slavery of your children
Africa tell me Africa
Is this you this back that is bent
This back that breaks under the weight of humiliation
This back trembling with red scars
And saying yes to the whip under the midday sun
But a grave voice answers me
Impetuous son that tree young and strong
That tree there
In splendid loneliness amidst white and faded flowers
That is Africa your Africa
That grows again patiently obstinately
And its fruit gradually acquires
The bitter taste of liberty.

THEMATIC ANALYSIS;
1. **EXPLOITATION;** There are evidences of exploitation in the poem in the fact that the poet expresses how the sweat of Africans was lost in vain.
   "The blood of your sweat
   He sweat of your work"

All this was done at a time when Africans were turned into slaves and worked for their masters without any benefit.

> "The work of your slavery
>> The slavery of your children"

2. **OPPRESSION AND HUMILIATION;** Oppression and humiliation were common practices in colonial time. They were used to force Africans work for colonizers without objection. This has left scars to Africa that we still depend on them even when they seem to mistreat us.

>> "This back that breaks under the weight of humiliation
>>> This back trembling with red scars
>>> And saying yes to the whip under the midday sun"

3. **IDENTITY AND AWARENESS;** The poet however seems to be aware of his identity as black African. Although he grew up in France he shows that black blood flows in his veins, which is to say he is still an African regardless of where he grew up.

>> "I have never known you
>>> But your blood flows in my veins"

The voice that answers Diop sums up his African identity.

>> "Impetuous son that tree young and strong
>>> That tree there
>>> In splendid loneliness amidst white and faded flowers
>>> That is Africa your Africa."

4. **EFFECTS OF COLONIALISM;** The poet concludes his poem by showing the effects that colonialism had on African continent. Nevertheless, he seems to be optimistic that at least Africa is growing up again just like a young tree.

>> "That is Africa your Africa
>>> That grows again patiently obstinately"

Figures of speech;

1. **Anadiplosis;** the repetition in which the last expression of one statement becomes the first expression in the following statement;

>> "The blood of your sweat
>>> The sweat of your work
>>> The work of your slavery
>>> The slavery of your children"

2. **Rhetorical question** a question that does not need a reply. *"Is that you this back that is bent"*

3. **Symbolism; e.g.** *Scars', 'whip' and 'blood'.* They stand for the torture that Africans went through in colonial time. *Black blood-* symbolizes African identity.

4. **Personification;** The poet addresses Africa as though it is a human being and has blood that flows, and can sweat etc.

5. **Alliteration-** repetition of similar consonant sounds at the beginning of consecutive words *"You beautiful black blood"*

6. **Repetition** (for emphasis).The word Africa is repeated 7 times throughout the poem E.g. **Africa my Africa.**

7. **Under exaggeration;** "*Your beautiful black blood*". This is under exaggeration because there is no black blood in color.

SUMMONS RY RICHARD MABALA

YOU ARE LOST by Isack Mruma

To you dada.
it's the days that matter,
for we are unable to chat
in the language we had.

When I look at you
and see my pay slip
in your eyes
I feel empty
and sapped.

Your glance, sister,
is to me the measure
of the heat of the dough
in my pocket.

Never are passions cool,
To you I am now a tool,
And all my wage is now the fare:
I ride on your throbbing kisses.

It is you I accuse,
Because your love is lost,
And you only touch me
With the tenderness that asks
Where my wallet is.

It is to you dada,
that my pen tears the pad,
For I only see your love
Focused on my purse
with your passions
chasing my bank account.

THEMATIC ANALYSIS

1. **HYPOCRITICAL LOVE;** The kind of love portrayed in this poem is not the trueone. It is a love focused on money. This girl kissesthe man only when she notices that he has money. Ifthe guy happens to have no money she minds her own business, then there is no love.

    Your glance sister,

Is to me the measure
Of the heat of the dough
In my pocket

The persona shows that the girl has turned him into the tool of production or the source of income. He works and his entire wage is claimed by the woman.

Never are passions cool
To you I am now a tool
And all my wage is now the fare
I ride on your throbbing kisses

2. **PROTEST/CONFLICT;** The man in the poem shows a sense of protestbecause he has realized that his mistress is not intrue love with him. The woman's love is focused onthe money she gets. When no money, no love. Sothe man is protesting against his mistress' behavior.

It is to you dada
That my pen tears the pad
For I only see your love
Focused on my purse (wallet)

3. **AWARENESS;** The man is aware that the woman is only exploiting her money in the name of love. Even when she pretends to touch him romantically, she just searches for the wallet. So the man has realized that her love was lost a long time ago, what makes it going is money. Here says the poet;

It is you I accuse,
Because your love is lost
And you only touch me
With the tenderness that asks
Where my wallet is

4. **PROSTITUTION;** The woman seems to be engaged in prostitutionbecause her love is for sale. She looks for peoplewith money and has no true love. This is a verydangerous behavior because it exposes her toterrible sexually transmitted diseases. The manshows that the woman is always chasing his bankaccount.

For I only see your love
Focused on my purse
With your passions
Chasing my bank account.

5. **EXPLOITATION;** The woman in this poem seems to exploit the man. He works hard but all he earns goes to the woman. As he says in the 3rd stanza

To you I am now a tool,
And all my wage is now the fare:
I ride on your throbbing kisses.

What lessons do you lean from the poem?

1. Prostitution is dangerous because it may expose someone to STDs.

2. Love based on money is not good. Because when one runs out of money love is lost altogether.
3. Hypocrisy in love should be discarded/discouraged.
4. Men should be aware of the tricks girls use to get their money.

FIGURES OF SPEECH;
1. **Barbarism;**
   To you dada
   It is to you dada
2. **Personification;**
   ... the tenderness that asks where my wallet is
   With your passion chasing my bank account.
3. **Exaggeration;** e.g.*When I look at you and see my pay slip in your eyes*
4. **Metaphor;** e.g.*To you I am now a tool,*
5. **Repetition;** e.g.*dada*

HOLLOW HEADS BY JWANI MWAIKUSA

Hollow heads torture me with ignorance,
Blind eyes harass me with darkness,
Deaf ears tire me with silence,
Dumb voices deafen me with gibberish,
Blank minds confuse me with emptiness,
And, above all,
There is power and command.

With wits and ears and eyes,
I have speech and a strong mind,
But I remain weak and powerless.
They oppress me, they torture me
They fight me, they kill me.
It's a fight to bring me down to silence,
To darkness and gibberish, to ignorance,
And through brainwashing to emptiness.

All right, my friends,
It's a battle and I'll fight it.
Ears and wits and eyes and speech,
And a strong conscience:
These are my weapons,

And I will fight to the last cell.

THEMATIC ANALYSIS;
1. **TORTURE AND OPPRESSION;** The persona complains for the torture and oppression he gets from those in power. Those in power are not intellectually powerful as thepersona

and he uses different images to describe their incompetence. These are blind eyes, deaf ears, dumb voices, blank mind etc all theseshow that he is fighting against empty-headed people who cannot reason properly. He says

"I have speech and strong mind,
But I remain weak and powerless,
They oppress me they torture me"

2. **INTELLECTUAL BATTLE/PROTEST;** The persona describes his opponents as empty-headed with brainwashing ideas. They want to silence him that he may not express himself. They even want to kill him as a way of silencing him. He raises an open protest against this oppression and torture from the ruling class.

All right, my friends,
It's a battle and I'll fight it.

Ears and wits and eyes and speech,
And a strong conscience:
These are my weapons

3. **SACRIFICE AND COURAGE;** The persona shows that although his opponents are powerful he is not going to retreat easily. He says it is a battle and he has to fight it even to the last cell. Sacrifice and courage are very important when dealing with brainwashing from the ruling class. In the last stanza the poet says;*And I will fight to the last cell*

4. **CONSCIOUSNESS;** The persona in this poem is aware of problems. He knows that ignorance tortures. He is also aware that the enemies surrounding him are strong. So there is a need for sacrificing. He is aware that all these evils have a negative effect to him. They torture, kill and silence him. In the second stanza he says:

"With wits and ears and eyes,
I have speech and strong mind,
But I remain weak and powerless"

FIGURES OF SPEECH;

1. **Irony:** All right my friends. (He calls his enemies his friends)
2. **Parallelism;** They oppress me, they torture me, they fight me ,they kill me
3. **Personification:** hollow heads, blind eyes, deaf ears blank minds, are personified that they can, torture, harass, tire, deafen and confuse, respectively.

What message does it carry?

1. There should be freedom of speech and conscience for intellectuals to give their views.
2. Sacrifice is important if you want to achieve a particular cause.
3. Oppression and ignorance are obstacles in the creation of ideal society and building the future.

LIVE AND LET DIE by KUNDI FARAJA

One says that
My children are dwarfs
That no one seems taller
Than the other.
That they never take a bath

That they are soiled.
That they eat lice
From their clothes
Let them eat, brothers,
Until the system changes,
Until exploitation ends;
Let them eat brother,
Because we are on the way
To build Ujamaa
But, at present,
The system has not changed.

Let them eat, brother,
Because the rich nations
Are not yet ready
To die a little
So that the poor nation may live:
Let them eat, brother,
Because the rich man
Is not yet ready
To die a little
So that the poor man may live

Let them drink water,
Let them eat air,
Let them digest the sunshine
Because that is what
I can afford to buy.
Meanwhile I wait
For Uhuru to flower,
For Uhuru to come
When the time is ripe.

Let them eat brother,
Because the rich man
Is convinced that
It's because I'm lazy
That they don't have food.
That they don't have good health.
That they wear rags.
And that their house
Is like an abandoned hut

Let them eat brother
Because the rich man
Thinks that it's because

I don't plan my family

Let them eat brother.
Because the rich man
Does not like to hear
That he is rich
Because of me
That I work hard,
But for him and
Not for myself
That it's only because
I'm a slave of a system
That I lead a poor life.

THEMATIC ANALYSIS;

1. **POVERTY;** The poem discusses how poverty dehumanizes the dignity of people and makes them slaves for the rest of their lives. The poet complains because people keep on mocking his/her children that they are dwarfs, dirty and hungry. However he shows that it is the exploitative system that keeps him/her at the bottom.

> Until the system changes,
> Until exploitation ends

He also shows that it is even harder to get food although he states it in a more exaggerated manner. He does all this however to show his dissatisfaction towards the system.

> Let them drink water,
> Let them eat air.
> Let them digest the sunshine
> Because that is what
> I can afford to buy

The excuses of the rich are that, the poor man is poor because he does not plan his family and is lazy.

2. **EXPLOITATION;** The poem shows that one of the reasons we have poor people is because the rich are feeding on their efforts and resources. In any society where the bourgeoisie class exploits the proletariats the poor live miserably. The poet shows that there is exploitation at individual level, national level and international level. At individual level the poet says

> That he is rich
> Because of me
> That I work hard,
> But for him and
> Not for myself

At national level he shows that the system of the country also exploits its citizens and there are no changes yet.

> Until the system changes,

Until exploitation ends

At international level he shows that the rich nations also exploit the poor nations.
>Because the rich nations
>Are not yet ready
>To die a little
>So that the poor nation may live

3. **CLASSES;** Another issue discussed is the issue of stratification on economic basis. The poet shows that there are two contrasting classes in this society-Therich and the poor. He goes a step ahead by showing that the poor are so because of the exploitative system that favors the rich at the expensesof the poor.He says:
>Because the rich man
>Is not yet ready
>To die a little
>So that the poor man may live

There are rich and poor people in the society. Nevertheless, these rich people have become parasites who feed on the blood of the poor. So the poor get poorer and poorer while the rich get richer and richer. The poet uses the figurative language that the rich ought to die a little that the poor may live. Actually he does not refer to death as we literally know it, but at least that the rich should be ready to consider the poor people by helping them to get their basic needs.

4. **NEO-COLONIALISM;** The poet shows the cases of neo-colonialism and how it has put a powerful influence on the poor nations. The poet shows that at international level there are also rich and poor nations. But the poor nations are in the state of poverty because the rich nations keep on exploiting them. The rich nations, like rich people are not read to sacrifice some of their demands so that the poor nations may rise out of poverty. The poet says
>Because the rich nations
>Are not yet ready
>To die a little
>So that the poor nation may live

5. **AWARENESS;** The poet is aware that his poverty is caused by exploitation by the rich people. He is aware that his efforts are wasted because he is not working for his own welfare but his efforts benefit the rich. However the sad thing is that he is not ready to do anything to change his current state. He is patiently and optimistically waiting for the system to change by chance. That is not a good approach for building the future. People must be active and take measures to solve the problems facing them.
>Let them eat, brothers,
>Until the system changes,
>Until exploitation ends

He believes that the time is not yet ready for him to enjoy the fruits of independence and he says.

> Meanwhile I wait
> For Uhuru to flower,
> For Uhuru to come
> When the time is ripe.

6. **BAD LEADERSHIP;** The poet has also discussed about bad leadership. Rich people especially leaders and rich nations have been exploiting the resources and efforts of poor nations but they claim that it's because poor nations are lazy, have no family planning etc that's why we are poor. They don't remember that they are rich because of exploiting our efforts and resources. He says

> Because the rich man
> Does not like to hear
> That he is rich
> Because of me
> That I work hard,
> But for him and
> Not for myself

7. **IRRESPONSIBILITY;** The ruling class is irresponsible as they exploit the efforts of the poor and claim that the poor are lazy and they don't plan their family that is why they are poor, have no food in the house, and have poor health and so on. Irresponsibility is also seen on the side of the citizens. While the persona knows that he is poor because of the rich person/nation. He is not ready to take any measures to change this status. This is irresponsibility. He believes that the time will come when the system will change automatically.

> Until the system changes,
> Until exploitation ends

8. **MALNUTRITION;** The children are suffering from malnutrition as a result they have impaired growth. They look like dwarfs and that no one looks taller than the other. This is a result of eating poor diet or lack of proper balanced diet. The poet uses strong images to show his dissatisfaction. He says

> Let them eat air,
> Let them digest the sunshine
> Because that is what
> I can afford to buy.

The fact that the persona says his children eat lice, air, and digest the sunshine, is an emotional appeal to show his deep dissatisfaction about the current situation.

9. **POOR LIVING CONDITIONS;** The standard of living among most Africans is below the average. Most people are living poor life. They do not get important and necessary services at better level, i.e. few schools, poor health centers, poor communication systems, etc. Due to this, children are getting Kwashiorkor as a result of underfeeding. The existing system has failed to solve problems in order to improve the living condition. The poet says,

one says that
My children are dwarfs
That no one seems taller
Than the other
That they never take a bath
That they are soiled

What lessons do you get?

1. The rich people should stop exploiting the poor people.
2. Classes are an obstacle to national development.
3. Poor countries should be careful with the tricks used by rich nations to exploit our resources.
4. The poor should take measures to change the system instead of waiting for the system to change automatically.
5. Bad leadership and irresponsibility are obstacles to individual and national development.

FIGURES OF SPEECH;

1. **Overstatement/exaggeration;** the poet exaggerates some facts in this way; that his children eat lice, air and sunshine.
   Let them eat air.
   Let them digest the sunshine
2. **Personification;** The rich and poor nations are regarded as people who can live or die.
   Because the rich nations/Are not yet ready/to die a little/ so that the poor nation may live
3. **Parallelism;**
   Let them drink water,
   Let them eat air.
   Let them digest the sunshine
4. **Simile;** e.g. And that their house is like an abandoned hut
5. **Barbarism** (using more than one language)
   - To build Ujamaa (Ujamaa is a Swahili word which means socialism)
   - For Uhuru to flower (Uhuru a Swahili word which means independence)
6. **Metaphor;** e.g.*I'm a slave of the system*
7. **Anaphora;**
   That they never take a bath
   That they are soiled.
   That they eat lice

DEVELOPMENT by Kundi Faraja

A man of the people
Enters his office
To sit on the throne
Of Party and State,
His stick of power
Across the table.

He looks into the files
To see the demands
Of the millions of people
Who for years since Uhuru
Have just managed to survive
They ring out one message
Man of the people
You have always been telling us
What we need…
Health centre,
More schools,
Clean water,
Better transport facilities,
Better living conditions.

Do you plead incapable
To bring about development?

I declare running
Better than walking
For a young and poor country;
I plead fighting underdevelopment
Tougher than fighting
A wounded buffalo
With a pocket knife;
I plead underdevelopment
Stronger than the blows of the sea
When the hurricane is at its height.

I plead fighting underdevelopment
Tougher than combating colonialism;
I see that it's more difficult
To maintain peace
Than to stop a coup d'état.

I plead the cry
Of the nation
More painful than the yell
Of a woman
As her husband dies in sickness;
It's more painful than the screams
Of a man
Dying in agony
In the coils of the greatest python
Found in the African forest.

How is development
To be brought brother
When the people to whom
We have entrusted power
Are corrupt?

I plead the stomachs
Of the privileged few
Greater than the Rift-Valley;
They cannot be satisfied
With a normal share.

I plead the thirst
Of the minority
Greater than that of the Sahara;
No rain can quench it.

I reckon the minority
More sensitive to egoism
Than to National Development ;
Nothing that is not theirs
Is of any interest.

Their response to egoism,
Is faster than camera film to light
But as slow as tropism
To nation-building.

The majority plead
Exploited,
Cheated,
Disregarded,
But, brother,
How is development to come?

THEMATIC ANALYSIS

1. **SELFISHNESS (EGOISM);** Most post-colonial African leaders are thinking in terms of me, myself and I. Although the resources of the country ought to benefit bothclasses, the lower class has remained spectators of the game. The high class misuses the national resources at the expenses of the lower. KundiFaraja criticizes the hypocritical behavior of most African leaders who think of themselves (being the minority) while the majority whoseefforts are wasted are disregarded. The national resources are not distributed equally anymore. Their selfish tendencies are expressed by thepoet in these terms.

   "I reckon the minority
   More sensitive to egoism
   Than to national development

Nothing that is not theirs
Is of any interest."

The issue of national development that was at the top of the agenda has now turned only a daydream. To the leaders he asks;
"Do you plead incapable
To bring about development?"

2. **CORRUPTION;** Shortly after independence in an attempt to lift ourselves up from the bottom of colonialism in which we had fallen unwillingly, the nation identified three enemies that we had to fight tooth and nail in order to stand on our own feet. These included; poverty, ignorance and disease. Nevertheless in the long run corruption emerged and added to their number and has since then become tougher than the first three enemies. It is however sad to note that it's not the common people who are at the forefront in giving and receiving corruption but the leaders. Critically speaking, the issue of development is even more complicated when we come to think of the fact that those to whom we have entrusted power are the same who are corrupt. Thus the poet comes to a point when he shows there is no way a country whose leaders have invested in corruption can develop. No way! He says
"How is development
To be brought brother
When the people to whom
We have entrusted power
Are corrupt?"

Implicitly, the poet is calling for action. Because we did a mistake in the first place by giving corrupt leaders the mandate to rule us, do we still need to continue with them even when we realize that they have hypocritically, betrayed our cause? Think of it.

3. **CLASSES AND MARGINALIZATION;** Practically speaking, classes in any society are inevitable. However, the sociological investment should be more of how to bring about a harmonious relationship among the existing classes than how to neutralize them. In most cases it has been evident that whenever these classes exist, the high class oppresses, exploits and marginalizes the lower. To show how detrimental class division can be in any society, the poet uses strong metaphorical comparisons to bring the message home. While the minority (whom he calls privileged few) enjoys the national cake, the majority have been marginalized and disregarded.
"I plead the stomachs
Of the privileged few
Greater than the rift valley
They cannot be satisfied
With a normal share."

Their thirst he compares with that of the Sahara desert which no rain can quench. In other words he is trying to say that there is no point they will be satisfied if at all the majority will stay staring at them waiting sympathetically for their turn. Never!

4. **EXPLOITATION;** Although exploitation was condemned in colonial time as being detrimental to the national development, it is wonderful that today it has been the major means of capital accumulation by the bourgeoisie class in the post colonial Africa. Evidences show that most leaders who climb up the leadership ladder, begin while they are as poor as flies but in no time they become distinguished petty bourgeoisies. In the poem, the poet continues to point a finger at the leaders who exploit the masses.

> *"The majority plead*
> *Exploited."*

5. **POOR SOCIAL SERVICES AND DISILLUSIONMENT;** One of the main topics that dominated political policies in colonial era was the improvement of people's ways of life after the attainment of Uhuru. Most people, regarding the suffering they had experienced in colonial time, and considering the fact that colonial social services wereprovided on the basis of color (race) and economic status, they fought for independence heart and soul. To their surprise, today the same leaders who promised to help the common people to improve their ways of life in their free countries, have betrayed their cause. This is to say, social services for the poor have remained as poor as before. Today the masses are disillusioned and they ask.

> *"Man of the people*
> *You have always been telling us*
> *What we need*
> *Health centers*
> *More schools*
> *Clean water*
> *Better transport facilities*
> *Better living conditions"*

This however, is not what turned out to be. The millions of people still live in the same lifestyle they lived before independence. To them, independence is but a change of color from white colonialists to black colonialists.

6. **AWARENESS;** The kind of awareness portrayed in the poem is that which the marginalized classes have towards the ruling class. The minority seems to be awareof everything that is taking place. In so far as the liberation of the oppressed is concerned, awareness is a very important step at least as the firstthing to start with. Additionally, it is a very vital step towards national development where the national resources will benefit both the ruling class and the masses. Because of this sense of awareness they ring out one message demanding for their right.

7. **IRRESPONSIBILITY;** This is a state whereby leaders are not thinking enough about the effects of what they do or not showing a feeling of responsibility. In this poem leaders are irresponsible. They are no longer concerned about the welfare of their people but they are caught up in the same evil lifestyle of their colonial masters. The majority has been left in the periphery while the minority is enjoying the national cake. That's why the majority class is asking?

> *"Do you plead incapable*
> *To bring about development?"*

This is to say the majority of people are now aware of their leaders' irresponsibility and triviality.

8. **BUILDING THE FUTURE/STRUGGLE FOR CHANGE;** The persona proposes several changes that have to be taken by poor nations if they need to realize sustainable development. Changes cannot be brought if the majority sits and waits for their time. He shows for instance that development cannot be brought by corrupt leaders. The implication is that they should change the ruling system. But also he declares running better than walking for poor nations. People must work harder than they are doing currently to fight for development.

> *"I declare running*
> *Better than walking*
> *For a young and poor country;*
> *I plead fighting underdevelopment*
> *Tougher than fighting*
> *A wounded buffalo"*

Therefore, as a matter of facts, irresponsible leaders, corrupt rulers and selfish behavior of the few, will still remain the obstacles to development if at all the masses remain passive. The end of the poem seems to have a sense of calling for action. He leaves the audience with the question for everybody to ask him/herself. "How is development to come?" Another similar question could be "Do we have to sit and wait for our turn? Think about it.

MESSAGES;

1. If the leaders are not careful with national development one day the majority might stage a revolution.
2. Awareness is an important tool in so far as the liberation of the oppressed is concerned.
3. Corrupt leaders are an obstacle to national development.
4. Bringing about development is not a simple task or a cheap commodity. It needs determination, dedication and focus.
5. Exploitation and misuse of public resources for private gain is also an obstacle to development.
6. Selfishness is not good if we need to bring about sustainable development.
7. The leaders should fulfill their promises to the majority when they get power.

FIGURES OF SPEECH;

1. **Barbarism.** Using more than one language in a literary work e.g. *"Who for years since Uhuru"*
2. **Parallelism;**
   > *"Health centers*
   > *More schools*
   > *Clean water*
   > *Better transport facilities*
   > *Better living conditions"*
3. **Rhetorical question**

> **Examples;**
> *Do you plead incapable to bring about development?*
> *When the people to whom we have entrusted power are corrupt?*
> *How is development to come?*

4. Hyperbole/exaggeration
Examples;
- I plead the stomachs of the privileged few greater than the rift valley.
- I plead the thirst of the minority greater than that of the Sahara.

5. **Simile;** e.g. *"But as slow as tropism to nation-building"*
6. **Imagery;** There are several images in this poem which the reader can imagine of in terms of; Visual image- this is an image of sight e.g.
   - Greater than the Rift-Valley;
   - Camera film to light, coils of the greatest python
   - Stronger than the blows of the sea
   - When the hurricane is at its height.
   - Organic image -this is image of feeling
   - Dying in agony
   - More painful than the yell
   - Audio image – this is an image of sound
   - The yell of a woman
   - I plead the cry of the nation
   - the screams of a man
   - Kinetic image -this is an image of motion.
   - Is faster than camera film
   - But as slow as tropism
   - I declare running
   - Better than walking
7. **Personification** has been used in this poem. This can be seen in the stanza fourteen when a country is given qualities of running and walking. The persona says:
   > *"I declare running*
   > *Better than walking*
   > *For a young and poor country..."*

SONG OF LAWINO AND OCOL by OKOT P'BITEK (UGANDA)
INTRODUCTION

- *Okot P'Bitek* (7th June, 1931 – 20th July 1982) was a Ugandan poet, who achieved wide international recognition for *Song of Lawino*, a long poem dealing with the tribulations of a rural African wife whose husband has taken up urban life and wishes everything to be westernized. *Song of Lawino* was originally written in the Acholi language, (*Wer pa Lawino*) self-translated to English, and published in 1966.
- It was a breakthrough work, creating an audience among Anglophone Africans for direct, topical poetry in English; and incorporating traditional attitudes and thinking in an

accessible yet faithful literary vehicle. It was followed by the pendant *Song of Ocol* (1970), the husband's reply. (Wikipedia)

- Both *Song of Lawino* and *Song of Ocol* are dramatic monologues. A dramatic monologue is like a play in which there are no actions or movements and only one person speaks. The poet pretends to be someone else and uses the voice of that person to tell the story or express the ideas he is interested in.
- So in *"Song of Lawino"* we only hear what Lawino has to say, whilst in *"Song of Ocol"* we only hear Ocol's voice. Both of these poems express a set of ideas rather than telling a story. All of the ideas that Lawino expresses are connected with her argument with Ocol which she tells us briefly in the first few lines of section 1.

CHAPTERS SUMMARY

CHAPTER 1

The first Chapter sets up the differences between Lawino andOcol. Ocol despises Black people and their traditional ways andhas adopted Europeans values. Because he works in thegovernment, he wants to modernize Africa in those values. Lawinodisagrees and implores her husband to stop hating his ownpeople:

«He says Black people are primitive
And their ways are utterly harmful
Their dances are mortal sins
They are ignorant, poor and diseased! ...»(SOL, P. 36).

In this Chapter, Lawino asserts that Ocol is rude and abusive bothto her and other people:

«My husband abuses me together with my parents
He says terrible things about my mother
And I am so ashamed! ...» (SOL, P.35).

CHAPTER 2

The Second Chapter addresses the issue of Ocol's new wife.Ocol's new wife, unlike Lawino, is thoroughly Europeanized. Herewe note that the attack starts as a fairly straight forward factualaccount of Lawino's husband's preference for a modern girl. Then

to enable Lawino to advance her argument forcefully, Okot givesher the gift of wit and employs Acoli poetic forms to produce apungent work of satire. She first displays her wit forcefully at thebeginning of Chapter two, where (she) Lawino makes a mockeryof modern notions of beauty, including the use of make-up andcosmetics, by comparing her rival, Clementine, the girl of modernways, to what in traditional Acoli Society must be regarded as theugliest and most weird of all creatures. That which is consideredmost beautiful by admires of European culture is made to appearabsurd and grotesque. We quote a long passage to show how shebuilds up her argument:

«Ocol is no longer in love with;
The old type;

He is in love with a modern girl;

The name of the beautiful one;

Is Clementine;

Brother, when you see Clementine!

The beautiful one aspires;

To look like a white woman;

Her lips are red-hot;

Like glowing charcoal;

She resembles the wild cat;

That has dipped its mouth in blood;

Her mouth is like raw yaws;

Tina dusts powder on her face;

And it looks so pale ;...»(SOL, P.37).

In the Second Stanza the tone changes dramatically to acontemptuous one: «Brother, when you see Clementine!» Thenthe criticism gathers momentum and builds up to a crescendo aswe get horrible image after horrible image in the process of whichClementine is disfigured and transformed from «the beautiful oneinto a veritable»guinea fowl». But that is not the end .BeforeLawino is done, she must demonstrate to us how she, Lawino, ispossessed by strange ghosts which make if necessary for a wholeritual to be performed before she can recover:

«The smell of carbolic soap;

Makes me sick;

And the smell of powder;

Provokes the ghosts in my head;

It is then necessary to fetch a goat;

From my mother's brother;

The sacrifice over;

The ghost -dance drum must sound;

The ghost be laid;

And my peace restored.»(SOL, P.37).

In this Chapter Two, Lawino is not unfair to Europeans. She is nottrying to impose her set of beliefs on them. She is using herprejudices in an argument with other Africans within Africa. Butshe is unreasonable in some of her criticism of Clementine and

Ocol. Some of her comments are little more than scandal-mongering for example when she first attacks Clementine, theclimax of her abuse is:

«Perhaps she has aborted many!

Perhaps she has thrown her twins

In the pit latrine!» (SOL, P.39).

In this same chapter we notice that Lawino is not only witty, shealso versatile, conjuring up all kinds of images to bring her goinghome. This talent is coupled with a sense of humour and an abilityto admit her weaknesses in a clever way, as in the followingpassage in which she cunning confesses that she is jealous of thewoman she ostensibly despises:

«Forgive me, broth

Do not think I am insulting

The woman with whom I share

My husband!

Do not think my tongue

Is being sharpened by jealousy

It is the sight of Tina

That provokes sympathy from

my heart.» (SOL, P.39)

Then the truth comes out:

«I do not deny

I am a little jealous

It is no good lying,

We all suffer from a little jealousy.

It catches you unawares

Like the ghosts that bring fevers;

It surprises people

Like earth tremors:

But when you see the beautiful woman

With whom I share my husband

You feel a little pity for her.» (SOL, P.39).

By the end of this section, Lawino turns on her attacks andexposes their own immorality and hypocrisy.

These attacks on Western ways are one of the reasons for thepopular success of the poem. Okot is making a number of veryserious points through Lawino's mockery of Westernized ways.Here, Lawino shows ways in which Western things can be dirty,

stupid or hypocritical. At the same time she shows how traditionalways of life allow her to express herself fully and freely as awoman. Both ways of life are open to criticism, both ways arevalid. If Lawino has learnt one way of life, why should she change?Why should the Massai wear trousers? The words like «Witch»,«Kaffirs» and «sorcerers» that Ocol throws at her don't answerthat question.

But Lawino does not believe that the two ways of life are equallyvalid for Africans, and neither does Okotp'Bitek. She thinks thecustoms of white probably suit white people. She does not mindthem following their own ways.

«I do not understand

The ways of foreigners

But I do not despise their customs» (SOL, P. 41).

The poet has used the proverb in closing this second chapterwhich is an Acoli proverb:

«The pumpkin in the old homestead

Must not be uprooted» (SOL, P.41).

According to Okot (1972:6) pumpkins are a luxury food. They growwild throughout Acoli land. To uproot pumpkins, even when youare moving to a new homestead, is simple wanton destruction. Inthis proverb, then, Lawino is not asking Ocol to cling to everything in his past, but rather not to destroy things for the sake ofdestroying them. In other words, what Lawino has to say wouldhave been better expressed by another Acoli proverb Doko abilani eye meni (Your first Wife is your Mother) (SOL,P.13).To meanthat you cannot abandon your first pot, for your first pot is alwaysthe best one.

CHAPTER 3

In Chapter Three, Lawino praises the cultural dances of herpeople:

«I cannot dance the rumba,

My mother taught me

The beautiful dances of Acoli.

I do not know the dances of white people.

I will no deceive you,

I cannot dance the samba,

You once saw me at the Orak dance

The dance for youths

The dance of our people» (SOL, P.42).

Accoding to p'Bitek, the «dirty gossip» of colonialists condemnedAfrican dances because of the immorality of nakedness. Lawinodoes not waste her time on a reasoned and balanced defence ofdancing naked. She presents the openness, liveliness andhealthiness of Acoli dance positively, without apology:

«When the drums are throbbing

And the black youths

Have raised much dust

You dance with vigour and health

You dance naughtily with pride

You dance with Spirit,

You compete, you insult, you provoke

You challenge all», (SOL, P.42).

Notice that the dramatic reversal of values is not limited tocosmetic and make-up. It is only a prelude to a more generalizedattack on European social and cultural values which go againsttraditional codes of behaviour. Imported forms of dancing, forexample, result in immoral behaviour when each man dances witha woman who is not his wife .Then, Lawino goes to attack:

«Each man has a woman

Although she is not his wife,

They dance inside a house

And there is no light

Shamelessly, they hold each other

Tightly, tightly,

They cannot breathe» (SOL, P.44).

Western dances are immoral because people embrace in publicand dance with anyone, even close relatives said p'Bitek. Apartfrom being immoral, their kissing and dancing are seen asgrotesquely ugly:

«You kiss her on the cheek

As white people do,

You kiss her open-sore lips

As white people do

You suck slimy saliva

From each other's mouths

As white people do.»(SOL, P.44).

CHAPTER 4

The Fourth Chapter details when Lawino was a young woman andhow Ocol once wooed and won her .While she remembers Ocol `swooing of her and the beauty of her home, Lawino's voice takeson a note of nostalgia:

«When Ocol was wooing me

My breasts were erect

And they shook

As I walked briskly, And as I walked

I threw my long neck

This way and that way

Like the flower of the lyonno lily

Waving in a gentle breeze.» (SOL, P.47).

Then after, Lawino laments because her husband does not loveher any more:

«My husband says

He no longer wants a woman

With a gap in her teeth,

He is in love

With a woman

Whose teeth fill her mouth completely

Like the teeth of war- captives and slaves» (SOL, P.49).

CHAPTER 5

Chapter Five looks at question of what is considered beautiful.Ocol thinks the way Lawino does her hair is ugly; then shelaments:

«He says that I make his bed-sheets dirty

And his bed smelly

Ocol says

I look extremely ugly

When I am fully adorned

For the dance!» (SOL, P.53).

On the other hand Lawino praises her beauty and the beauty ofher people:

I am proud of the hair

With which I was born

And as no white woman

Wishes to do her hair

Like mine,

Because she is proud

Of the hair with which she was born.» (SOL, P.56)

Then after Lawino criticizes Ocol's wife's hair and that of hispeople:

«When the beautiful one

With whom I share my husband

Returns from cooking her hair

She resembles

A chicken

That has fallen into a pond;

Her hair looks

Like the python's discarded Skin.» (SOL, P.54).

In the previous paragraphs, it is said that Lawino is proud; she isproud; not only of her beauty, but of every aspect of her way oflife. From this position of pride she attacks:

«I have no wish

To look like a white woman.» (SOL, P.56).

Now Lawino makes the argument here that Ocol should not try tobe something he is not:

«No leopard

Would change into a hyena,

And the crested crane

Would hate to be changed

Into the bold-headed,

Dung-eating vulture,

The long-necked and graceful giraffe

Cannot become a monkey.

Let no one

Uproot the pumkin.» (SOL, P.56).

The message conveys by Lawino in this section is that Africanwomen are invited to run away from artificial and European waysof cooking hair for their beauty. They must remain natural. Theycould not abandon their traditions. The poem becomes an

argument honoring the traditional African values.

Along this Chapter, we also see Lawino's wit at work when shegives an account of the differences between European and Africantraditions and values. Ostensibly, her argument is that Europeanculture is good for Europeans and African culture good forAfricans, but in an apparently objective comparison she usessubtle animal imagery to portray a negative picture of things forEuropean and a positive picture of African values. This isparticularly striking in this Chapter Five, where the dominant motifis the comparison of the «graceful giraffe», which symbolizes thebeauty of the African Woman, and the «monkey» which stands forthe Ugliness of white women and those who ape whites bywearing white people's wigs: See the example given above fromsong of Lawino page 56.

CHAPTER 6

Chapter Six deals with food and Ocol criticizes his wife for notcooking white people's meals:

«Ocol says

Black people's foods are primitive,

But what is backward about them?

He says

Black people's foods are dirty:

He means,

Some clumsy and dirty black women

Prepare food clumsily

And put them

In dirty containers.» (SOL, P.62).

Lawino again argues that the food that is native to her people isbest for them:

«Look,

Straight before you

Is the central pole

That shiny stool...

At the foot of the pole

Is my father's revered stool.

Further on

The rows of pots

Placed one on top of other

Are stores

And cupboards.

Millet flour, dried carcasses

Of various animals,

Beans, peas

Fish, dried cucumber...» (SOL, P.59).

Ocol criticizes the improved stove and Lawino praises it; Ocolgives his point of view of that improved stove:

«I really hate

The charcoal stove!

Your hand is always

Charcoal-dirty

And anything you touch

Is blackened;

And your finger nails

Resemble those of poison woman.» (SOL, P.57).

Now Lawino reacts:

«I am terribly afraid

Of the electric stove,

I do not like using it

Because you stand up

When you cook.» (SOL, P.58).

She points out another disadvantage of electric stove and sheapologizes that she has no notion about cooking white food.

«The electric fire kills people:

They say

It is lightning...» (SOL, P.57)

In this passage she accepts that she does not know such acooking:

«I do not know

How to cook

Like white women;

I do not enjoy

White men's foods;

And how they eat

How could I know?

And why should I know it?» (SOL, P.62).

In the closing lines of the poem of this section, the poet gives hispoint of view throughout Lawino that:

«I do not complain

That you eat

White men's foods

If you enjoy them

Go head

Shall we just agree

To have freedom

To eat what one likes?»(SOL, P.63).

He also shows the importance of the traditional cooking stove inmany societies which is improved for domestic cooking. So thepoet shows Lawino's weakness for not being to school to learnhow to use white men's cooking stoves. Lawino confesses:

«I confess,

I do not deny!

I do not know

How to cook like a white woman.» (SOL, P.57)

CHAPTER 7

The Seventh Chapter deals with the issues of time. In this section,Ocol puts accent on the respect of time. His wife Lawino reactsthat Ocol abuses of the way of using time because of hisarrogance for he loses his dignity. He is always in a hurry. He isalways ruled by time. Everything he does must take place at afixed time:

«If my husband insists

What exact time

He should have morning tea

And break fast,

When exactly to have coffee.»(SOL, P. 64).

Lawino doesn't understand the need for these set times. She doesthings when she wants to. Children are fed or washed when it isnecessary and:

«When sleep comes

Into their head

They sleep,

When sleep leaves their head

They wake up.»(SOL, P. 69)

If visitors come when you are doing something, you stop and enjoytheir visit. But Ocol has no time to enjoy anything:

«He never jokes

With anybody

He says

He has no time

To sit around the evening fire.» (SOL, P. 67)

All Ocol`s life is haunted by his fear of wasting time. For him, timeis a commodity which can be bought and sold. It must not bewasted because:

«Time is money» (SOL, P. 67);

While for Acoli time is not a commodity that can be consumed untilit is finished:

«In the wisdom of the Acoli

Time is not stupidly split up

Into seconds and minutes

It does not flow

Like beer in a pot

That is sucked

Until it is finished.» (SOL, P. 69).

Ocol in his arrogance does not know how to welcome visitors.When they appear at his door he tries to get rid of them quicklywith the question:

«What can I do for you?» (SOL, P. 68)

And even the crying of children makes him wild with rage becauseit interrupts his work:

«He says

He does not want

To hear noise,

Those children's cries

And coughs disturb him!» (SOL, P. 67).

Despite his high opinion of himself, he is no more than a servant oftime:

«Time has become

My husband`s master» (SOL, P. 68).

No one likely to respect him because of his unkindness, andbecause he:

«...Runs from place to place

Like a small boy,

He rushes without dignity» (SOL, P. 68).

In addition to investing Lawino with a witty mind, a sense ofhumour capacity for dramatization, Okot p`Bitek has the ability tomake use of traditional troupes and modes of expression in amanner which enriches his poetry and lends it a peculiarfreshness. Comparing the modern technological concepts of timewith Acoli concepts, Lawino describes the Acoli idea of latemorning in the following terms:

«When the sun has grown up

And the poisoned tips

Of its arrows painfully bite

The backs of the women weeding or harvesting

This is when

You take drinking water

To the workers »(SOL, PP 64- 66).

To end this section, it is seen that Ocol is governed by time, oftenstating the hour whenever the sun rises. Lawino does notunderstand the importance of being led by such strict definitionsand thinks everything happens in its own time without forcing it.

This idea is followed into Chapter Eight when Lawino also arguesthat breast feeding isn't something you can hold strictly to time.When children are hungry, then they will be breastfed. To do it byOcol's way, children should be fed even if they are not hungry.

Religion, healthcare, politics are also dealt with.

CHAPTER 8

In Chapter Eight and Twelve, we have Lawino's explanation ofwhat has gone wrong. Ocol's teachers were like Lawino's teacherin the evening speaker's class. If Ocol had run from them to thedance as Lawino did he would have learnt things that meantsomething to him:

«We joined the line of friends

And danced among our age- mates

And Sang songs we understood.

Relevant and meaningful songs,

Songs about ourselves» (SOL, P.79).

Ocol wants Lawino to be christened, but she says that her eldersister was a protestant and she suffered bitterly in order to buy thename Lawino joined the catholic evening Speaker' class, but shedid not stay long in, she ran away:

«I ran away from shouting

Meaninglessly in the evenings

Like parrots

Like the crow birds

The things they shout

I do not understand»(SOL, P.75).

They do not understand what they shout and the teacher of theevening class controls them only by anger. It seems as if Ocol isstill like a parrot, boasting in the market place and condemningeverything that the white priests told him to condemn, instead ofpicking out the good from both African and European ways.Now Lawino is obliged to leave evening speaker's class:

«Anger welled up inside me

Burning my chest like bile,

I stood up

And two other girls stood up

We walked out

Out of that cold hall» (SOL, P.79).

To end this section, Lawino argues that their spiritual beliefs arejust as valid as Catholicism, but also points out the ignorance andarrogance of priest and nuns who run the missionaries in theirvillages.

CHAPTER 9

In Chapter Nine we see another aspect of Ocol's arrogance. HereLawino asks questions in a genuine mood of enquiry. She doesnot ask silly questions:

«Where is the pot?

Where it was dug,

On the mouth of which River?» (SOL, P.87).

Somewhere in Chapter Three, Lawino has spoken aboutimmorality in the dances of white men. The same question ofsexual morality is involved in her late comments on catholic priestand nuns. The tradition of priestly celibacy has a long history inEurope. There is also a long tradition of priestly hypocrisy, and ofliterary mockery of this hypocrisy. To Lawino the whole idea iscompletely incomprehensible. So when the Padré and the Nunshout at her, it must be their sexual frustration expressing itself:

«They are angry with me

As if it was I

Who prevented them marrying» (SOL, P.85).

Again no priest can possibly discipline his sexual desires. They are teacher from the evening speaker's class follows her to the dance.And every teacher must be like this:

«And all the teachers

Are alike

They have sharp eyes

For girls' full breast

Even the padres

Who are not allowed

To marry

Are troubled by health» (SOL, P.81).

To conclude this section, let us write that the problems of whocreated the creator and the mystery of the virgin birth areproblems which better educated people have found to be barriersto Christian belief. An educated Christian like Ocol ought to haveconsidered them. If he were really interested in knowledge, hewould be willing to discuss these things. But Lawino does not thinghe is really interested in knowledge. She wishes she had someoneelse to ask:

«Someone who has genuinely

Read deeply and widely

And not someone like my husband

Whose preoccupation

Is to boast in the market place...» (SOL, P.90).

Brief Lawino really makes us wonder whether this progressive andcivilised man deserves any respect with all his status. He surelyought to have a little more dignity. Above all he ought to treat hiswife, his parents and his home community with a little morerespect.

CHAPTER 10

Chapter Ten deals with Lawino's culture and its values. In thisChapter we are given further examples of Ocol's intolerance. Ocolwill let neither Lawino's relatives, nor his own relatives into hishouse because they might make it dirty or give diseases to hischildren.

«My husband complains

That I encourage visitors

Who should not

Come into his house,

Because they bring dirt and house-flies!» (SOL, P.91).

Ocol condemns all traditional medicines:

«He says

The medicine gourds are filthy,

And the herbs

Are drunk from unhygienic cups

My husband agrees

That sometimes by accident...»(SOL, P.93)

Again he condemns all traditional religious beliefs, because he isan educated man and a Christian. In the years since Uganda'sindependence, there has been a great deal of reassessment ofmissionaries views of African traditional beliefs by AfricanChristians .Ocol's attitudes have not changed at all. For himtraditional beliefs are no more than foolish superstitions:

«He says

No such things exist

It is my eyes

That are sick

And only foolish superstitions.»(SOL, P.92).

Ocol not only rejects these superstitions himself, he wants to wipethem out. He prevents Lawino from visiting the diviner priest ormaking sacrifices when she is in trouble:

«My husband has threatened

To beat me

If I visit the diviner- priest again.» (SOL, P.93)

When his father was alive, he:

«Once smashed up the rattle gourd

Cut open the drum

And chased away the diviner priest

From his late father's homestead.» (SOL, P.95).

He later tried to destroy the tree on father's shrine. Ocol is areligious man yet. Lawino must not wear charms, yet he wears acrucifix:

«My husband wears

A small crucifix

On his neck»(SOL,P.93).

For him prayer can be effective:

«It is stupid superstition superstition

To pray to our ancestors

To avert the smallpox,

But we should pray

To the messengers of the hunch back

To intercede for us.»(SOL, P.93).

Ocol sees no similarity between the two sorts of charms or the twosorts of prayer. Ocol continues to praise White man's medicines.Since the time of patient has not yet come to death every medicinecures him says Lawino:

«It is true

White man's medicines are strong,

But Acoli medicine

Are also strong.

The sick gets cured

Because his time has not yet come.»(SOL, P.101).

Once the time comes, the death knocks at your door, there is nostop. Whatever medicine cannot cure the sick. Even crucifixes,rosaries, toes of edible rates,...none of them can block the path ofno return (SOL, P.102)

«When death comes

To fetch you

She comes unannounced

She comes suddenly

Like the vomit of days...»(SOL, P.102).

Lawino says that Ocol should be tolerent for, once mother deathcomes, there is no excuse, neither black nor white it calls themand they have no power on it:

«White diviner priest,

Acoli herbalists,

All medicine men and medicine

Are good, are brilliant

When the day has not yet dawned

For the great journey

The last safari

To pagak.» (SOL, P.103).

CHAPTER 11

Brief you may be the man of whatever rank, you cannot resistwhen death comes to fetch you. Chapter Eleven ofSong ofLawinois a very rich poem, Addressing important issues affectingpost-independence Africa. The poem is a satirical comment on theneo-colonial mentality of the African petty bourgeoisie-theintellectuals and political leaders of Africa. The target of Lawino'scriticism, Ocol, is the representative of this class. He is both anintellectual and politician an embodiment of the disease Lawino

diagnoses in her song, satirizing the ills of Africa leaders describedelsewhere by Okot in an essay entitled «Indigenous social Ills», inwhich he refers to them as culturally barren ladies and gentlemen.Ocol's behavior does not lift up him before the leaders of his party.He behaves like: ... a newly-eloped girl (SOL,P.108) he says in hisspeeches that he is lighting for national unity:

«He says

They want to unite the Acoli and Lango

And the Madi and Lugbara

Should live together in peace!

The Alur and Iteso and Baganda

And the Banyankole and Banyoro

Should be united together» (SOL, PP.103-104).

However, his political energies do not really seem strong forbringing about unity, national or local. Most of his time as apolitician is taken up with condemning other people.Ocol says that the Congress Party is against all Catholics, and thatthey will steal all their property:

«The Congress Party

Will remove all Catholics

From their jobs

And they will take away

All the land and schools

And will take people's wives

And goats, and chickens and bicycles,

All will be came the property

Of the congress people.» (SOL, PP.105-6).

And it is not only the other party that he condemns. When he talksto the party leaders, he accuses other party:

«Everybody else is us

He alone

Is the hard working...?» (SOL, P.108).

The most destructive result of his political activity is its effect onhis own family. Ocol's brother is in the congress party. His thinkshis brother wants to murder him. Now is this the unity of Uhuru? Isthis the peace that Independence brings? (SOL, P.105). Heforbids Lawino to talk to the man who may one day become herhusband.

Okot does not ignore economic problems in his poems. In thissection of song, Lawino criticizes Ocol and the African politicalelite for political ineptitude and economic mismanagement. Shelashes out at corruption, points out that many politicians joined thecampaign for material gain:

«Someone said

Independence falls like a bull buffalo

And the hunters

Rush to it with draw knives,

Sharp shining knives

For carving the carcass.» (SOL, P.107).

Using political power for personal wealth is a common feature ofpetty bourgeoisie in developing countries, for in these countriesthere is no true national bourgeoisie, as in the USA or EUROPE,which derives its economic power from is the only means by whichthe political elite can acquire substantial wealth. Lawino speaks inironic terms when she says:

«The stomach seems to be

A powerful force

For joining political parties,

Especially when the purse

In the trouser pocket

Carries only the coins

With holes in their middle.» (SOL, PP.108).

Lawino is not blind to the fact that, while politicians are fighting toenrich their own pockets and inter-party strife rages, the commonpeople suffer, for they bear the hardest part of the economicproblems due to the ineptitude of the political elite:

«And while the pythons of sickness

Swallow the children

And the buffaloes of poverty knock the people down,

And ignorance stands there like an elephant,...»(SOL,P.111).

Politics has destroyed the unity of home and brought miserymember of it:

«The women there

Wear mourning clothes

The homestead is surely dead.» (SOL, P.111).

Now, where is peace of Uhuru when there is no harmony andconfidence at home?

«Where is the peace of Uhuru?

Where the unity of independence?

Must it not begin at home?

And the Alico and Lango

And the Madi and Lugbara,

How can they unite?

And all the tribes of Uganda

How can they become one?»(SOL, P.107).

This view of African petty bourgeoisie in control of political poweris corroborated in song of Ocol by Ocol. First, he is so thoroughlycolonized that he hates himself for being black:

«Africa

This rich granary,

Of taboos, customs,

Traditions...

Mother, Mother,

Why,

Why was I born?

Black?» (SOO, P.126).

Accordingly, he and his fellow members of the elite want todestroy all things African, anything that reminds them their Africanpast. Instead, they will erect monuments to the architects ofAfrican colonialism-Bismarck-David Livingstone, Leopold ofBelgium and others:

«To the gallows

With all the Professors

Of anthropology

And teachers of African History,

A bonfire

We'll destroy all the anthologies

Of African literature

And close down

All the schools

Of African studies.» (SOO, P.129).

Secondly, Ocol lends weight to Lawino's view that themisdemeanours of Africans politicians lead to the impoverishmentof workers.The power of the song of Lawino is due in large measure to theauthor's successful portrayal of an authentic spokesperson, anuneducated woman who has become highly aware of thenecessity for her race to preserve its own culture and identity. Sheis a vivid and memorable character. At first she may appearlighthearted and flippant, but in fact she advances a sound seriousargument. Unlike the negritude poets, she does not overtly claim that African culture is superior to European culture.Her central argument is summed up at the end of chapter Two:

«Listen Ocol, my old friend,

The ways of your ancestors

Are good,

Their customs are solid

And not hollow

They are not thin, not easily breakable

They cannot be blown away

By the winds

Because their roots reach deep into the soil.

I do not understand

The ways of foreigners

But I do not despise their customs.

Why should you despise yours?» (SOL, P.41).

The politicians, Okot mentions in this section are too busy fightingone another. Certainly Ocol sees no reason to do anything inChapter Six of Song of Ocol, he asks the voters to agree thatbecause he has worked harder for Uhuru he deserves:

Some Token Reward (SOL, P.139).

He is not responsible for the sufferings of the waters, although hewas rewarded of a large house in the town and a big form incountry:

«Is it my fault?

That you sleep

In a hut

With a leaking thatch?»(SOO, P.139).

Song of Ocol again confirms Lawino's opinions. In Chapter TwoOcol trots out for us the attitudes to Africa that he as a politicianhas swallowed whole from the missionaries:

«What is Africa?

To me

Blackness,

Deep, deep fathomless

Darkness...» (SOL, P.125).

Second is thequotation taken from Okot p'Bitek's bookSong of Lawino and songof Ocol (1972):

«I do not understand

The way of foreigners

But I do not despise their customs.

Why should you despise yours?

Listen, my husband,

You are the son of a Chief.

The Pumpkin in the Old homestead

Must not be uprooted!»(SOL, P. 41).

Both quotes impress on Afrocentricism. Particularly, the p'Bitek'swritten discourse introduces an interesting dialogue betweenhusband and wife. The wife in this case reminds her husbandabout his Africaness. Our feeling is that we cannot avoid dealingwith these bipolar realities that is being African in the currentsituation that is moved by continuous on a daily basis. This change manifests in many ways; political, social, and economic,spiritually, biotechnologically to name only these. In this regard,

the African image and mind wrestle to find place and space. SinceAfrocentricism is concerned, we can raise the questions:Who is an African? Do we need African centers in Africa? AreAfricans in a foreign continent? How can they sing being in aforeign land?How foreign is Africa to Africans? Africa needs toassert itself within the context of its diversity.

In Chapter Three ofSong of Ocol, Ocol condemns all efforts tofind reasons for pride in Africa's past. He would prefer to forget hispast:

«Smash all these mirrors

That I may not see

The blackness of the past

From which I came

Reflected in them.» (SOO, P.129).

In other words, Ocol wants to deny his Africanness. These feelingswring from him the cry of anguish which ends Chapter Two ofSong of Ocol.

«Mother, mother

Why

Why was I born?

Black?» (SOO, P. 126).

CHAPTER 12

In Chapter Twelve, Lawino summarises what has happened toOcol. «Ocol has read many books among white men and he isclever like white men» (S.O.O.p113). This section, from which theabove quotation is taken, constitutes the climax of Lawino'sargument and demonstrates Okot p'Bitek's use of Apostrophe. Thesection falls into three major subjections if we go by Lawino'ssubject matter and her audience. In the first subjection Lawinoaddresses her clan men. The subject matter is her husband's darkforest of books. Although Ocol has read many books among whitemen those books has not helped him. Instead he has lost hishead:

«Listen, my clansmen,

I cry over my husband

Whose head is lost

Ocol has lost his head

In the forest of books.» (SOL, P.113).

This as we shall see, is at the heart of her argument. In the secondsubsection she addresses Ocol in the words quoted above anddoes not mention books at all. Then she ends the section by goingback to address the clansmen and returning to the subject ofbooks. And in the end the books have destroyed him:

«... the reading

Has killed my man,

In the ways of his people

He has become

A stump» (SOL, P. 113).

Ocol still has the roles of husband and head of household, but heis no longer able to perform them. Instead he has become:

«A dog of the Whiteman!» (SOL, P. 115).

The Whiteman is his ultimate master, acting on him through hiscontinuing cultural and economic influences. Ocol obeys hismaster's call and is pleased only by those things that belong to hismaster. Ocol no longer owns anything. Every thing he usesbelongs to his master:

Aaa! A certain man

Has no millet field

He lives on borrowed foods

He borrows the clothes he wear

And the ideas in his head

And his actions and behaviour

Are to please somebody else

Like a woman trying to please her husband!

My husband has become a woman! (SOL, P.116).

And many young men are the same. Lawino calls on her clansmento weep for them because:

«Their manhood was finished

In the classrooms

Their testicles

Were smashed

With large books!» (SOL, P.117).

Here Lawino is mocking all those Olcols who are carrying the habitof slavish imitation of white men they leant in the mission schoolinto every sphere of their lives in the new nations of Africa. Forher, this is not the last word. She thinks there is still hope for Ocol.

Ocol only needs treatment to rid him of his disease.

In Section Thirteen, the last section, Lawino's whole approach,manner and tone of voice change: She tones down the bitternessin her voice and instead of lampooning her husband she cajoleshim, coaxes him like a loving wife, even advising him to buyclothes, beads and perfumes *«for the woman with whom I shareyou»* (SOL, P.120). She assumes the role of both a teacher and aloving wife.

CHAPTER 13

In Section Thirteen, she does not address her clansmen at all.First she recommends physical remedies to Ocol. Ocol's throat isblocked by the shame that has been choking him for so long:

«The shyness you ate in the church...» (SOL, P.118).

It must be cleaned out by traditional foods and herbs. His ears areblocked by the things he has heard from priest and teachers. Theymust be cleaned. His eyes, behind his dark glasses, are blind tothe things of his people. They must be opened. His tongue is dirtywith the continuous flow of insults he has been pouring on hispeople. It must be cleaned.

When the physical remedies have been completed, Ocol will beready for the real cure. He will be ready to regain his roots amonghis own people. Lawino explains how he nearly lost those roots:

«When you took the axe

And threatened to cut the Okango

That grows on the ancestral shrine

You were threatening

To cut your self loose,

To be tossed by the winds

This way and that way...» (SOL, PP. 119-120).

For this real cure, Ocol must beg forgiveness of all those heinsulted. But he must also seek the blessing of the elders and begforgiveness from the ancestors, because:

«... when you insulted me

Saying

I was a mere village girl,

You were insulting your grandfathers,

And grandmothers, your father

and mother!»(SOL, P. 119).

If he does all these things he will become a man again, theancestors will help him recover:

«Ask for a spear that you will trust

One that does not bend easily

Like the earth-worm

Ask them to restore your manhood!» (SOL, P. 119).

Lawino's final appeal concerns her domestic situation. She wantsthings to be normal in the household again. She wants Ocol tobehave like her husband. And when he is recovered, if he onlygives her:

«... One chance» (SOL, P. 120).

She is certain that things will become normal. When his ears areun-blocked he will hear the beauty of her singing. When hisblindness is cured, he will see and appreciate her dancing:

«Let me dance before

My love,

Let me show you

The wealth in your house...» (SOL, P.120).

In Chapter Three of Song of Ocol, Ocol briefly, but effectively,comments on traditional medicine. However foolish he might be incondemning all traditional remedies it is difficult not to share someof his horror at the scene he describes:

«That child lying... A gift of death»(SOO, P. 127).

Traditional remedies should have some place here in Africa, butthey cannot solve all her medical problems.

In Chapter Four of Song of Ocol, Ocol considers the position ofwomen in traditional societies. It is interesting to compare hisdescription of the walk to the well. Lowino is happy with hertraditional role, but she does have to work rather hard:

«Woman of Africa

Sweeper

Smearing floors and walls

With cow dung and black soil

Cook, ayah, the baby tied on your back

Vomiting

Washer of dishes,

Planting, weeding, harvesting,

Store-keeper, builder,

Runner of errands,

Cart, lorry

Donkey...» (SOO, P.133).

And in some ways here status is rather low:

«In Buganda

They buy you

With two pots

Of beer,

The Luo trade you

For seven cows...» (SOO, P.134).

Really, if we read carefully Section Thirteen, Lawino does notaddress her clansmen. In Section Twelve, however, her clansmenoccupy the center of subject matter which becomes even moreapparent when it is compared with Song of prisoner, whosedensity of texture is sustained throughout and whose language ispacked with emotion and feeling.

Some of the traditional modes of expression Okot employs inSong of Lawinodo not come off-at least for those readers who donot understand Acoli. In this connection, the proverb which saysthe *«Pumpkin in the old homestead should not be uprooted»*occurs frequently, and is clearly meant to play a key role inconveying Lawino's message. But to the author of this thesis, towhom Acoli is a strange language, the proverb conveys little or nomeaning. This is also true of some of Okot's imagery. Consider, forinstance, the fallowing lines from Section Two where Lawinointroduces the conceit of Clementine as the woman with whomshe shares her husband:

«Her body resembles

The ugly coat of the hyena;

Her neck and arms

Have real human skins!

She looks as if she has been struck

By lightning;

Or burnt like the Kongoni

In a fire hunt». (SOL, P.37).

This is far from being as effective as the description of Clementinewhich occurs at the beginning of the same section and which wasquoted earlier in the chapter.

There are also some inconsistencies and contradictions in song ofLawino. As a character, Lawino sometimes gets out of hand andOkot is not able to control her and shape her plausibly. WhatLawino says in Section Eleven is out of character. Her analysis ofbehaviour of politicians in Uganda is so sophisticated that onewonders whether she is the same woman who is at one timeamazed at the ticking of Ocol's clock (section7).

In Section Eleven Lawino does not strike the reader as a simplewoman commenting in a simple way about political rivalry.Naturally, we are not suggesting that peasants cannot be politicalanalysts. They can in fact be more revolutionary than theintelligentsia; but the problem here is that Okot presents us with aseemingly simple peasant woman and then turns her into apolitical scientist without creating the circumstances that give riseto such a transformation.

To conclude this Song of Lawino and Song of Ocol, in the lastchapter of the book, the core of Ocol's speech is his expression offaith in the urban future of Africa, and in the foundations of thatfuture laid by Europeans. Naively and improbable he promises to:

«... Erect monuments

To the founders

Of modern Africa:

Leopold II of Belgium,

Bismarck...» (SOL, P .151).

However, most of the speech is in the form of challenges tovarious people in positions of influence in Africa to explain theAfrican foundation of their activities. Okot is mocking the borrowedplumes of all these dignitaries and challenging them to justify their

borrowings.

Why should lawyers and bishops wear long robes as the Englishdo? Why the African legal system should be based on English LawReports? Why should all officials in local government take theirnames from English equivalents (Mayors, councillors, Town

clerks). Okot's most serious challenge is to the scholar:

«Can you explain

The African philosophy

On which we are reconstructing

Our new societies...» (SOO, P.150)

Okot has made the foundation on which he wishes to build Africannations abundantly clear throughout his poems,Song of LowinoandSsong of Ocol. He wants to challenge all concerned withnation building to make their own activities in light of his ideas. Ifthey do not accept the challenge, then like Nyerere and Sengorwho are looking for an African mould for nation-building will beutterly defeated by the continuing cultural influence of Europe on Africa.

CHARACTERIZATION

1. **LAWINO:** she isAn African woman who lacks formal education. She is not converted to Christianity. She is a responsible mother who loves and cares for her family.
2. **OCOL:** He is an African man who has got western education. He imitates the white men in everything. He despises all traditional ways of life. He is arrogant. He is hypocrite politician (leader of DP).
3. **CLEMENTINE:** She is a modern girl. She is Ocol`s girl friend. She is a westernized woman. She imitates the white women. She is arrogant.

THEMATIC ANALYSIS

1. **ARROGANCE AND PREJUDICE;** Ocol treats Lawino with prejudice just because she's never been to school and is not westernized. That is not a reason strong enough to make him despise her, who was once his beloved wife. This is very common among the Africa educated elites who mistakenly think that the western education they received elevated them higher and gave them the right to look down upon those uneducated counterparts who did not have that privilege. Lawino says;

   He abuses me in English
   And he is so arrogant.

He claims to be a modern, civilized and progressive man who has read extensively and widely and can no longer live with a thing like Lawino. His arrogance is not confined to his wife alone but he extends it to the parents who are supposed to be his parents-in-law. She laments;

   My husband abuses me together

   With my parents

   He says terrible things about my mother

   And I am ashamed.

2. **MENTAL COLONISATION;** Ocol is mentally colonized and has a slave mentality but he has no idea about it. He praises everything that is western whether good or bad and

despises everything that is African whether good or bad. Little does he realize that he cannot become a white man just by fallingin love with European culture.He despises Lawino just because she cannot play the guitar; she cannot read, cannot hear a single foreign word and cannot count the coins. This proves that the kind of education Ocol received was just education for alienation, subordination and creation of mental confusion. Since his education has failed to transform him into a civilized man nothing is expected out of that knowledge to transform his traditional society into a modern one he wishes to see.

3. **HYPOCRISY;** Ocol professes to be a man of God but his tongue proves the opposite. He cannot claim to be a God-fearing fellow and all he has got to say about his people is that they are "all Kaffirs". He says that they do not know the ways of God and the Gospel. He portrays an open hypocrisy because God loves the sinners and the lost but Ocol in Lawino's account she says;

He says we are all Kaffirs

We do not know the ways of God

We sit in deep darkness

And do not know the Gospel

He says that my mother hides the charms

In her necklace

And that we are all sorcerers

With these words no one can see God whom Ocol claims to worship, as a result people find it better remaining that they are, than becoming what Ocol has become, thus no any transformation is required.

4. **BETRAYAL AND LOSS OF IDENTITY;** Ocol has betrayed his African identity and his fellow Black People. It is no wonder that Lawino compares him with *"a hen that eats its own eggs"*. He despises the things that were and are still part of him and by so doing he loses his identity and becomes a completely uncivilizedman while he claims to be one. Expressing this detrimental situation Lawino says:

He says Black People are Primitive

And their ways are utterly harmful

Their dances are mortal sins

They are ignorant poor and diseased.

5. **AFRICAN TRADITION;**
   - **POLYGAMY;** Lawino being an African woman she knows that it is impossible to stop men from wanting women and so she is familiar with polygamy. So in this respect, she is not completely jealous of Clementine in a narrow sense of desiring

to have sole possession of Ocol (though she partly claims to be a bit jealous) but she is simply annoyed that Ocol prefers a woman who is no younger than her and can match her in none of her womanly accomplishments. Lawino is okay with this form of marriage because she knows that a man's heart is won through nice meals, a hot bath and sour porridge when he returns home from the field or from the hunt. She declares;

> *The competition for a man's love*
> *is fought at the cooking place*
> *when he returns from the field*
> *or from the hunt*
> *you win him with a hot bath*
> *and sour porridge.*

This gives Lawino much confidence because she sees herself better qualified in these womanly accomplishments that her rival. A woman who would be jealous in such cases is the one who is slow, lazy, shy, cold, weak and clumsy.

- **SACRIFICIAL RITES;** In African setting Sacrifice is a necessary rite when one wants to deal with any unpleasant situations. Lawino evokes this point when she suggests that only sacrifice can restore her peace that has been seriously damaged by Clementine's sight. She says:

  > *It is then necessary to fetch a goat*
  > *From my mother's brother,*
  > *The sacrifice over*
  > *The ghost-dance drum must sound*
  > *The ghost be laid*
  > *And my peace restored.*

- **AFRICAN DANCES;** Lawino defends African dances as compared to European dances. The Whites condemned African dances because of immorality of nakedness. Lawino doesn't waste time in a reasoned and balanced defense of dancing naked. She presents the openness, liveliness, and healthiness of the Acoli dance positively without apology.

  > *When the drums are throbbing*
  >
  > *And the black youths*
  >
  > *Have raised much dust*
  >
  > *You dance with vigor and health*
  >
  > *You dance naughtily with pride*
  >
  > *You dance with spirit*
  >
  > *You compete, you insult, you provoke*

You challenge all.

- **BRIDE PRICE;** Bride price is another aspect of African tradition that emerges in this section. Although Okot does not explain in detail the expected bride price of cattle, he knows that this will not present any difficulty to Africans to understand. In African context it is common when one has a beautiful daughter to prepare the kraal in anticipation of the bride price of cattle when men will come proposing to marry his daughter. She says;

    For my breasts shook

    and beckoned the cattle

    And they sang silently

    Father prepare the kraal

    Father prepare the kraal

    The cattle are coming

- **TRADITIONAL HEALING;** Moreover, Lawino shows how Africans used to deal with different social and natural phenomena. Although it might seem as a kind of incantation, it helped to deal with unusual misfortunes. For example she says if a ring-worm has eaten the little girl's hair, all they do is put hot porridge on the head, hold a dance, sing a song, and then the hair grows again. This traditional ritual is still relevant to some societies today.

- **DEATH RITUALS;** It is common in African set up for people to do certain practices when death has occurred, believing that it would help in purifying the homestead and clearing the bad luck brought by the death. While in some societies they shave their hair, in Acoli they leave their hair uncombed and remove all the beads and necklaces as a sign of mourning. So a woman who adorns herself in the middle of such a crisis is considered to be the killer and she just attends the funeral to congratulate herself.

- **WITCHCRAFT/SUPERSTITIOUS BELIEFS;** In African traditional setting, many happenings are linked to witchcraft or superstitious beliefs. For example, the ghosts of the dead people are thought to have interactions with the living beings and can cause some things to happen in human life. Lawino for instance Believes that the wigs that Tina puts on her head are the hair of some dead white women who died long ago and that alone qualifies her to be a wizard. As one night the wig fell down, Lawino comments that it was the ghost of a dead woman that did the pull. She says;

    One night the ghost of the dead woman
    Pulled away her hair
    From the head of the wizard

The fact is that Lawino portrays her ignorance about the wigs technology and overstates the matter as a way of showing her anger and discontent with Tina's rivalry in her marriage.

- **EATING ETIQUETTE/MANNERS;** In traditional communities eating manners are strictly observed by all members of the family in respect to gender and age and the Acoli are no exception. Young boys have to sit cross-legged and the girls are required to sit carefully on one leg and only the father sits on a stool. The eating process itself is done by simply washing the hands and attacking the loaf from all sides. It should also be noted that when eating only the right hand is used even when someone is left handed. Lawino wonders why she should sit on chairs - which she describes as trees - like monkeys. (*This after all isn't bad*). She wonders why knives should be used in cutting the millet bread and eating using the left hand is considered to be bad manners and the one who eats using the left hand is considered to be rude.

- **TABOOS;** Lawino introduces one of the serious taboos in their culture in as much as family planning is concerned. It is a serious taboo for a woman to turn her back to her husband a sign that can be translated as she is not ready to make love with him. This can only be permitted when the baby is toothless for it is believed that if the couples make love when the baby is still toothless, then it becomes sickly, thin, and the stomach swells as that of a pregnant woman.

- **TRADITIONAL MARRIAGE;** In Acoli it is possible for a girl to visit the man whom she is betrothed to in his bachelor's hut so as to try his manhood before marriage. Lawino makes this point to contrast what she was taught about the virgin birth, that Mary did not know any man when she gave birth to Jesus while she was betrothed to Joseph. It doesn't make sense to her, how this virgin birth took place. She says;

  Among our people

  When a girl has

  Accepted a man's proposal

  She gives a token

  And then she visits him

  In his bachelor's hut

  To try his manhood (p.90)

- **WIDOW INHERITANCE;** Lawino points out that in their tradition if a brother dies, then, the young brother has the right to inherit his brother's properties including his wife and children. Lawino wonders why Ocol insults and prohibits her to talk and joke with a man who may one day become her husband when he dies. Lawino says;

  But I know that if Ocol dies

  His mother's son, whom he now hates so much

  Will inherit all Ocol's properties

The goats, the chicken and the bicycles

And I will become his wife

And my children will become his children.

6. **AWARENESS AND IDENTITY;** Lawino is surer of her identity and wishes not to compete with Clementine by beautifying herself the way she does. Being aware of herAfrican identity she knows that there are ornaments suitable for Black skins and ones for White skins. She says;

> *I do not like dusting myself with powder*
>
> *The thing is good on pink skin*
>
> *Because it is already pale*
>
> *But when a black woman has used it*
>
> *She looks as if she has dysentery.*

This is one reason why Lawino would rather remain a typical African woman than try to beautify herself to please her husband.

7. **SYMPATHY AND JEALOUSY;** While Lawino admits to be a bit jealousy of Clementine, she goes a step ahead to claim that it is rather sympathy and not jealousy that drives her to speak what she says about Clementine. She sees Clementine as a person who deserves out pity and sympathy because she has lost her identity unawares. Lawino says;

> *But when you see the beautiful woman*
>
> *With whom I share my husband*
>
> *You feel a little pity for her*

8. **EFFECTS OF GLOBALIZATION;** Additionally, in the poem Lawino continues to pour attacks on white man's dances but she adds some important details to make her point. Not only are the dances immoral but the actions accompanied with the dances sum up the immorality of the dances. Nevertheless, these actions are done by Africans who have been affected by globalization and they copy western mode of life. Lawino pinpoints some of these practices.

> *They drink white men drinks.*
>
> *Each man has a woman although she is not his wife.*
>
> *They kiss each other on the cheek as white people do.*
>
> *You kiss her open-sore lips as white people do.*
>
> *You suck slimy saliva from each other's mouth as white people do.*

They dress up as white men as if they are in white men countries.

They wear dark glasses and neck-ties from Europe.

You smoke cigar like white men.

9. **PROTEST;** Lawino shows an open protest against European culture that is invading African culture. She does all it takes to educate African women to love and care for what they have, believe in who they are, and what they want to do with their lives. She protests doing her hair like white women. She says;

> *It is true*
>
> *I cannot do my hair*
>
> *As white women do*

Lawino's final words conclude her stand and protest against her husband's suggestions when she declares:

> *The long-necked and graceful giraffe*
>
> *Cannot become a monkey*
>
> *Let no one*
>
> *Uproot the pumpkin.*

10. **IGNORANCE;** Traditionally it is believed that lightning and thunder are caused by a giant reddish-brown bird (Rain-Cock) that is almost identical withthe domestic fowl. When it opens its wings, lightning flashes and thunder is caused when it strikes with its powerful bolt. The Acoli have this belief and they attribute it to the actions of electricity.

> *The electric fire kills people*
>
> *They say*
>
> *It is lightning*
>
> *They say the Whiteman has trapped*
>
> *And caught the Rain-Cock*
>
> *And imprisoned it*
>
> *In a heavy steel house.*

This is a portrayal of Lawino and the Acoli's ignorance of the advancement in modern technology. Her description of the electric stove by linking it to local beliefs on one side and her ignorance of how to use it on the other side tell it all. She rejects the use of the electric stove simply because she has no idea how to use it but she attaches some empty and unfounded claims to justify her protest. She gives complaints such as it is not proper to cook while standing and the fact that she is afraid of touching the deadly tongue of the Rain-Cock.

11. **EXPLOITATION;** The protestant teachers and Catholic priests made the people work for them by telling them that it is the only way to acquire a Christian name. They made their converts work for them while they themselves did none of the works. The young girls had to draw water, grind millet and simsim, hoe their field, split firewood, cut grass for thatching and for starting fires. They had to smear their floors and harvest their crops. This is the highest level of exploitation that was wrapped by the trick of acquiring a Christian name.

12. **SELFISHNESS;** Ocol is partly haunted by the spirit of selfishness, one must admit. Although he gives many excuses why both his relatives and Lawino's should not visit him, a careful examination reveals that he has inherited the selfishness of his missionary teachers. Africans have a long standing history of hospitality to both relatives and strangers. Ocol has betrayed the "Ubuntu" philosophy and he does not welcome visitors even when the weather does not permit them to leave. Lawino says;

> *And when the storm is threatening*

> *He says*

> *There are no beds*

> *In his house*

> *For villagers.*

He claims that they will soil his bed sheets and ruin his nicely polished floor. He segregates his own mother and locks the door for her. He needs one to write him a letter before they pay a visit to his house. He even prohibits his children from visiting their grandmother. Only a selfish person can justify these practices and find them genuine.

13. **UNITY AND DISUNITY;** Ocol says in his speeches that they want to bring national unity that will unite all the tribes of Uganda; the Acoli, Lango, Madi, Lugbara, Alur, Iteso, Baganda, and Bunyoro. They should be united together and live in peace. If you look very closely his political Movements don't really seem to be geared at bringing about unity, be it local or national. Most of his time as a politician is taken up with condemning other people. He says that the Congress Party is against all the Catholics and they want to steal people's properties if elected (communism). He says

> *The congress party*

> *Will remove all the Catholics*

> *From their jobs*

> *And they will take away*

Ocol's brother who belongs to the Congress Party also condemns the Democratic Party that it belongs to the Padres, fools and block heads and they receive their orders from the Italian Fathers. He claims that the DP will sell the land to the poor White men who came to their country. This political division confuses Lawino completely when she comes to think that the people who are talking about unity are the ones who are dividing the society further apart. She doesn't see how the idea of unity will be achieved while the two parties have failed to join their parties with a common aim. Both are talking about bringing unity and independence but they are fighting separately with great enmity against each other as shown in these lines;

It appears to Lawino that it is poverty that drives them into power and not unity and independence as they claim.

14. **CONFLICTS;**
   a) **Intrapersonal conflict;** Lawino suffers from intrapersonal conflict because of several reasons;
- She wonders how Ocol and his brother will manage to bring unity and peace out of the insults they heap on each other.
- She doesn't understand most of their political policies like Communism, and how these people will take properties from the people. She wonders that Ocol calls the white people poor and says they will buy the land from the Congress Party. It seems to her like a contradiction since a poor person cannot afford to buy the land.

b) **Political conflict;** Ocol and his brother belong to two different political parties Democratic Party and Congress Party respectively. Politics has destroyed the unity of the home and has brought misery to every member of it. Ocol's political activities have only created new conflicts without settling the old ones. The main source of this conflict is the material benefit that might partially compensate for these new conflicts. In their political activities you will never think of the fact that they slept in the same womb. Ocol insults his brother in one meeting and his brother does the same in the other. Lawino fails to see the point how these two will succeed to unite the country while they themselves are not at peace. Their political conflicts seem to hold much promise to only few, those who are strong; Lawino says

If your chest

Is small, bony and weak

They push you off (p. 107)

Lawino believes it is the money and competition for position that drives the political leaders to hate one another and quarrel on the platforms.

c) **Family conflicts;** Politics has brought a serious gap in Ocol's family and has become one of the major sources of conflict in the family. Ocol and his brother are not in good terms as though they did not share the womb.
- Ocol does not enter his brother's house.
- He hates his brother and calls him a liar and a fool
- He has sternly warned Lawino never to joke with him because the strong gum of the joke will reconnect the snapped string of brotherhood.
- He accuses his brother that he wants to kill him.
- Ocol's brother also insults Ocol and his followers that they are fools.

So Lawino wonders whether this is what the unity, peace and Uhuru mean. This family quarrel confuses her so much that she says:

Others carry pieces of stones

On their necks

And call them heads.

d) **Cultural conflict;** Lawino shows an open cultural clash between the culture of her people and that of the Whites. She shows the differences that existbetween Acoli's culture and European culture in almost all walks of life and she finalizes by showing that the only way to end thesupposed controversy is by retaining her culture. She says

I do not enjoy

The fact that Ocol abuses African foods by calling them primitive and backward does not move or shake her in any way. She continues to insist that African foods have made her strong enough to dance all night long and thus she gives her credit to it. To resolve this conflict she advises;

My husband

I do not complain

that you eat

White men's foods

if you enjoy them

****

go ahead

shall we just agree

to have freedom

to eat what one likes?

This is to say Ocol should not dictate his wills upon others but should leave the chance to exercise their own freedom of choice.

15. **CLASSES;** This is one of the biggest divisions brought by the political activities which followed Uhuru. The newly attained independence has ever since produced a class of rich people who got the political positions and enjoyed the favors that came with it and a class of poor people whose life has remained the same as in colonial time. Lawino shows this state of hopelessness among the members of the poor class;

And those who have fallen into things

Throw themselves into soft beds

But the hip bones of the voters

Grow painful, sleeping on the same earth

So the politicians are not doing anything to help their voters improve their standard of living but they are busy fighting one another.

16. POSITION OF WOMEN IN THE SOCIETY:
- **A woman is portrayed as an oppressed, humiliated and alienated** due to the belief that she is uncivilized, uneducated, static and unchanging woman such as Lawino.
- **A woman is portrayed as a mother who is responsible member of her society** such as Lawino.
- **A woman is portrayed as a strong representative of tradition** such as Lawino and Clementine.
- **Women lack formal education such** as Lawino.

FIGURES OF SPEECH

1. Similes;
- Some stand there tall and huge like the *tido* tree. (p.113)
- You behave like a dog of the white man. (p.115)
- His name still blows like a horn. (p.116)
- Dancing silently like wizards. (p.47)
- Your sick stomach that has swollen up like that of a pregnant goat. (p.50)
- A white woman's hair is soft like silk. (p.51)
- Lurking in the shades like the leopardess with cubs. (p.53)
- He hisses like a wounded ororo snake. (p.54)
- Hot and steaming like the urine of the elephant. (p.55)
- The head of the beautiful one smells like rats. (p.55)
- The thing roars like a male lion. (p.57)
- It tastes like earth. (p.58)
- The stoves are flat like the face of a drum. (p.59)
- They are like pawpaw. (p.60)
- They burn like paper. (p.60)
- The smoke it produces is like a spear. (p.60)
- Three mounds of clay shaped like youthful breasts full of milk. (p.61)
- Ocol storms like a buffalo. (p.67)
- His eyes were like rotting tomatoes. (p.76)
- His hair resembled the elephant grass. (p78)
- And his cheeks were rough like the tongue of the ox. (p.78)
- My name blew like a horn among the payira (p.48)

2. Personifications;
- The reading has killed my man. (p.113)
- The stench from the latrine knocks you down, from afar. (p.46)
- All the tribes of human dung. (p.46)
- And the different smells wrestle with one another. (p.55)

- (The hair) it cries aloud in a sharp pan as it is pulled and stretched. (p.54)
- My stomach rebels and throws its contents out. (p.57)
- The winds go off to visit their mothers-in-law. (p.57)
- And the stove has many eyes. (p.58)
- The mother stone has a hollow stomach, a strange woman she never gets pregnant. (p.59)
- Even if the world has boxed him. (p.99)
- And her daughter sitting in her belly. (p.59)
- You hear the song of stones.
- You hear the song of the grains. (p.60)
- (The clock) Its large single testicle dangles below. (p.63)
- A hunger begins to bite people's tummies. (71)
- (The moon) it elopes, climbs the hill and falls down. (p.70)
- The heads of the young men reject the pillows and prefer the arms of their lovers. (p.80)
- When all the diseases have fallen in love with him. (p.96)
- When mother death comes she whispers come. (p.102)
- When death comes to fetch you, she comes unannounced. (p.102)
- Her ripe breasts lift up their hands. (p.97)

3. **Metaphors;**
   - My husband has become a woman. (p.116)
   - I am a mere dog, a puppy. (p.49)
   - The time has become my husband's master. (p.68)
   - It is my husband's husband. (p.68)
   - Buffaloes of poverty. (p.111)
   - The pythons of sickness. (p.111)

4. **Exaggeration/hyperbole;**
   - My husband's tongue is bitter like the roots of the lyonno lily. (p.35)
   - It is hot like the penis of the bee. (p.35)
   - My head he says is as big as that of an elephant but it is only bones there is no brain in it. (p.36)

5. **Anaphora;**
   - *A lazy* youth is rebuked,
   - *A lazy* girl is slapped
   - *A lazy* wife is beaten
   - *A lazy* man is laughed at (p.69)
   - …*even if* your father is totally blind
   - *Even if* his ears are dead
   - *Even if* the world has boxed him
   - *Even if* his legs are dry like firewood (99)
   - *You* do not resist
   - *You* must not resist
   - *You* cannot resist (p.102)

6. **Parallelism;**
   - I know their names and their leaves and seeds and barks. (p.60)
   - Lunch-time, tea-time and supper time (p.64)
7. **Alliteration;**
   - The wild white lilies. (p.53)
   - Women weeding or harvesting.(p.64)
   - The sister stone (p. 60)
8. **Onomatopoeia;**
   - It goes tock-tock-tock-tock. (p.63)
   - The cock must crow. (p.64)
   - It makes no crackling sound (p. 58)
9. **Rhetorical questions;**
   - Didn't the Acoli have adornments?
   - Didn't black people have their ways?
   - Is lawala not a game?
   - Is cooro not a game? (p.49)
   - Whoever cooked standing up? (p.58)
   - Where is the peace of Uhuru? Where the unity of independence?
   - Must it not begin at home? (p.107)
10. **Oxymoron;**
   - The wild white lilies are *shouting silently* (p.53)
11. **Irony:** e.g.Ocol calls himself "A modern man, progressive and civilized" but his life proves the opposite.
12. **Euphemism;**
   - When a young girl has seen the moon for the first time (p.70). It is a sign that the *garden* is ready for *sowing* and when the *gardener* comes carrying two *bags* of *live seeds* and *a good strong hoe* the *rich soil swells with a new life*. (She describes the act of making love euphemistically) And the *spears* of the lone hunters, The trusted right-hand spears Of young bulls Rust in the dewy cold (p.80)
13. **Reiteration;** e.g.Slowly slowly (p.117)
14. **Sayings and proverbs;**
   - Let no one uproot the pumpkin. (p.56)
   - Who has ever prevented the cattle from the salt link? (p.79)
   - The last safari to Pagak. (p.91) Pagak is the place of no return or death's homestead.
   - He behaves like a hen that eats its own eggs. (p.35)
15. **Consonance;**
   - You cannot wield the shield. (p.50)
   - Women weed*ing* or harvest*ing*.(p.64)
   - Sow*ing*, weed*ing*, harvest*ing*. (p.71)
16. **Symbolism;** *The Pumpkin* represents African (Acoli) culture which cannot be easily destroyed by Ocoli and his fellow educated elite.
   - *The graceful giraffe* = black people
   - *The monkey* = white people

- When a young girl has seen the moon for the first time (p.70) It is a sign that the *garden* is ready for *sowing* and when the *gardener* comes carrying *two bags* of *live seeds* and *a good strong hoe* the *rich soil swells with a new life.*
- The garden represents the womb.
- Sowing means conceiving.
- Gardener represents a male partner.
- Two bags of live seeds represent the testicles carrying sperms.
- A good strong hoe represents an erected and functioning penis.
- The rich soil means the womb.
- Swells with a new life means become pregnant.
- And the young men sleep alone cold like knives without handles (p.80) And the *spears* Of the lone hunters, (p.80)
- The spears represent the penis of young boys.

17. **Imagery;** The most important influence Acoli songs have had on *Song of Lawino* is in the imagery Okot uses. Okot has completely avoided the stock of common images in English literature through his familiarity with the stock of common images in Acoli literature. This gives the poem a feeling of freshness for every reader and a sense of Africanness for African readers. These images are found in the songs that are set out as quotations in the poem. These are found in pages 60; 62; 66-67; 76-78; 98; 101; 115; and 120. For example;

> Odure *come out*
>
> *From the kitchen*
>
> *Fire from the stove*
>
> *Will burn your penis!*

Odure is a nickname for small boys who are fond of sitting in the house when his mother is cooking. It is derived from a small boy of that name whose penis was burnt by fire from the stove.

CHAPTER 6

VOCABULARY

USING OF A DICTIONARY

DICTIONARY;

It is a kind of book or reference that containing words of a language, arranged alphabetically, showing class and uses.

Importance of a dictionary book;
1. It gives meaning of words.
2. It shows words of the same meaning (synonyms)
3. It shows words which mean the opposite (antonyms)
4. It shows the classes of word (verb, noun etc)
5. It shows how words are used
6. It shows how words are made
7. It shows how words are pronounced

GIVING DIRECTIONS;
Example;
Rehema; Excuse me could you tell me the way to the pharmacy?

Suzy; Yes, it's the way, just go straight away after two houses turn to the left; it's on the corner opposite the post office

Rehema; Thanks

WAYS USED TO ASK OR SHOW DIRECTIONS;
- Can you direct me to…?
- Turn left/ right and go straight to… at zebra
- Crossing and take a bus to… on your left follow Jacaranda street and then keep right

TALKING ABOUT FAMILY;
FAMILY;
Is a smallest social unit which consists of father, mother, children and relatives.

Vocabulary;
1. **Uncle;** the brother of your father or mother.
2. **Cousin;** the child of your uncle or aunt.
3. **Nephew;** the son of your brother or sister.
4. **Niece;** the daughter of your brother or sister.
5. **Father-in-law;** the father of your wife or husband.

6. **Mother-in-law;** the mother of your wife or husband.
7. **Brother-in-law;** the brother of your wife or husband.
8. **Sister-in-law;** the sister of your wife or husband.
9. **Aunt;** the sister of your father or mother.
10. **Grandfather;** the father of your father or mother.
11. **Grandmother;** the mother of your father or mother.

VOCABULARY (1)

1. **Vendor;** is a person who sells commodities such as food stuffs and clothes by walking with them around the streets looking for customers.
2. **Tour guide;** is a person who directs and instructs tourists when they are going for a tour.
3. **Cyclist;** is a person who rides a bicycle or a motorcycle.
4. **Foreman;** is a person who supervises others in performing a certain task or activity.
5. **Lawyer;** is a person who advises clients on legal matters.
6. **Chef;** is a person who cooks in a hotel or restaurant.
7. **Keeper;** is a person who administers the property, house and finances of another.
8. **Grocer;** is a person who sells household items.
9. **Deacon;** is a person whose rank is immediately below a priest.
10. **Dean;** is a person who is a chief administrator of a college or university.
11. **Guardian;** is a person who looks after someone.
12. **Trader;** is a person who is engaged in commercial purchase and sale.
13. **Thief;** is a person who takes other people properties without permission.
14. **Artist;** is a person who paints pictures, signs and composes poems.
15. **Tenant;** is a person who pays rent for the use of a room, building or land to the person who owns it.
16. **Accountant;** is a person whose job is to keep or check financial accounts.
17. **Sibling;** is a brother or sister.
18. **Shirt;** is a garment worn on the upper part of the body, usually having sleeves and buttons.
19. **Skirt;** is a garment hanging from the waist.
20. **Legible;** that is clear enough to be read easily.
21. **Audible;** that can be heard.
22. **Edible;** good or safe to eat.
23. **Illegible;** difficult or impossible to read.
24. **Portable;** that can be moved or carried easily.
25. **Blouse;** is a cloth like a shirt.
26. **Bridegroom;** is a man on or just before his wedding day.
27. **Bridesmaid;** is a woman or girl who helps a woman on her wedding day.
28. **Tailor;** is a person whose job is to make clothes like suits for an individual customer.
29. **Airhost;** is a male flight attendant.

30. **Customer;** is a person that buys something from a shop or business.
31. **Inspector;** is a person whose job is to visit schools, factories to check that rules are being observed, obeyed and that standards are accepted.
32. **Librarian;** is a person who is in charge of or works in a library.
33. **Authoress;** is a woman who writes books.
34. **Electrician;** is a person whose job is to connect, repair electrical equipment like cables, wires in a house, car or machine.
35. **Swarm;** is a large group of insects especially bees.
36. **Flock;** is a number of sheep.
37. **Audience;** a number of people listening to a concert or lecture.
38. **Spectators;** a number of people looking on at a football match.
39. **Clump;** is a number of trees.
40. **Set;** is a collection of tools.
41. **Bunting;** is a collection of flags

VOCABULARY (2);

1. **A crowd** of people
2. **A chest** of drawers
3. **A flock** of sheep/ birds
4. **A gang** of thieves/ bandits
5. **A constellation** of stars
6. **A board** of directors
7. **A choir** of singers
8. **A plague** of insects/ locusts
9. **A school** of whales/ dolphins
10. **A bunch** of keys/ roses
11. **A swarm** of bees
12. **A troop** of lions/ monkeys
13. **A hand** of bananas
14. **A herd** of cattle/ buffaloes
15. **A crew** of sailors
16. **A pack** of cards
17. **A band** of musicians
18. **A brood** of chickens
19. **A kindle** of kitten
20. **A bevy** of beautiful girls
21. **An anthology** of poems
22. **A bouquet** of flowers
23. **A fleet** of ships
24. **A stack** of wood

25. **A pencil** of rays
26. **A clutch** of eggs
27. **A set** of tools
28. **A host** of angels
29. **A nest** of mice/ rabbits
30. **A staff** of teachers
31. **A team** of horses/ players
32. **A troupe** of dancers
33. **A cluster** of stars
34. **A horde** of children
35. **Spectators;** In football field
36. **Audience;** in a concert
37. **Mob;** in a riot
38. **Crowd/ throng;** in a street
39. **Assembly;** in a meeting
40. **Congregation;** in a church
41. **Patients;** in hospital
42. **A bale** of cotton
43. **A lump** of sugar
44. **A gallon** of oil
45. **A meter** of cloth
46. **A piece** of bread
47. **A sheet** of paper
48. **A tone** of coal
49. **A bar** of chocolate
50. **An acre** of land
51. **A loaf** of bread
52. **A block** of ice
53. **A slice** of bread
54. **A speck** of dust
55. **A cloud** of mosquitoes
56. **A fleet** of cars
57. **A bundle/ heap** of clothes
58. **A panel** of judges
59. **A crop** of apples
60. **A contingent** of soldiers
61. **A team** of researchers
62. **A company** of players
63. **A bundle** of sticks
64. **A bunch** of bananas

65. A deck of cards

66. A pile of papers

67. A pack of flies

68. An array of facts

69. A fleet of buses

SOUNDS OF ANIMALS;

1. Sheep- bleat
2. Snake- hiss
3. Tigers- roar/ growl
4. Tortoise- grunt
5. Hares- squeak
6. Hippos- bray
7. Horses- neigh/ whinny
8. Hyena- laugh
9. Kittens- mew
10. Lions- roar
11. Mice- squeak
12. Monkeys- chatter/ gibber
13. Parrots- talk
14. Pigs- grunt/ squeal/ squeak
15. Rhinos- snort
16. Blackbirds- whistle
17. Bulls- bellow
18. Calves- bleat
19. Cats- meow/ mew/ purr
20. Chickens- peep/ cackle
21. Cocks- crow
22. Cows- low
23. Dogs- bark
24. Dolphins- click
25. Doves- moan
26. Ducks- quack
27. Eagles- scream
28. Elephant- trumpet
29. Flies- buzz
30. Foxes- bark/ yelp
31. Frogs- croak
32. Giraffe- bleats/ grunts
33. Grasshoppers- chirp/ pitter

34. Donkey- bray
35. Rabbit- grunt
36. Bees- buzz/ murmur
37. Beetles- drone
38. Birds- sing/ chirp
39. Apes- gibber
40. Rat- squeak
41. Man- speak
42. Hen- clucks

WRITTEN BY JOHN EDWARD (BAED-HONS)
PHONE; 0757189316
E-MAIL; johnedwardmej@gmail.com

REFERENCES;

Ndambo, S (2008). "English Language for Advanced level"
 Dar es Salaam: Afroplus Industries LTD

Kadeghe, M (2001). "English for Advanced level- Book 2"
 Dar es Salaam: University of Dar es Salaam

Nyamsenda, S (2008). "Advanced English language Paper 1"
 Dar es Salaam: University of Dar es Salaam

University of Nairobi (1988). "English structure"
 Nairobi: University of Nairobi

Maghway, J.B (1996). "Linguistics and the study of Language"
 Dar es Salaam: The Open University of Tanzania

Okombo, O (1988). "Linguistics- study of English IV"
Nairobi: Univerity of Nairobi

Obado, E.T (1988). "Linguistics study of English III"
 Nairobi: University of Nairobi

Okolo, B.A (2008). "Introduction to Syntactic Models"
 Lagos: National Open University of Nigeria

Murthy, J.D (1998). "Contemporary English Grammar"
 New Delhi: Book Palace

"Three Suitors One husband". Play Anaylsis
Accessed on March 16, 2019.https://samwiterson.blogspot.com/2018/05/three-suitors-one-husband-analysis-by.html

"The Lion and the Jewel". Play analysis
Accessed on January 5, 2019. samwiterson.blogspot.com/2019/04/the-lion-and-jewel-by-wole-soyinka.html

"Introduction to Literature". Theory of Literature
Accessed on May 8, 2019 samwiterson.blogspot.com/2018/05/introduction-to-literature.html

"Passed like A shadow". Novel Analysis
Accessed on March 16,209.https://samwiterson.blogspot.com/2018/05/passed-like-shadow-analysis-by-samson.html

"Summons" Poems Analysis
Accessed on April 8, 2016.http://ttbinvestment.blogspot.com/2016/05/poemsanalysissummons.html

"Growing up with poetry". Poems Analysis
Accessed on April 8, 2016.http://ttbinvestment.blogspot.com/2016/05/growingupwithpoetrydrubadiri.html

www.ingramcontent.com/pod-product-compliance
Lightning Source LLC
Chambersburg PA
CBHW081302250726
48662CB00008B/2356